Growing Strong, Growing Apart

SUNY series, James N. Rosenau series in Global Politics

David C. Earnest, editor

Growing Strong, Growing Apart

The Erosion of Democracy as a Core Pillar of
NATO Enlargement, 1949–2023

EYAL RUBINSON

SUNY
PRESS

Published by State University of New York Press, Albany

Printed in the United States of America

For information, contact State University of New York Press, Albany, NY
www.sunypress.edu

Library of Congress Cataloging-in-Publication Data

Name: Rubinson, Eyal, 1986– author.
Title: Growing strong, growing apart : the erosion of democracy as a core
    pillar of NATO enlargement, 1949–2023 / Eyal Rubinson.
Description: Albany : State University of New York Press, [2024]. | Series:
    SUNY series, James N. Rosenau series in global politics | Includes
    bibliographical references and index.
Identifiers: LCCN 2023036256 | ISBN 9781438497310 (hardcover : alk. paper) |
    ISBN 9781438497334 (ebook) | ISBN 9781438497327 (pbk. : alk. paper)
Subjects: LCSH: North Atlantic Treaty Organization—Membership. | Democracy.
Classification: LCC UA646.3 .R83 2024 | DDC 355/.031091821—dc23/eng/20231117
LC record available at https://lccn.loc.gov/2023036256

10 9 8 7 6 5 4 3 2 1

Contents

Preface

In the global landscape of post–World War II multilateral security alliances, the North Atlantic Treaty Organization (NATO) stands out as a tremendous success story. In fact, it is an international security unicorn, the only one of its kind left standing on the global arena. Over seventy-four years since its inception in 1949, NATO has outlasted its competition—most notably, the Warsaw Pact, which slowly but surely disappeared into the abyss in the aftermath of the Cold War. It is not surprising, therefore, that NATO has received enduring scholarly attention across issue areas, analyzing the multitude aspects that underpin the Alliance's prosperity. A substantial piece of NATO's resilience puzzle is vested in the organization's remarkable ability to continuously expand its membership. From an original group of twelve founding Allies in 1949, during the Cold War the Alliance integrated Greece, Turkey, and West Germany, and added Spain to its ranks. Afterward, as global security architecture was swiftly shifting, NATO expanded by another fourteen members in several waves, eventually bringing its current strength to thirty-one Allies, with Finland's accession in 2023, and Sweden as a forthcoming Ally. However, unlike the United States Declaration of Independence, which famously stipulates that *all men are created equal*, the nineteen member states which had joined the Alliance throughout its history were not made equal. In fact, they vary greatly in numerous attributes, including the prevalence of democracy in their governing systems and the extent of their domestic democratic traditions—a notion NATO holds particularly dear as part of its membership criteria. Nonetheless, NATO's recent enlargement waves—particularly those preceding the 2022 war in Ukraine—had proven increasingly incompatible with the most prevalent attributes of democracy, as defined in the international relations (IR) literature. Against this backdrop, this book pursues a research agenda connecting my primary scholarly emphasis on multilateralism and international security with the notion of diminishing levels of democracy among NATO members. Over this intellectual journey, many have partaken in the realization of this project. The idea for this book first materialized during my tenure as Mediterranean Dialogue Fellow at the NATO Defense College in Rome in 2019, where I was given an insider's glimpse of the intricate mechanisms of NATO enlargement. Many brilliant researchers and academics based in Rome contributed to my comprehension of the topic and its countless facets. These include, among others, Thierry Tardy, Marc Ozawa, Andrea Gilli, Chloe Berger, Christine Whitecross, Stephen J. Mariano, Francesco Cherubini, Christian Leuprecht, Katarina Đokić, Eugenio Mengarini, and Flaminia Del Monte. I also gained invaluable feedback from Frank Schimmelfennig and the participants of the ETH Zürich European Politics Research Group, faculty members at the International Relations Division at Haifa University, and at the Department of Middle Eastern Studies and Political Science at Ariel University. Participants of the International Studies Association (ISA) annual meeting in 2021 also helped materialize this project. A remarkably devoted and impressive cadre of policy makers at the NATO Headquarters in Brussels helped shed light on the topic from the organizational perspective. Of those, I'm particularly indebted to Petr Chalupecky, Benedetta Berti, Tanya Hartman, Steffen Elgersma, and Nicola de Santis. I had also gained priceless feedback from the editorial team and anonymous reviewers at the *Journal of International Relations and Development*, where an introductory version of this research first appeared in March 2021. The referees and editorial team at SUNY Press likewise provided vital advice and insight throughout the book's materialization. Gadi Hitman was also instrumental in pushing me to take on this project and bring it to fruition. My mentor and friend Tal Sadeh inspired me and provided invaluable personal guidance in the process. Last but not least, I am endlessly indebted to my wife Mica, whose advice, patience, and selflessness made all this possible, and to my extended family for their support. I dedicate this book to them.

Introduction

The primary purpose of this book is to explore the role of democracy in NATO enlargement decisions throughout its history, and to offer an assessment of how the notion of democracy is expected to navigate decision making about future expansion. The principal puzzle that the book tackles is vested in the question of why NATO admits new member states that fall short of the organization's robust expectations of democracy, as stipulated in an elaborate scheme of texts, speeches, and statements set forth by the Alliance throughout its history. In pursing this perspective, the book sheds light on the multilateral/institutional framing of the enlargement process: how NATO bureaucrats and officials opened the gate for further expansion. The NATO story is not merely about the domestic conduct and decision making of each Ally—whatever large and central—but rather it is a tale of an international organ with a unique viewpoint. It is about the meaning and role of the *O* in *NATO*—an international *organization*, that took upon itself the grand historic mission of anchoring and preserving the postwar rules-based multilateral order, a calling that looms large in the aftermath of Russia's full-scale invasion of Ukraine in February 2022. To address the puzzle of NATO's diminishing democratic threshold, the book maintains that this policy results from gradual erosion in the prominence of democratic discourse within the organization, normalizing deviations from previous optimistic expectations that became increasingly unsustainable in recent decades. During this hopeful period, NATO turned to expand into former Soviet Republics and ex-Communist regimes, quickly exhausting its democratic pool. To ensure the preservation of the expansion train—which provides an invaluable lifeline for every international organization (IO)—NATO was willing to overlook the democratic deficiencies among aspiring member states. The analysis of NATO's conduct in this regard builds on archival research and interviews with NATO officials and senior

1

member states representatives, complemented by detailed case studies that scrutinize the genuine role of democracy in organizational decision-making on enlargement throughout the Alliance's history.

The book is structured as follows. chapter 1 unpacks the roots and causes of enlargement in IOs—formal institutions established by legally binding treaties incorporating three states or more. In the post-war global order, IOs have become broadly prevalent for a myriad of functions, with recent accounts identifying more than five hundred and sixty formal IOs, and another two hundred informal IOs (frameworks for global cooperation, such as the G7 group of states). IOs are often negotiated and formed by a collection of like-minded states around a particular issue area or boarder purpose, and expand their membership over time, as other states join their founding treaties. With the slow widening of organizational membership, the rules and norms that underpin the IO's operations become more prevalent in the global system. All types of IOs are equipped with administrative resources and structures (most commonly, secretariats and plenary organs) to realize their purpose, coordinating the mechanisms for enlargement. IOs seek expansion for several reasons. First, IOs are fundamentally international bureaucracies, for whom expansion constitutes an organizational lifeline: admitting more members requires additional resources, creates jobs, and generates growth. Indeed, IO bureaucracies are vast powerhouses. NATO, the focus of this book, entails a substantial bureaucratic chain, encompassing around 4,000 employees and national delegates in its Brussels headquarters alone. In the long term, these immense structures and their employees develop strong multinational identities that sometimes transcend the domestic mind-set, creating a group identity that contributes to expansion pressures. The appropriate proceedings for IO enlargement are defined in their founding treaties, which specify the mechanisms and requirements for expansion. In procedural terms, the actual moment of IO enlargement is preceded by a demanding and sometimes lengthy process, over the course of which the candidate state is scrutinized, required to meet various criteria the IO had put in place—a process known as membership conditionality. Some IOs—typically those where membership entails genuine financial, administrative, or military implications—are notoriously arduous in the process of vetting new members. Subscribing to this approach, NATO's membership conditionality involves a multifaceted set of requirements on several realms, including a strong commitment to democracy—a key pillar that constitutes the theme of this book. Over the course of NATO accession talks, experts and representatives from the candidate state and the Alliance meet in several sessions, attending to the political and military criteria, as well as to the technical, legal and procedural matters. The candidate state then provides a letter of intent to NATO's secretary general, outlining the schedule for the conclusion of all required reforms. A satisfactory implementation of all agreed modifications is considered a prerequisite for accession, enabling progress toward membership invitation—followed with signing accession protocols, and finalized with unanimous Allied domestic ratification. The domestic ratification phase can become stained due to political circumstances and considerations, as exemplified by Turkey's delay of the ongoing process with regard to Finland and Sweden's accession.

After laying out the theoretical foundations of IO enlargement and surveying the mechanics of NATO expansion, chapter 2 extensively outlines the central role democracy had played in the formation of the Alliance, demonstrating how pivotal this notion has been in enlargement decisions throughout its history. Since its establishment, the Alliance issued numerous documents, declarations, and communiqués that underlie the importance of democracy for NATO's mission. In the midst of the Cold War, NATO strove to enhance political cooperation among its member states—with democracy as an organizing principle. In the final years of the Soviet Union, with its grasp on Europe quickly eroding, the Alliance increasingly referenced the necessity for West-East dialogue. The chapter reveals the narrative aimed to bring the newly established Central and Eastern European states closer to the Western set of values, based first and foremost on adherence to democracy, framing the core purpose of the Alliance around this theme. As rapprochement toward the East became a core mission, in November 1991, NATO adopted a new Strategic Concept, followed with the establishment of the North Atlantic Cooperation Council (NACC)—a forum for dialogue with ex–Warsaw Pact states (later replaced with the Euro-Atlantic Partnership Council—EAPC). A crucial step in the preparations for NATO's Eastern enlargement took place in January 1994, with the formation of the Partnership for Peace (PfP) program—a tailor-made instrument to facilitate a bilateral partnership with participating states. At its core, the PfP was designed as a preparatory mechanism for future membership, with the stated aim of consolidating the democratization of civil-military relations. Shortly afterward, NATO released its most significant document to clearly define the various aspects of enlargement—the 1995 Study on NATO Enlargement. This formative text leads with the notion of advancing democratic values as one of the defining features for progress, grounding NATO expansion in the principles of the UN Charter. Following the 1999 enlargement round, integrating Poland, Hungary, and the Czech Republic, NATO approved a new Strategic Concept, emphasizing the Alliance's commitment to remain open to consider new candidates, famously stressing that no European *democratic* country will be excluded from consideration. Ever since, this wording will have accompanied the vast majority of NATO statements and speeches on enlargement. In practice, in 1999, the Alliance's Washington Summit charted a way for future enlargement, introducing a carefully tailored new mechanism—the Membership Action Plan (MAP), created to assist aspiring members to meet NATO's expectations. To date, eleven aspirant countries that took part in the MAP were ultimately able to gain full membership (Bulgaria, Estonia, Latvia, Lithuania, Romania, Slovakia, Slovenia, Albania, Croatia, Montenegro, and North Macedonia), with Bosnia and Herzegovina remaining the sole active participant. At the Brussels Summit meeting in June 2021, the Alliance commissioned the formation of a new Strategic Concept, finalized and introduced during the June 2022 NATO Summit in Madrid, sustaining the reliance on the notions of democracy, the rule of law, and respect for human rights as the core instruments shaping the Alliance. Against the backdrop of the dramatic events of Russia's invasion of Ukraine in February 2022, and the tragic war that ensued, NATO's compass—emphasizing democratic values and credibly committing to defending these values—remains the guiding principle for the Alliance's future in the decades to come. The 2023 accession of Finland (and the much-anticipated Swedish membership)—represents a powerful signal for the attractiveness and relevance of the Alliance by two of the most robust and vigorous European democracies, which for decades maintained a policy of military nonalignment.

After the first two chapters provide a comprehensive account of the centrality and importance of the notion of democracy for the structure, cohesion, and enlargement conditionality of the Alliance over its history, chapter 3 connects these dots with the occasionally painful reality of enlargement. How did NATO translate this ironclad commitment to democratic values into its enlargement decision-making over the years? And what are the consequences for the future of NATO expansion? To assess this theme, chapter 3 first dives into the conceptualization of democracy in modern political science, touching on the various ideational and empirical aspects of this term, in an attempt to offer a multifaceted framing for the analysis. This is performed by harnessing methodological and conceptual insights from leading global democracy indices—complex structures that connect the theoretical language to real-world measurement. A sober evaluation of the actual state of democracy in the ranks of the Alliance, and particularly among its newest pre-Ukraine members, is crucial for understanding whether NATO's democratic conditionality indeed has been rigorously applied throughout its expansion history. Undeniably, this assessment paints a somewhat gloomy picture, detached from the optimistic expectations reflected in the Alliance's inaugural texts and speeches—demonstrating that NATO has been experiencing democratic backslide. Then, the chapter introduces a new theoretical framework to explain this phenomenon, building on the constructivist school of thought in the study of international relations (IR). This conceptual approach suggests that the desire to expedite the historic process of NATO enlargement encouraged long-term organizational behavior that eroded original organizational norms, diminishing—over time—the key tenet of uncompromising importance of a robust democracy, a process known as normalization of deviance. This term was devised as part of an analysis of the organizational culture in the National Aeronautics and Space Administration (NASA) in the period before the 1986 *Challenger* crash, in an attempt to investigate the structural behavior that contributed to the negligence that underpinned the disaster. The chapter then proceeds to apply the notion of normalization of deviance to NATO's enlargement practices, using a wide array of originally performed interviews with NATO officials presently or previously involved in the various aspects of enlargement decision-making. This effort lays the groundwork for the next chapters, which offer elaborate case studies on every enlargement round in the history of the Alliance, including the most recent process concerning Sweden and Finland, while also aiming to identify the prospects for future enlargements.

In accordance with this line of investigation, chapter 4 surveys internal NATO deliberations and decision-making rationale vis-à-vis the Alliance's early enlargements states—Greece and Turkey (1952), West Germany (1955) and Spain (1982)—in the context of democratic membership conditionality. This task entails harnessing archival evidence and historical accounts to assess the genuine role played by adherence to democracy in NATO's enlargement decisions throughout the internal deliberation and bargaining process. Relying on the prominent democracy indices available for the period, Polity IV and V-Dem, these enlargements vary in their accession-day levels of democratic consolidation. While Greece and Turkey were dubbed electoral autocracies or borderline democracies, West Germany's reintegration into the family of nations brought into the Alliance a full-fledged liberal democracy. Spain, another European postfascist giant, also held quite robust democratic characteristics on accession day, while not as comparatively inclusive as West Germany. The chapter thoroughly fleshes out NATO's perspective on these three enlargements rounds.

Chapter 5 takes on the journey of post–Cold War enlargement. The collapse of the Soviet Union saw NATO's transformation into a centerpiece mechanism of the newly established unipolar American-led global order. Absent its core founding military mission of protecting European democracies from a possible Communist invasion or threat, NATO willfully embraced the endeavor to facilitate and promote democratization in Eastern Europe, positioning itself as a lighthouse for projecting democratic norms toward its East. A meeting of the North Atlantic Council (NAC) in July 1990 best exemplifies how essential it was for NATO to provide Eastern Europe with the chance to integrate itself into the Western sphere of influence: "NATO must evolve and it must look back to its origins. It is a defensive Alliance of free and democratic nations on both sides of the Atlantic which is adapting to a new European reality. . . . East European countries have expressed their will to adopt a new way of life shaped by the common denominators of the Alliance such as pluralistic democratic administration, supremacy of law and free market economy."[1] Correspondingly, this chapter investigates this transformation, harnessing archival material to flesh out the role of democracy in post–Cold War expansion decisions. This account includes a discussion of the 1999 enlargement round, incorporating Poland, the Czech Republic, and Hungary, followed with an assessment of the massive 2004 expansion round (Bulgaria, Estonia, Latvia, Lithuania, Romania, Slovakia, and Slovenia). To conclude, the chapter also attends to the accession of Croatia and Albania (2009), Montenegro (2017), and finally, North Macedonia in 2020. Large-scale analyses of the levels of democracy in all post-Communist NATO members demonstrate that democratic regime characteristics are positively associated with the prospects for NATO accession.[2] However, while the 1999 enlargement round was relatively strong in terms of democracy rankings, further enlargements—in particular those of the recent decade (Albania, Montenegro, and North Macedonia)—were increasingly unable to uphold the same standards, effectively lowering the democratic entry bar. Hence, a more fine-grained breakdown of the role of democracy in NATO accession is essential to further flesh out the dynamics behind enlargement decisions, helped by an analysis of how processes of domestic liberalization unfolded in aspiring states, and in turn perceived by NATO.

Chapter 6 offers an assessment of the future of NATO expansion, and the role democracy is expected to play in enlargement decisions. Following the Finnish and Swedish dramatic decision to pursue NATO membership in the aftermath of the February 2022 Russian full-fledged invasion of Ukraine, three countries formally remain in the running for future membership: Georgia, Ukraine, and Bosnia and Herzegovina. The potential candidacy of Georgia and Ukraine has been mulled over by the Alliance since the late 1990s, but has become significantly strained over their recent military confrontations with Russia. These wars—that is, Russian military campaigns in Georgia (2008) and in Ukraine (2014 and 2022)—had left parts of these countries' territory under Russian occupation or separatist rebel rule, rendering their future membership immensely challenging. A substantial portion of this challenge is derived from NATO's policy, according to which prospective members should put to rest any existing territorial disputes before finalizing their membership. The 1995 Study on NATO Enlargement determines that "States which have ethnic or external territorial disputes . . . must settle those disputes by peaceful means [and] . . . resolution of such disputes would be a factor in determining whether to invite a state to join the Alliance."[3] Similarly, the 1999 MAP framework also references territorial disputes, emphasizing that their resolution is *expected* from aspirant members.[4] This reality considerably strains Georgia and Ukraine's NATO membership bids, but the tensions with Russia are not the sole delaying factor. As the book exemplifies, the democratic record in candidate countries is vital for an aspirant nation to be considered suitable for NATO membership, albeit the importance of this notion has been gradually eroding. However, Ukraine's democratic ranking reflects a partly free hybrid regime nature (also referred to as an Open Anocracy in the Polity IV index), a sharp decline since 2014, after Russia's annexation of Crimea, placing it below the expected NATO threshold. Georgia's rankings had steadily improved since 2004, yet it is still struggling to maintain the ability to meet the Alliance's expectations, while currently still dubbed partly free and hybrid. As Ukraine struggles for its mere survival and existence, Ukrainian President Zelensky acknowledged the challenges for Ukraine's possible NATO membership, yet still formally submitted an application for NATO membership, requesting an accelerated ascension into the Alliance, backed by NATO's Eastern Flank countries. The chapter assesses the future scenarios for NATO's relations with Ukraine and Georgia. The third potential candidate—Bosnia and Herzegovina—fares worse than Ukraine and Georgia on all existing indexes, also defined as a partly-free hybrid-regime. It is not, however, presently involved in international disputes or conflicts over its own territorial borders, rendering it as a more feasible candidate compared to the former group. Considering the gloomy developments in NATO's relations with Russia, the Alliance cannot allow Sarajevo to become the next victim in its struggle with Moscow over regional influence on its Easter Flank. The chapter assesses the possible constellation for Bosnia and Herzegovina's membership bid.

Then, chapter 6 provides an assessment of the circumstances that had led to the historic Finnish and Swedish membership bid. The two Nordic states are among the world's most robust democracies, with a rich history of exemplary respect for the rule of law, human rights, and individual freedoms. Their momentous decision to pursue membership is the direct result of enhanced security concerns in the aftermath of Russia's 2022 invasion of Ukraine, which changed the security architecture of the entire region and indeed, the post–Cold War order. The chapter details Sweden and Finland's road to membership. As both states rightfully expected swift vetting procedures in the Alliance's internal consultations, eyeing a possible integration as early as June 2022, the Alliance's domestic ratification process proved more stubborn. Nevertheless, this step, in which thirty Allies ratify Finland and Sweden's accession to the Alliance, turned out to be quite lengthy and strained—contrary to the preliminary optimistic expectations—and resulted in Finland's accession in April 2023, as well as a significant delay over Sweden's membership (driven by Turkey and Hungary). The chapter explains Turkey's opposition, stemming from its demands to comprehensively halt all forms of support of Kurdish elements deemed terrorist organizations by Ankara, and assesses the future role of both Nordic countries within the Alliance. Finally, the chapter lays out the intricate history behind the notion of nonalignment in Europe, and surveys the current state of affairs with regard to the chances that other traditionally neutral states (such as Austria, Ireland, and Malta) would opt to pursue full membership in the future. It also identifies those European states that presently seem highly unlikely to pursue a membership path, most prominently Belarus, and explores the current positioning of Armenia, Azerbaijan, Kosovo, and Cyprus in this complex web of political-military interests and preferences.

Chapter 7 concludes, developing a discussion of NATO's present-day increasing role and visibility in global affairs, and considers what this reality could mean for the cohesion and structure of the Alliance in the decades to come.

Chapter 1

The Roots and Causes of
NATO Enlargement

The Essentials of NATO Enlargement: Why IOs Seek Growth?

A central tenet of IOs' rationale on expansion is rooted in their fundamental composition as international bureaucratic entities. Expansion constitutes an organizational lifeline for IOs: admitting more members requires additional resources, creates more jobs, and effectively moves the IO's administrative wheels forward and generates growth. According to this approach, narrow membership is detrimental to the purpose of organizational development, and may lead to long-term stagnation. IOs, like every bureaucracy, seek to maximize their ability to exploit existing resources and acquire new ones. This narrative builds on the bureaucratic politics model in political science, and the sociological approach, which focuses on outputs that result from bargaining processes between bureaucratic actors, rather than political leaders, and attributes significant powers to IO administration, and in particular IO secretariats.[1] The model presumes that organizational interests drive actors, rendering decisions as outcomes of interactions between competing policy preferences, exerting power and influence by leveraging their resources.[2] This school of thought conceives of IO secretariats' power as a slippery slope that—once granted certain amount of autonomy—is expected to grow in its capacity to influence and gain further traction in decision making and agenda setting.

Indeed, IO bureaucracies are vast powerhouses. The UN, with its network of affiliated organizations, employs nearly 37,000 people in 193 locations, including four global offices (UN headquarters in New York,

Geneva, Vienna, and Nairobi). Its massive bureaucratic structure involves, among other things, the UN Secretariat (with geographically diverse employees, aimed to fairly represent the distribution of member states), dedicated UN programs (e.g., UNICEF and UNDP), and specialized agencies and affiliated entities, some of which operate as fully autonomous IOs. The UN also operates peacekeeping operations, special political missions, and regional economic/social commissions across the globe. The EU boasts an even larger bureaucratic mechanism, with around 55,000 employees from among its twenty-seven member states, of whom nearly 33,000 work at the European Commission (usually on a tenure-based contract, designed to ensure their objectivity and autonomy from their home member states), and around 7,000 at the European Parliament. Other key structures include the European Council, the Council of the EU, the European Court of Justice and the EU Court of Auditors and the European Central Bank. According to the European Council, the bloc's 2021–2027 multiannual financial framework (MFF), coupled with the COVID-19 NextGenerationEU recovery instrument, encompass over €1.8 trillion of funding for EU long-term priorities and policy areas.[3]

NATO also entails substantial bureaucratic chain of decision making—encompassing more than 4,000 employees and national delegates in its Brussels headquarters alone. The Alliance is structured around a multifaceted logic of political/civilian and military components, all well-equipped with personnel and resources to cope with an ever-rising Russian threat on its Eastern flank, and an emerging Chinese challenge. Suffice it to mention the complex civilian structure, which includes, among other offices, the Political Affairs and Security Policy Division (responsible for several liaison offices in Europe), the Operations Division, an Emerging Security Challenges Division, the Defence Policy and Planning Division, the Defence Investment Division, Public Diplomacy Division and a Joint Intelligence and Security Division. The Alliance also operates special educational programs such the NATO School Oberammergau (NSO), the NATO Defense College in Rome, the NCI Academy in Mons, and others, and facilitates vast outreach mechanisms. The Alliance's immense military structure consists of, among other things, the International Military Staff; the Allied Command Operations (ACO), with its many permanent military headquarters, groups, and country offices; the Allied Command Transformation (ACT) and several other Command and Staff organizations, such as the Combined Joint Planning Staff (CJPS). These and other permanent mechanisms that underpin the everyday function of the Alliance were gradually established in the early 1950s (after the appointment of the first secretary general in 1951), as NATO's preliminary composition concentrated on the traditional military aspects, with little formality in coordination mechanisms between the original founding members. Over time, and as the Alliance grew in membership, NATO transformed into its current form.[4] This institutional setting accounts for at least part of the reason why NATO remained viable and functioning after the Cold War, as bureaucratic structures are extremely difficult to disentangle.[5]

In the long term, these massive IO bureaucratic structures and their employees develop strong multinational identities that sometimes transcend the domestic mind-set (e.g., a Portuguese citizen working for the European Central Bank in Frankfurt, or a Turkish citizen working at the NATO headquarters in Brussels). The supranational outlook strengthens their cosmopolitan identity and potentially weakens the bond between them and their original nation-states, as IO bureaucrats often enjoy distinguished salaries and a system of tenure (or other forms of permanent employment), and become strongly associated with their IO.[6] This association may eventually contradict the policy interests of their original member states, as IO employees become committed to the norm of impartiality and see themselves as dedicated international civil servants.[7] This self-acquired community identification (e.g., "Europeanness" in the case of the EU[8]) is helped by further economic and political integration, and most notably by deepening expansion. IO enlargement strengthens the real or imagined newly formed group identity, as it physically connects staff from new member states with officials from other member states working at the IO's various locations, creating a sense of diversity and growth. That is part of the reason why large IOs such as the EU, the UN, and NATO opt to concentrate their operations in megahub cities, the most notable of which is Brussels—hosting the EU Commission, the Council of the EU, NATO headquarters, and many other smaller IOs. Other IO city-hubs include Geneva, Washington, DC, the Hague, and Paris.

Naturally, however, IOs' bureaucratic interests and objectives differ at times from those of the principal member states, and when significant questions like enlargement arise, IO officials may possibly frame and address them in a manner that is not necessarily beneficial to the core policy interests of their member states. This derives from a rationalist perception of utilitarianism, profit-seeking approach as traits that best describe IO bureaucracies, seen as political structures that serve the self-interest of their employees. This school of thought views inspirational values like advancement of the global well-being with some suspicion, as IO bureaucracies seek to expand and grow in resources, delegated authority, and overall autonomy.[9] But though IOs' bureaucracy and appointed officials are generally tasked with making recommendations on enlargement and drafting advisory opinions vis-à-vis candidate states, eventually it is up to the delegating member states to decide on expansion. This derives from the nature of IOs as agents and member states as principals, bearing in mind that member states normally hedge against undesired fundamental shifts in the nature of these IOs, including their membership architecture. Hence, while NATO may aspire to grow its membership, contradicting domestic interests may drive member states to effectively veto the prospects for expansion (e.g., Turkey's politically driven objection to integrate Cyprus into the Alliance, on account of its long-standing conflict with the island state and Greece over its status). One of the most central mechanisms to preserve control over IO enlargement—which is enshrined in NATO's founding Washington Treaty as well—is a requirement for domestic ratification, via the member states' internal protocols. Different member states feature divergent mechanisms for this task. For instance, the US Constitution determines that treaties require a majority of two-thirds of the senators, and in practice treaties are brought before the Senate Committee on Foreign Relations, followed by a vote on approval. In the UK, treaties are brought before the Parliament for twenty-one sitting days before ratification by the government, but there is no legal requirement for a Parliamentary debate or vote. These procedural variations may at times be translated to significant delays in the NATO membership ratification process. This notion has been particularly evident in the case of Finnish/Swedish ratification process in 2022, as both countries were issued a formal membership invitation in June 2022, with accession protocols signed in early July. Within one month, their accession was ratified by Canada, Iceland, Norway, Estonia, the UK, Albania, Denmark, Germany, the Netherlands, Luxembourg, Bulgaria, Latvia, Slovenia, Croatia, Poland, Lithuania, Belgium, Romania, North Macedonia, Montenegro, and the US, while others (e.g., Spain and Slovakia) required nearly two months to complete the process. Eventually, Finland has been granted full membership in April 2023, while Sweden's membership has been delayed even further, driven by Turkish demands to sever its alleged ties with Kurdish elements, and Hungarian accusation of Swedish interference with domestic Hungarian issues, while playing an active role in initiating EU sanctions over Hungary.

Enlargement can result in further "character" change, as new members often inadvertently or intentionally inject the IOs with their own sets of values and characteristics, particularly when questions of norms related to rule of law, democracy, and human rights are at stake. One of the most prominent examples for this phenomenon is NATO's (and the EU's) eastward enlargement in 2004, taking in several former Soviet states that significantly differ in their political culture compared to its membership at the time. This rapid enlargement pace entails complex sociological, political, and cultural consequences on the organizational nature, which may eventually produce new policy directions and ideas, not necessarily supported by the original pre-enlargement membership landscape. IO culture is central to its operations, since organizations build on their expert and moral authority to frame, construct, and shape their future policy interests and desirable toolkits.[10] This endeavor may produce outcomes that conflict with some member states' views, thereby potentially leading to a confrontational dynamic within the organization. This corresponds to the principle of transaction costs, under which IOs may act autonomously by advancing policies undesirable by the member states, or even attempt to assert a more proactive role in strategic decision-making.[11] IOs' interests do not necessarily converge with member state views, and they may be inclined to slip from original mandates by overperforming, or alternatively underperform (shirk), where states interests are unclear or weak, and the ambiguity serves various IO interests.[12] For example, while some NATO officials may hold the view that Ukraine and Georgia should join the Alliance as full members, these two countries constitute a major geopolitical challenge vis-à-vis Russia, as both fell victim to the latter's military campaigns (Georgia in 2008, and Ukraine in 2014 and 2022), which left parts of their territory under Russian occupation. This state of affairs entails a myriad of political complexities and military challenges, which could be perceived in an entirely diverse fashion between Washington, London, Paris, or Berlin, and NATO officials in Brussels. As alluded to by US Secretary of State Blinken in June 2021, on the issue of possible NATO membership for Ukraine, "MAP itself would have to be done in full consensus with other NATO members . . . [and] I think there are some countries that are less supportive than others of that right now."[13] This stance, communicated before Russia's invasion of Ukraine in February 2022, has only substantialized as the ramifications of this devastating war continued to unfold. After Ukrainian President Zelenskiy applied for fast-track membership in September 2022, US National Security Adviser Jake Sullivan responded that Washington believes Ukrainian membership is not to be pursued at the current stage, pouring cold water on Kyiv's membership bid: "Right now, our view is that the best way for us to support Ukraine is through practical, on-the-ground support in Ukraine and that the process in Brussels should be taken up at a different time."[14] From an IO standpoint, keeping its member states satisfied with the organization's work is an imperative for long-term survival. IOs that experience extreme internal instability may eventually dissolve or cease to operate properly,[15] with their resources slowly cut back by the member states, until they ultimately become unviable.[16] This notion is particularly true with regard to the larger member states, as these usually account for a majority of financial contributions to the IO's budget (e.g., in the case of the UN system, the US accounts for about 22 percent of the organization's regular operating budget, while Russia accounts for nearly 2 percent and India for less than 1 percent). This divergence is likely to translate into IO decision-making prioritization and strategic planning when matters concerning the core policy interests of large member states are at stake. In a notable recent example, through President Trump's tenure, the US has significantly increased its funding for the European Deterrence Initiative, from $800 million in 2016 to as much as $6.5 billion in 2019, driving considerable White House criticism.[17] According to Schuette, in order to address Trump's concerns, NATO Secretary General Stoltenberg helped broker a new common funding formula for the Alliance's budget, significantly boosting German defense spending. In an additional example from another realm, in 2018 the US halted funding to the UN Relief and Works Agency (UNRWA) assisting Palestinian refugees—requiring a thorough reexamination of its operations and finances,[18] before later announcing a restoration of aid to the agency.[19]

Like other IOs, NATO heavily relies on its organizational reputation—a set of beliefs about its capabilities, history, mission, and intentions.[20] Organizational reputation can be either "won" or "lost," and entails a variety of audiences, including the NATO's member states (as well as other IOs and the general public). A successful track record of institutional professionalism is crucial to build reputation and institutional power, and is likely to attract states to delegate more resources and responsibilities—a goal also supported by IO enlargement.[21] A respectable reputation is also important to persuade member states to invest funds multilaterally (rather than via bilateral defense aid), thereby supporting the emergence of new issue areas of responsibility, and eventually enabling expansion. To attract new members, IOs also attempt to project morality and signal their responsiveness to existing member states and to their general public, in a manner that they hope would eventually translate into bureaucratic gains and further delegation, and invest significant resources in outreach and public relations schemes, to help brand their policy recommendations as trustworthy. In NATO's context, this notion has been widely demonstrated after Russia's invasion of Ukraine in February 2022, during which the NATO Press Office and its virtual "newsroom" became an indispensable source of information on the Alliance's response and policy throughout the crisis. As NATO's Secretary General's Annual Report for 2021 testifies, throughout that year NATO's digital communication channels (broadcast, social media, and the NATO website) "continued to reach existing and new audiences . . . with notable growth on all social media platforms."[22]

NATO also makes use of external actors to facilitate the relationship with its target audiences—a process called orchestration.[23] These intermediaries may include private actors and institutions, and sometimes even certain cooperative member states, recruited to help the organizations advance their goals. A prominent example can be found in national NGOs who aim to independently promote NATO's values and goals, such as the NATO Association of Canada (NAOC), and the Atlantic Treaty Association of the United Kingdom (ATA UK). Given a necessity or relative advantage, following the theoretical principles of resource exchange—NATO can also opt to collaborate with other IOs, seeking to maximize their perceived value in the eyes of their member states, in a fashion that may yield reputational gains. That, in turn, may also foster enlargement, as result-driven cooperation between IOs may appeal to potential stakeholders, and prospective candidates 'sitting on the fence.' A prominent example of such cooperation is NATO's relations with the UN. Among other areas, NATO provides support for UN-sponsored operations in the field of disaster relief, acute food shortages, and field hospitals (collaborating with the World Food Programme).[24]

Ultimately, NATO, like other prominent IOs on the world stage, is found in constant tension between its desire for further expansion, and the uncertainty that this policy may bring for the organization's functionality, day-to-day dynamic or even long-term survival. Diverse membership—an inevitable byproduct of expansion—may cause destabilization in decision making and social dynamics.[25] And yet, as NATO enlargement in recent decades has repeatedly demonstrated, the Alliance is bound to grow, pushed by bureaucratic and organizational powers, constantly evolving over NATO's continuous enlargement.

The Mechanics of Enlargement in International Organizations: NATO Enlargement Unpacked

The proceedings for enlargement are defined in the founding treaties of every IO, specifying—in varying levels of detail—the mechanisms and requirements for expansion. Throughout their lifetime, some IOs adopt either binding or noncompulsory guidelines for enlargement, through dedicated documents or declarations, aimed to outline a tentative vision and at times, laying down certain conditions for expansion (amendments to the founding treaty may also apply). The actual moment of enlargement is preceded by a demanding and sometimes lengthy process, over the course of which the candidate state is scrutinized and required to meet various criteria that the IO had put in place—a process known as accession conditionality. NATO, similarly to other substantial IOs on the global arena such as the EU and the OECD, where affiliation entails genuine financial, administrative, or military implications—is notoriously arduous in the process of vetting new members. These accession criteria entail complex military, political, legal, administrative, and institutional/domestic processes and reforms, followed by a (typically) extensive period of membership negotiations. Eventually, an official membership invitation is issued, requiring the unanimous domestic ratification of all existing Allies, as well as the candidate's.

More specifically, NATO's membership conditionality involves a multifaceted set of requirements on several realms: commitment to democracy, human rights, and the rule of law—a key pillar that constitutes the theme of this book; a potential for a military contribution to the Alliance's strategic posture—a core component, rendered vital for a demonstration of objective added value; financial, legal, and administrative domestic conditions, including sufficient civilian supervision of the military—a central collection of indicators that signals material and logistical preparedness. During NATO's founding years, expansion was (at least de jure) dominated by Article X of the inaugural North Atlantic Treaty (the Washington Treaty) of 1949, which determined that "the Parties may, by unanimous agreement, invite any other European State in a position to further the principles of this Treaty and to contribute to the security of the North Atlantic area to accede to this Treaty." By adopting this framing, the Alliance's founding charter had purposely left plenty of room for maneuver for freely interpreting which candidate is in a position to "further the principles of the treaty," and even what "European" means (as evident in the case of NATO's first expansion in 1952, integrating Turkey and Greece).

In modern days, however, NATO enlargement is more comprehensively conceived and legally grounded. The criteria for expansion were first laid out in an explicit manner in the 1995 NATO Study on Enlargement.[26] To foster enlargement, Allies agreed that aspiring candidates must be able to contribute to the collective defense, democratic composition, consensus decision-making and the overall cohesion of the Alliance. This set of principles was further developed in 1999, as NATO launched its Membership Action Plan (MAP)—an institutional framework designed to guide candidate states through the necessary reforms in the political, legal, and military realm, albeit without commitment for eventual guaranteed membership. States participating in the plan submit annual national reports, and hold periodic meetings and workshops with NATO officials to oversee the candidate's progress toward full membership.[27] Currently, after North Macedonia's accession in March 2020, Finland's successful bid to join the Alliance in April 2023, and Sweden's forthcoming accession, Bosnia and Herzegovina remains the sole participant in the MAP framework, having been associated with the program in 2010. While MAP is the most comprehensive cooperative framework leading toward accession, NATO also operates other lower-scale forms of cooperation with interested partners, the most prominent of which is the Partnership for Peace. This program entails bilateral cooperation with NATO on a variety of aspects, designed to strengthen the trust, security, and build a more effective connection between the parties, which may lead to a more enhanced dialogue further down the road.[28] Currently, twenty states take part in the PfP, including neutral EU states such as Austria, Malta, and Ireland.

In procedural terms, the road toward NATO membership begins with a formal dialogue between the aspiring candidate and the Alliance, which may then lead to enhanced ties, specialized engagement, and to the creation of dedicated bilateral bodies. As this association process reaches fruition, an official invitation to join the MAP would be extended on NATO's behalf. As the aspiring state is evaluated by NATO to meet all necessary prerequisites underpinning the preliminary membership criteria, the Alliance can decide to start formal accession talks. Over the course of accession talks, experts and representatives from the candidate state and the Alliance meet in two sessions—the pivotal one attends to the political and military criteria, and the other deals with technical, legal, and procedural matters. The candidate state then provides a letter of intent to NATO secretary general, outlining the schedule for the conclusion of all remaining reforms (if applicable).[29] A satisfactory conclusion of the all modifications agreed on under the various facets of the negotiation process is a key a prerequisite for accession, enabling progress toward the final stage of membership invitation. At this stage, NATO and the new forthcoming member sign the amended accession protocol, to be submitted for unanimous Allied domestic ratification. A fundamental principle of the entire enlargement process is the understanding that its completion crucially corresponds to a political will within the Alliance. This notion reflects the nature of the Alliance as a predominantly political project, as barring the appropriate partisan constellation—even a significant progress in the MAP shall not suffice. Since a unanimous ratification is obligatory,[30] it is indeed crucial to understand at an early stage whether some members may oppose expansion on political grounds. Corresponding to this rule, Greece had blocked North Macedonia's NATO membership for years, until the latter agreed to change its official name from the Republic of Macedonia to the Republic of *North* Macedonia in early 2019, resulting in its swift accession to NATO. Similarly, Turkey is consistently blocking Cyprus's membership on account of its dispute with Greece over the final status of the island, and exerted significant pressure during the ratification process for Sweden and Finland's membership bid in 2022–2023, on account of their perceived support of the Kurdistan Workers Party (PKK)—a movement defined as a terrorist entity by Ankara. Over the course of negotiations between Turkey, Sweden, and Finland, the former even reportedly demanded the extradition of dozens of suspects residing in both candidate states, exercising tremendous political pressure on Stockholm and Helsinki in order to advance in its domestic ratification process. Moreover, while it was ultimately satisfied with Finland's approach and ratified its membership status, Ankara consistently maintained its opposition to Swedish membership, on account of what it perceives as insufficient flexibility within Stockholm's political circles to accommodate Turkish demands. Hence, political clarity is a crucial benchmark for embarking on the road for expansion.

Chapter 2

Democracy as a Founding Principle of the Alliance

Democracy as NATO's Founding Principle

An inseparable element of the post–World War II US-led liberal international order, democratic principles stood at the heart of NATO's founding philosophy. Since its establishment in 1949, the Alliance issued numerous documents, declarations and communiqués which repeatedly underlie the importance of democracy, the rule of law and the preservation of human rights to the Alliance's core mission—creating and maintaining a stable and peaceful order in the North Atlantic region. While this massive body of historic Allied resources represents an official narrative, and may not fully uncover various understandings left beneath the surface, it is a vital outlet that demonstrates the formal judgment of the Alliance as a whole, adopted after numerous internal deliberations. As such, it speaks mostly of the consensual organizational line, which is eventually projected by the Alliance on behalf of its member states. First and foremost, the Alliance's establishing document—the 1949 North Atlantic Treaty (also known as the Washington Treaty)—touched on the theme of democracy with reference to the Charter of the United Nations (UN):[1] "The Parties to this Treaty reaffirm their faith in the purposes and principles of the Charter of the United Nations . . . determined to safeguard the freedom, common heritage and civilization of their peoples, founded on the principles of democracy, individual liberty and the rule of law" (preamble). The final communiqué of the first Session of the North Atlantic Council (NAC) in September 1949 reiterated this notion, by stating that the founding treaty was indeed designed to collectively "safeguard and preserve the parties' common heritage of freedom."[2] The first draft of the Alliance's Strategic Concept, submitted in November 1949 to the North Atlantic Military Committee (initially titled the Strategic Concept for the Defense of the North Atlantic Area), stressed the inseparable connection between achieving the founding goal of the Treaty and maintaining the principles of democracy, liberty and the rule of law.

> The attainment of the objectives of the North Atlantic Treaty requires the integration by the parties of those political, economic, and psychological, as well as purely military means, which are essential to the defense of the North Atlantic area. Of particular significance is the requirement that the objectives of the Treaty be accomplished in accordance with the purposes and principles of the Charter of the United Nations. The parties to the Treaty have declared they are determined to safeguard the freedom, common heritage, and civilization of their peoples, founded on the principles of democracy, individual liberty, and the rule of law.[3]

In November 1949, at the first meeting of NATO's Military Production and Supply Board, US representative N. E. Halaby emphasized the democratic roots of the Alliance, stating it will "bring together the munitions power of twelve great democracies . . . and in a very real sense we will be building an arsenal for the democracies—a bulwark of freedom."[4] A consultation between the members of the North Atlantic Defence Committee in October 1949 further emphasized this theme. The British representative, A. V. Alexander, stressed the defining and unifying democratic nature of the peoples that comprise the North Atlantic Pact, and the need to persuade large audiences in the Alliance of its benefit: "It is absolutely essential that . . . we should have to be able to satisfy, because of the whole democratic basis of every one of the nations that we have represented here, our parliaments and our people. . . . We can have plans and machinery and everything else, but if we can't carry the people with us, we won't be successful."[5] The following NAC meetings further fortified this conception. At the fourth session of the NAC in London in May 1950, the Allies contemplated the purpose and meaning of democratic values under the treaty, concluding the following:

The Foreign Ministers . . . reaffirmed the adherence of their governments to the principles which inspire the United Nations Charter and their conviction that common action under the Treaty is an integral part of the effort which all free nations are making to secure conditions of world peace and human welfare. . . . Freedom means the independence of nations, the respect for spiritual values, and the dignity of man. Only a free society can guarantee to the individual, the benefits of economic and social betterment.[6]

In a note by NATO Executive Secretary N. E. P. Sutton (NATO acting administrator in chief, in lieu of an official Secretary General) in September 1951, he emphasized that "the peoples of the North Atlantic Community are united under the Treaty to preserve their freedom and to develop their common heritage of democracy, liberty and the rule of law."[7] These principles were cemented into NATO's newly altered organizational structure, transformed at the 1952 NAC meeting in Portugal from an informal ministerial session into a permanent organ with Allied delegates (i.e., permanent representatives), chaired by a Secretary General.[8] As the first NATO Secretary General, British General Hastings Lionel Ismay was a strong proponent of NATO expansion, said to support a so-called umbrella approach, to grow NATO's membership until it covered the entire free world.[9] In his 1960 memoir, Ismay wrote that the post–World War II global architecture—with the swift division between the free world and those behind the iron curtain—made the development of an Alliance of democracies fairly inevitable: "By the end of 1947, Bulgaria, Romania, Hungary, Eastern Germany, and Poland were all behind the iron curtain, and in February 1948 a coup d'état in Prague resulted in the enslavement of Czechoslovakia. The mortal danger to Western democracies was now only too obvious."[10] Ismay also emphasized that the Alliance has become the best possible way to protect the Western way of life and the freedom of the countries that comprise the free world, hence stressing the core tenet of the Alliance's democratic nature. Shortly afterward, in December 1952, the NAC underlined that "Our work will be greatly inspired if we realize what fate our concept of democratic rights and liberties might suffer without this great Alliance. . . . We felt that very strongly when we signed the North Atlantic Treaty."[11] Less than two years after Ismay assumed his position, the Alliance held the 1954 London Conference of Nine Powers—a multilateral assembly that discussed the most pressing issues facing the West, with the participation of Belgium, Canada, France, the Federal Republic of Germany, Italy, Luxembourg, the Netherlands, the UK, and the US. In the meeting, NATO adopted a concluding document known as the Final Act, that stressed the importance of the democratic component of European integration in the strengthening of the Alliance—eventually allowing to facilitate Germany's accession[12] (for a detailed account of Germany's accession process, see chapter 4). At the same time, despite the emphasis on the merits of democracy, the Alliance was well aware of the shortcomings of the democratic system in competing with the Soviet Union throughout the cold War. A November 1954 report by the Military Committee, titled *The Most Effective Pattern of NATO Military Strengths for the Next Few Years*, emphasized the implications of these deficiencies in the military realm: "The Soviet political system, with its power of immediate decision and its advantage of strict security, as compared with the free and democratic system of the NATO type which must obtain decisions through group action, provides an initial advantage of great importance in achieving surprise."[13]

As the Cold War loomed large, NATO strove to enhance the non-military cooperation among its member states, to better cope with the Soviet threat. A December 1956 report underscored the importance of democracy as a core component in developing the Alliance's strategic goals in that regard.

> The common cultural traditions, free institutions and dem-
> ocratic concepts . . . are things which should also bring the
> NATO nations closer together, not only for their defence
> but for their development. This brings us to the second and
> long-term aim of NATO: the development of an Atlantic
> Community whose roots are deeper even than the necessity
> for common defence . . . the permanent association of the free
> Atlantic peoples for the promotion of their greater unity and
> the protection and the advancement of the interests which, as
> free democracies, they have in common.[14]

In the course of NATO's strategy formation as part of the Cold War, the Alliance gave a great deal of importance to highlighting the conceptual and ideological differences between the two camps—with the notion of democracy as centerpiece. In a December 1957 communiqué, NATO

Secretary General P. H. Spaak restated the democratic nature of the means that Allies were willing to undertake to contain the Soviet threat: "Within The North Atlantic Treaty there is no place for the concept of world domination. Firmly believing in peaceful change through democratic means, cherishing the character of our peoples and vigilant to safeguard their freedom, we will never yield to such a threat."[15]

After the accession of West Germany in 1955, the volume of discussions and deliberations on the role of democracy has somewhat decreased, as no new expansion was on the horizon for the foreseeable future. Over these formative years, NATO was consumed with building capabilities and improving its interoperability in the face of the peak of the Cold War. However, as the Alliance matured and expanded its operations and bureaucratic capacity, its commitment to democratic values remained a steadfast component in all its major texts. Closing down on its twentieth anniversary, an April 1969 Communiqué stated: "The Alliance was established to safeguard the freedom, common heritage and civilization of its peoples, founded on the principles of democracy, individual liberty and the rule of law, and in response to a common fear that without an effective security system, another war might erupt in a divided Europe. The Alliance continues as the expression of common purposes and aspirations."[16]

In June 1974, the NAC Ministerial Session adopted the Ottawa Declaration on Atlantic Relations, commemorating the Alliance's twenty-fifth anniversary. The document speaks volumes as to the centrality of democracy as part of the NATO mentality: "They have proclaimed their dedication to the principles of democracy, respect for human rights, justice and social progress, which are the fruits of their shared spiritual heritage, and they declare their intention to develop and deepen the application of these principles in their countries."[17] The concluding statement of the NAC Ministerial Session also commended the regime change in Portugal, which after several years did eventually lead to the full restoration of democracy in the country. Portugal, a founding member or the Alliance, was ruled by the authoritarian government of Antonio Oliveira Salazar between 1932 and 1968 (known as the Estado Novo regime), and final reinstitution of democracy in the country came only in 1976, following the adoption of a new constitution. According to Kay, Portugal's initial inclusion was highly contested among several founding members of the Alliance. Canada in particular held fundamental reservations about the presence of Portugal, led by then Secretary of State for External Affairs Lester B. Pearson, who is known for his vast contribution to the political development of NATO as an Alliance of like-minded states.[18] Taking these concerns into account, it became increasingly difficult to defend the stance according to which operational and geopolitical advantages (e.g., the centrality of Azores airfields in a future military campaign) could at times overshadow normative considerations in Alliance decision-making. However, as noted by van Dijk and Sloan, "the damage to the treaty by not including Portugal would be far outweighed by the political issues involved in its accession."[19] Gheciu explained that Portugal's geopolitical position was crucial for the North Atlantic system of defense against a possible Russian assault, a fact that eventually persuaded those initially opposed to its inclusion, expressing opaque hopes that the Portuguese won't "undermine the broader goal of liberal community building embedded in the treaty."[20] This early anecdote in the Alliance's life may perhaps offer premature clues for what will turn out to be a slow and gradual, yet steady, erosion in the role of democratic considerations in its enlargement decisions. Nonetheless, the nature of Portugal's regime has been for more than two decades a source for embarrassment for NATO, and the organization's foreign ministers at the 1974 NAC meeting were relieved to receive the news of Portugal's reforms: "The Minister of Foreign Affairs of Portugal gave a report on developments in his country since the change of regime. NATO Ministers welcomed the evolution towards the establishment of democratic and representative government in Portugal."[21] In May 1975, the NAC meeting in Brussels (with the participation of NATO heads of state and government) provided another hint at the future plans for integration of the entire North Atlantic region around common organizing values, centered on the notion of democracy.

> The Allied leaders . . . recall that the future of democracy and freedom throughout the world is closely linked to the future of those countries whose common heritage embraces these ideals. . . . They unanimously affirm that they will enhance the effectiveness and vitality of their association within the framework of the North Atlantic Treaty, which is fundamental not only to the security of the Allied nations but also to the preservation of the values to which they are deeply attached.[22]

Three years later, the 1978 NAC meeting in Washington, DC took another step forward in defining the democratic component as the most crucial element that binds the Alliance together: "Its [the Alliance's] fundamental vitality lies in the fact that all Allied countries enjoy democratic systems of government. The Allies remain convinced that these systems provide the most humane and effective means of organizing society to deal with the challenges of the modern world."[23]

In the following year, the December 1979 NAC meeting in Brussels took this conviction one step further, publicly expressing concern and alarm over violations of human rights and fundamental civilian freedoms in the Alliance's neighborhood: "Because their governments are based on the consent of their peoples, on democratic institutions, and on the principle of equality and the rule of law, the members . . . noted with concern that in certain countries the situation remained unsatisfactory or had even deteriorated as regards respect for human rights and fundamental freedoms, including cases where citizens continue to be subject to harassment and imprisonment."[24] The NAC Ministerial Session held in Ankara in June 1980 referenced the 1975 Helsinki Final Act (also known as the Helsinki Accords)—a multilateral agreement signed by thirty-five countries, which addressed a variety of global issues, including the respect for human rights and the founding principles of democracy.[25] NATO foreign ministers emphasized the concern over interference and harassment of groups in European countries that wished to uphold the principles of the Final Act: "They considered it particularly important . . . to reaffirm their determination to work together for the achievement of the fundamental ideals and aims of the Atlantic Alliance: national independence, security, human rights, democracy and the rule of law . . . [and] deplored the increased suppression in certain countries of human rights and fundamental freedoms and the harassment, imprisonment, internal exile and banishment of those who strive for implementation of the Final Act."[26]

In the last decade of the Cold War, Allies increasingly referenced the necessity for West-East dialogue, aimed to bring those interested parties closer to the Western set of values and norms, based on adherence to democracy, rule of law, and respect for human rights. The December 1982 Bonn Summit called to support such dialogue, and to uphold an internal debate on the shifting character of the Alliance: "The Allies are committed to the preservation of democracy and to building the foundations for peace. The Allies expressed their collective determination both to maintain adequate military strength and political solidarity and to seek more constructive East-West relations whenever Soviet behavior makes this possible. . . . Ministers also welcomed the growing public debate in the West about how best to preserve peace with freedom over the coming years."[27] A year later, after a 1983 meeting of the NATO Nuclear Planning Group (NPG) held in Portugal, the concluding statement framed the core purpose of the Alliance around the notion of maintenance of democracy, shoulder to shoulder with the prevention of war and promoting peace: "The main purpose of the Alliance is to prevent war, safeguard democracy and build the foundations of lasting peace."[28]

The following year, in May 1984, NATO foreign ministers restated their intention to improve East-West relations by holding dialogues on the most pressing matters underpinning democracy, including matters related to human rights. Ideally, the Alliance could expect this framework to eventually translate into possible integration, ultimately expanding its membership.

> The Allies . . . would like to see the benefits of peace, stability, human rights and freedom from interference which they themselves have enjoyed for over 35 years secured in other areas of the world as well. . . . The Allies reaffirm their offers to improve East-West relations . . . [and] propose that particular efforts be devoted to the dialogue, cooperation and contacts at all levels on the full range of questions between East and West—including political, security problems and human rights.[29]

This narrative was further enhanced as the Cold War was approaching its end. At a May 1988 NAC meeting, NATO heads of state and government underscored the centrality of East-West dialogue to achieve lasting political stability.

> Our Alliance is a voluntary association of free and democratic equals, united by common interests and values . . . dedicated to preserving peace and freedom. . . . It remains valid in political solidarity and adequate military strength, and, on that basis, the search for constructive dialogue and co-operation. . . . The ultimate political purpose of our Alliance is to achieve a just and lasting peaceful order in Europe. . . . The resolution of East-West differences will require progress in many fields . . . [and] must be firmly based on full respect for fundamental human rights.[30]

NATO Secretary General Wörner, in a statement in May 1988, echoed this view, emphasizing that "NATO is essentially a political Alliance, forged as much to consolidate the battered democracies of post-war Europe as to defend against the communist threat of aggression."[31] While this blunt ideological representation of the Alliance seems slightly more natural from a modern post–Cold War perspective, Wörner's expression of the prominence of the political-democratic component in NATO's mission was indeed extraordinary, yet imperative in building its future character. The following year marked NATO's fortieth anniversary, and the Alliance reflected on the consequences of the historic change the world was witnessing with the end of the Cold War quickly approaching. A May 1989 NAC declaration offered some insight as to how the underlying importance of democracy must persist to serve as the chief compass to guide the Alliance into the future.

> Our meeting takes place at a juncture of unprecedented change and opportunities. This is a time to look ahead, and to set our agenda for the future. In our rapidly changing world, the strength and accomplishments of democracy and freedom are increasingly apparent. . . . We welcome the progress in Eastern Europe towards establishing more democratic institutions, freer election, greater political pluralism and economic choice. Our vision of a just, humane and democratic world has always underpinned the policies of this Alliance . . . [and we are now] closer to the realization of this vision.[32]

A December 1989 communiquéby Secretary General Wörner praised the ousting of Romania Communist Party notorious General Secretary Nicolae Ceausescu's, once again prompting that "the power of the ideals of freedom and democracy for which this Alliance stands are now ascendant in Central and Eastern Europe."[33] In July 1990, the language transition seems to have completed, as NATO heads of state and government issued the Declaration on a Transformed North Atlantic Alliance, fully internalizing the perception that Eastern Europe is taking on the long journey toward freedom and democracy. But more importantly, the text emphasized that NATO has a role to play in facilitating democratization via amplified involvement in this endeavor, thereby inducing yet another political role for the Alliance, affecting its fundamental purpose.

Europe has entered a new, promising era. Central and Eastern Europe is liberating itself. . . . The walls that once confined people and ideas are collapsing. Europeans are determining their own destiny. They are choosing freedom. They are choosing economic liberty. This Alliance must and will adapt. It has done much to bring about the new Europe, yet it must be even more an agent of change. It can help build the structures of a more united continent, supporting security and stability with the strength of our shared faith in democracy, the rights of the individual, and the peaceful resolution of disputes. We reaffirm that security and stability do not lie solely in the military dimension, and we intend to enhance the political component of our Alliance.[34]

In reflecting on the shift toward Eastern Europe, Ronald D. Asmus, US deputy assistant secretary of State for European Affairs in the 1990s, wrote in 2002 that the strategic purpose of NATO enlargement was "consolidating democracy in Central and Eastern Europe . . . implying that the Alliance would eventually embrace much, if not all, of the eastern half of the continent,"[35] predicting that its final membership composition shall include between twenty-five and thirty members. Nearly twenty years later, Asmus's forecast withstood the test of time, as current membership reached thirty states in 2020, and is expected to reach thirty-two in the near future, with the accession of Finland and Sweden.

Democracy as a Prerequisite for NATO Membership in the post–Cold War Era

In the early 1990s, NATO was a transformed Alliance, whose primary Cold War–era purpose of maintaining a Western-led democratic order while containing the Soviet pole has seemingly become redundant. The Alliance's survival, with its complex web of organizational structures and mechanisms, depended on its ability to reinvent itself and construct, define, and reframe its underlying principles in the direction of facilitating a novel vision of European security that embraces the newly established democracies in Central and Eastern Europe. In the words of former NATO senior official LTG Michel Yakovleff, after the Cold War NATO "decided to stay together, [and] having started as an Alliance against—NATO became an Alliance for," with a new founding idea of befriending former foes.[36] The November 1990 Charter of Paris for a New Europe—adopted at the CSCE Summit of heads of state or government (Conference on Security and Cooperation in Europe, later renamed the Organization for Security and Cooperation in Europe [OSCE]), powerfully emphasized the centrality of democracy in rebuilding Europe after the Cold War:[37] "This is a time of profound change. We declare that henceforth, our relations will be founded on respect and co-operation. . . . The courage of men and women . . . opened a new era of democracy, peace and unity in Europe. Ours is a time for fulfilling the hopes and expectations cherished for decades: steadfast commitment to democracy based on human rights and fundamental freedoms; prosperity through economic liberty and social justice." In June 1991, setting in motion a process which has been in the works since the early 1980s, NATO issued a statement on the partnership with the countries of central and eastern Europe, paving the way for close dialogue and exchange of ideas. According to the statement, this newly created discourse is to be based on NATO's long-lasting commitment to democratic norms.

> The long decades of European division are over. We welcome the major increase in the contacts by the Alliance with the Soviet Union and the other countries of Central and Eastern Europe . . . [and] the progress made by the peoples of these countries towards political and economic reform. We seek to build constructive partnerships with them to promote security and stability. Our own security is inseparably linked to that of all other states in Europe. The consolidation and preservation of democratic societies is therefore of direct and material concern to us . . . [and] we will continue to support reforms undertaken to establish democratic systems of government based on the rule of law and the respect for human rights.[38]

As the Soviet Union formally collapsed, NATO issued a statement on the situation in the Soviet Union, emphasizing that "In the space of only a few short years, Europe has been transformed. The historic events . . . heralded a new era of European democracy, peace and unity based on the rule of law," particularly stressing the necessity to sustain the newly elected democratic regimes in Eastern Europe.[39] In November 1991, NATO adopted an updated Strategic Concept—the Alliance's fundamental strategic document reflecting on its purpose, nature and concurrent challenges, first introduced in October 1949 and regularly revised since. Aside from the repeating commitment to a democratic way of life, the document reiterated the notion of rapprochement toward the East: "All the countries that were formerly adversaries of NATO have dismantled the Warsaw Pact and rejected ideological hostility to the West. They have, in varying degrees, embraced and begun to implement policies aimed at achieving pluralistic democracy, the rule of law, respect for human rights and a market economy."[40] As the document conceives a new strategic environment for the Alliance that is favorable in terms of conventional military threats, it makes an attempt to imagine how the post–Cold War constellation may morph into new challenges for NATO, and how these relate to the founding principles of democracy, rule of law, and peaceful dispute settlement.

> Alliance security interests can be affected by other risks of a wider nature, including proliferation of weapons of mass destruction, disruption of the flow of vital resources and actions of terrorism. . . . Based on common values of democracy, human rights and the rule of law, the Alliance has worked since its inception for the establishment of a just and lasting peaceful order in Europe. This Alliance objective remains unchanged . . . to provide foundations for a stable security environment in Europe, based on the growth of democratic institutions and commitment to the peaceful resolution of disputes.

Immediately afterward, NATO's November 1991 Declaration on Peace and Cooperation (Rome Declaration) commended the progress made by the newly formed Eastern European democracies in the direction of democratic reform and institutions-building. The wording demonstrated how closely the Alliance has been following the nuts and bolts of this endeavor, signaling the general vector of long-term integration.

> We have consistently encouraged the development of democracy in the Soviet Union and Central and Eastern Europe. We applaud the commitment of these countries to political and economic reform. We will support all steps towards reform and will give practical assistance to help them succeed in this

difficult transition. The Alliance can aid in fostering a sense of security in these countries . . . and make democratic change irrevocable. This is a dynamic process: the growth of democratic institutions throughout Central and Eastern Europe now calls for our relations to be broadened, intensified and raised to a qualitatively new level.[41]

A watershed moment in building NATO's post–Cold War agenda has been the establishment in December 1991 of the North Atlantic Cooperation Council (NACC)—a forum for dialogue with ex–Warsaw Pact states (officially dissolved in February 1991), that embodied an earlier July 1990 call for a new cooperative framework with Central and Eastern Europe states.[42] As the forum's creation paralleled the collapse of the Soviet Union, all eleven former republics were invited to take part in the NACC, expressing the Alliance's desire to facilitate a wide-scale discussion. The first NACC Ministerial session, held in December 1991, brought together all NATO member states, and the representatives of the former Soviet republics, the three Baltic states, Poland, Czechoslovakia, Hungary, Bulgaria, and Romania.[43] While the consultations that took place at the forum mostly concentrated on military coordination and management of post–Cold War movement of forces, it managed to deliver a first-time venue for deliberations and interpersonal exchanges, formally enhancing newly elected democratic institutions in Eastern Europe and supporting reforms. In 1997, the NACC was officially replaced by the Euro-Atlantic Partnership Council (EAPC), a multilateral forum for consultations on political and security-related issues between NATO member states and twenty partner countries, usually held on a monthly basis at the level of Ambassadors.

The next step in East-West NATO integration came in January 1994, with a declaration of the heads of state and government on the introduction of the Partnership for Peace program, a major milestone for incorporating these states into NATO further down the road. The program's rationale was derived from the Alliance's goal to foster ties with the newly established democratic regimes in Eastern and Central Europe, with an outlook on future integration.

We wish to strengthen ties with the democratic states to our East. . . . We expect and would welcome NATO expansion that would reach to democratic states to our East, as part of an evolutionary process. We have decided to launch an immediate program that will transform the relationship between NATO and participating states . . . beyond dialogue and cooperation. . . . Active participation in the Partnership for Peace will play an important role in the evolutionary process of the expansion of NATO.[44]

The PfP was tailor-made to facilitate a bilateral partnership between NATO and the participating states, including the formation of a new military coordination mechanism—Partnership Coordination Cells in Mons, Belgium—eventually succeeded by the Military Cooperation Division at the Supreme Headquarters Allied Powers, Europe (SHAPE). As testified in the Declaration of the Heads of State and Government, the program was designed to best reflect the unique needs and requirements to deliver on the promise of integration: "NATO will consult with any active participant at . . . a pace and scope determined by the capacity and desire of the individual participating states, we will work in concrete ways towards transparency in defence budgeting, promoting democratic control of defence ministries, joint planning, joint military exercises, and creating an ability to operate with NATO forces."

NATO's January 1994 Initiation Document reiterated the expectations for the program's contribution to eventually integrate into the Alliance those PfP members that demonstrated their democratic capacity: "We expect and would welcome NATO expansion that would reach to democratic states to our East, as part of an evolutionary process, taking into account political and security developments in the whole of Europe. . . . The Partnership will expand and intensify political and military cooperation . . . by promoting the commitment to democratic principles that underpin our Alliance."[45]

In June 1994, the Ministerial Meeting of the North Atlantic Cooperation Council mirrored the principles of the newly established PfP, emphasizing its commitment to democratic values: "Partnership for Peace is based on the commitment to democratic principles and human rights, to the preservation of democratic societies, their freedom from coercion and intimidation and the maintenance of the principles of international law. Twenty countries have already joined the PfP . . . [and] we look forward to others joining, including other CSCE states which are not members of the NACC."[46] At its core, the PfP was designed as a preparatory mechanism for future membership, as the US and other key member states had crossed the threshold for imagining NATO's future enlargements. Among other aims, it was designed to consolidate the democratization of civil-military relations in newly democratized Central and East Europe, and instill a culture of enhanced transparency and civilian control over the local military establishments. In May 1995, NATO heads of state and government expressed their confidence in the PfP, describing the program as a core bridge to integrate Eastern Europe into the Alliance, stressing that solely democracies shall be invited to partake in the program: "[NATO Heads of State] . . . strengthened NATO's outreach to its East by adopting the Partnership for Peace initiative and inviting all the new democracies to join us in new political and military efforts to work alongside the Alliance. They also decided that the Alliance expects and would welcome NATO enlargement that would reach to democratic states to our East, as part of an evolutionary process, taking into account political and security developments."[47] Shortly afterward, NATO released its seminal and most significant document to clearly define, outline and discuss the various aspects of enlargement for the coming decades—the 1995 Study on NATO Enlargement. This formative text recognizes the opportunity created by the end of the Cold War to reshape Europe's security environment, and leads with the notion of democratic values as one of the defining features for progress: "Enlargement will contribute to enhanced stability and security by . . . reinforcing the tendency toward integration and cooperation in Europe based on shared democratic values . . . encouraging and supporting democratic reforms."[48] The document grounds NATO's enlargement endeavor in the principles of the UN Charter, including its commitment to democratic values, freedom and peaceful resolution of international disputes, but states that ultimate decisions on expansion shall be based on the judgment of member states as to whether admitting an aspiring candidate contributes to regional security and stability: "There is no fixed or rigid list of criteria for inviting new member states. . . . Enlargement will be decided on a case-by-case basis and some nations may attain membership before others. Ultimately, Allies will decide by consensus whether to invite each new member to join according to their judgment of whether doing so will contribute to security and stability in the North Atlantic area."

Gebhardt von Moltke, then NATO assistant secretary general for Political Affairs, stressed in a January 1996 article the importance of the notion of democracy and its fundamental values as a core tenet of this program: "We need to create a continent that is increasingly united by a shared commitment to open, democratic societies, respect for human rights, and market economies. In a Europe which is growing together, international institutions, such as NATO and the European Union, have to be open to membership of countries of Central and Eastern Europe which share the same values and the same geographic and economic space."[49] Later on, however, the document clarifies that security and stability also entail promoting and sustaining democracy, and that NATO enlargement is aimed at "like-minded" democracies: "We want to develop further our relations with all newly independent states, whose independence and democracy constitute an important factor of security and stability for Europe." Furthermore, while the document repeatedly claims lack of fixed criteria, it does ascribe a tentative list of so-called membership expectations, including—and starting with—firm commitment to democracy, individual liberty and the rule of law. This reality strongly signals that respect for democracy constitutes one of the most important measures of membership.

> Possible new member states will be expected to conform to basic principles embodied in the Washington Treaty: democracy, individual liberty and the rule of law; Accept NATO as a community of like-minded nations; Commit to good faith efforts to build consensus within the Alliance; Commit to resolution of ethnic disputes, external territorial disputes or internal jurisdictional disputes by peaceful means; Show a commitment to promoting stability and well-being by economic liberty, social justice and environmental responsibility and established appropriate democratic and civilian control of the defence forces.

Several years before the introduction of NATO's Membership Action Plan in 1999, the Study on NATO Enlargement endorsed the PfP as the main institutional framework toward enlargement, enshrined in protecting and building democratic capacity among candidate states: "PfP will help partners undertake necessary defence management reforms as they establish the processes and mechanisms necessary to run a democratically controlled military organization . . . [and] assist possible new members to develop well-established democratic accountability and practices and to demonstrate their commitment to internationally-accepted norms of behavior." This framework was also inspired by the renewed spirit of democracy across the various regional and EU-related multilateral bodies, most prominently the Vienna Declaration of the Council of Europe in October 1993, stipulating that "the end of the division of Europe offers an historic opportunity to consolidate peace and stability on the continent. All our countries are committed to pluralist and parliamentary democracy, the indivisibility and universality of human rights, the rule of law and a common cultural heritage enriched by its diversity."[50] In the following years, key documents, concluding communiqués, and statements repeatedly cement the notion of promotion of democracy as a core purpose of the Alliance, as evident in a December 1996 NAC meeting in Defence Ministers session: "The Alliance's fundamental objective remains the creation of a Europe whole and free, through the promotion of peace, democracy, security, stability and cooperation."[51]

A few months later, at the NATO Summit that took place in Madrid in July 1997, optimism and confidence in the vision of a new democratic European order appeared to have peaked, as Allies were said to be "moving towards a realization of the vision of a just and lasting order of peace for Europe as a whole, based on human rights, freedom and democracy."[52] The democratic consolidation of Europe was celebrated as a core Alliance mission, with expectations to expand the circle of membership further beyond the Czech Republic, Poland, and Hungary, with democracy as a core concept in the process: "The considerations set forth in our 1995 Study on NATO Enlargement will continue to apply. . . . No European democratic country whose admission would fulfill the objectives of the Treaty will be excluded from consideration. . . . We recognise and take account of the positive developments towards democracy and the rule of law in a number of southeastern European countries, especially Romania and Slovenia." Following the 1999 enlargement round, NATO approved a new Strategic Concept, which stressed that "The Alliance remains open to new members . . . [and] no European democratic country whose admission would fulfil the objectives of the Treaty will be excluded from consideration."[53] Ever since, this wording will accompany the vast majority of NATO statements, speeches, and minutes regarding the notion of enlargement, and become a jargon-familiar catchphrase, sending an evergreen message that expansion is never off the table. In practice, the Washington Summit Communiqué charted the way for future enlargement rounds with the help of a carefully tailored new mechanism—the Membership Action Plan, adopted in April 1999. The MAP was created to assist aspiring members meet NATO's expectations for membership, with annual individual reports, consultations, and dialogue on the various political, military, bureaucratic, and logistical aspects of membership. The Communiqué alluded to the following expectations:

> The Alliance expects to extend further invitations in coming years to nations willing and able to assume the responsibilities and obligations of membership. . . . We welcome the aspirations of the nine countries currently interested in joining the Alliance . . . [and] approve a Membership Action Plan which includes: the submission of individual annual national programs; a focused and candid feedback mechanism on aspirant countries' progress; a clearinghouse to help co-ordinate assistance by NATO to aspirant countries; a defence planning approach for aspirants.[54]

The document is divided into five main chapters, each covering an important aspect of enlargement: political and economic issues, military and security matters, and issues related to resources and legal matters. As for the political and economic issues, the MAP directly highlights adherence to democratic principles: "Future members must conform to basic principles embodied in the Washington Treaty such as democracy, individual liberty and other relevant provisions, . . . settle their international disputes by peaceful means, . . . demonstrate commitment to the rule of law and human rights, . . . establish appropriate democratic and civilian control of their armed forces [and], . . . promoting stability and well-being by economic liberty, social justice and environmental responsibility."[55]

For all MAP participants, NATO has held annual and ad-hoc training sessions, seminars, workshops and reform consultations, accompanied by Alliance policy and military experts, who were tasked with promoting best practices among the aspiring countries. To date, seven NATO aspirant countries that took part in the MAP were able to ultimately gain full membership—Bulgaria, Estonia, Latvia, Lithuania, Romania, Slovakia, and Slovenia (2004); Albania and Croatia (2009); Montenegro (2017); and North Macedonia (2020). Bosnia and Herzegovina remains the sole participant in the MAP, having joined the program in 2010. At the NAC ministerial meeting in December 1999, member states committed to remain open to additional enlargement rounds, repeating the well-known mantra in Alliance documents and oral statements—NATO's intention to eventually include all European democracies: "The Alliance expects to extend further invitations in coming years to nations willing and able to assume the responsibilities and obligations of membership, and as NATO determines that the inclusion of these nations would serve the overall political and strategic interests of the Alliance. . . . No European democratic country whose admission would fulfil the objectives of the Washington Treaty will be excluded from consideration."[56]

As the Alliance was preparing for the adoption of a new Strategic Concept in 2010, the organization sanctioned a report by a group of experts titled "NATO 2020: Assured Security, Dynamic Engagement." The report, published in May 2010, widely discusses the Alliance's Open-Door Policy, underlying the primacy of democracy and the rule of law as the guiding principles of the enlargement process. "Since 1995, the process of enlargement has been guided by certain principles, including . . . Democratic values and full support for NATO's political vision, . . . the fair treatment of minority populations, . . . [and] peaceful resolution of domestic and international disputes."[57]

At the Lisbon Summit, NATO heads of state and government adopted the Alliance's new Strategic Concept, which has been in preparation and formation for several years. The document, titled Active Engagement, Modern Defence, lays the foundations for the Alliance's decision-making vis-à-vis enlargement in the second decade of the century. It praises the enlargement process for boosting Allied security, reiterates that NATO's door remains open, and highly acclaims the role of democracy, human rights, and the rule of law that underpin the Alliance.

> The door to NATO membership remains fully open to all European democracies. . . . We are determined to continue renewal of our Alliance so that it is fit for purpose in addressing the 21st century security challenges . . . because it is based on common values of individual liberty, democracy, human rights and the rule of law, and because our common essential and enduring purpose is to safeguard the freedom and security of its members. These values and objectives are universal and perpetual.[58]

In June 2021, NATO heads of state and government adopted the secretary general's agenda for NATO 2030—the fruit of a two-year consultation process among independent and organizational experts, mapping global challenges to the Alliance for the coming decade.[59] The document attributes a central role to democracy as the backbone of the Alliance's future, while acknowledging the internal domestic challenges to democracy: "Inside NATO, societal divisions have arisen and representative democracy is being challenged. In many ways, the Alliance could be said to be . . . far from invulnerable to such political turbulence. Now, as then, Allies have remained bound together by a combination of shared principles, democratic institutions, and the benefits of collective security." Identifying the need to protect the member states' democratic way of life, the document suggests enhancing the political component of the Alliance, while "bolstering the political dimension of NATO, including its foundations of shared democratic principles, and political tools." NATO's foundation mission to safeguard the freedom and common heritage of its members, while shielding the principles of democracy and individual liberty, remains extremely present throughout the document. Against this backdrop, the report recommends that the Allies "redouble their commitment to the democratic principles enshrined in the North Atlantic Treaty, with all Allies free to shape their own destinies within these bounds." The willingness to reassert NATO's core identity as a club of like-minded of democracies received institutional expression in the report's recommendation to establish a Center of Excellence for Democratic Resilience. A proposal first raised by NATO Parliamentary Assembly president in 2019, since its inclusion in the NATO 2030 report, the Assembly formed a dedicated working group, followed by the Assembly's Standing Committee recommendation in February 2022 to integrate the Center in the Alliance's new Strategic Concept.[60] At the Brussels Summit meeting in June 2021, the Alliance commissioned the formation of a new Strategic Concept, which—like its predecessors—aims to define NATO's mission statement and the overarching means by which it is to cope with the challenges that the future may hold. The document was finalized and released in tandem with the NATO Summit in Madrid, in June 2022. With the dramatic events of Russia's war in Ukraine in mind, the new Strategic Concept continues to build on the notions of democracy, the rule of law, and respect for human rights as the core instruments shaping the Alliance.[61] The document frames the Alliance's modern role around safeguarding democracy as a shared value underpinning NATO: "We remain steadfast in our resolve to protect our one billion citizens, defend our territory and safeguard our freedom and democracy. We will reinforce our unity, cohesion and solidarity, building on the . . . strength of our shared democratic values." The document also determines that all members are "bound together by common values: individual liberty, human rights, democracy and the rule of law," and that the current international architecture is characterized by authoritarian actors that challenge the NATO democratic way of life, referencing recent events in Ukraine. Finally, the most recent concept too adheres to the tradition of "open-door" politics, signaling openness for enlargement, by stating that "our door remains open to all European democracies that share the values of our Alliance, which are willing and able to assume the responsibilities and obligations of membership, and whose membership contributes to our common security."

Approaching the July 2023 NATO Summit in Vilnius, the NATO Parliamentary Assembly advised the Alliance to uphold the commitment to democratic values, as laid out in the new strategic concept, by establishing a NATO Center for Democratic Resilience in Brussels: "Urging the Heads of State and Government of the North Atlantic Alliance at their Summit in Vilnius . . . to operationalize the commitment to shared democratic values reaffirmed in the new Strategic Concept, including by establishing a Centre for Democratic Resilience at NATO Headquarters."[62] The Vilnius Summit declaration followed these footsteps, emphasizing that "Democratic values, the rule of law, and domestic reforms . . . are vital for regional cooperation and Euro-Atlantic integration,"[63] reaffirming the Alliance's commitment to protect the freedom and democracy of its one billion citizens.

Chapter 3

The Erosion of NATO's Democratic Tenet

Measuring the Democratic Composition of the Alliance: When the Numbers Tell a Story

How does the organizational emphasis on democratic norms, values, institutions, and adherence to the rule of law manifest in existing academic indices? Many empirical studies in political science and IR literature attempt to offer reliable data to build an answer for this puzzle. These data sets attend to a myriad of attributes that comprise the multifaceted concept of democracy, as it is broadly defined in the literature. To understand this important avenue of research methodology, a discussion of the conceptualization of democracy is warranted. The most rudimentary understanding of democracy has come to be famously described as "rule by the people," in a context of sovereign polities. Hence, a rather minimalist approach for operationalizing democracy is expected to focus on the notion of free and fair elections—coding states according to the characteristics of their electoral systems and procedures, examining whether elections are carried out peacefully and without interference, and eventually lead to a peaceful transition of power. Recent scholarship affiliated with this approached viewed the concept of democracy as a "set of political institutions in which properly contested, repeated elections are free and fair—as assessed by international observers from democratic countries."[1] This definition builds on earlier representations of democracy as "a regime in which governmental offices are filled as a consequence of contested elections,"[2] or more simply put—when incumbents actually step down when defeated. As noted by the latter, this state of affairs entails an active challenge posed by opposition forces to other political factions under the auspices of a competitive election process, in which outcomes are unknown in advance and are fully respected in the aftermath of events. However, as frequently claimed in various critiques of this approach, a plain definition focusing on the nature of the election process may not be theoretically sufficient to conceptualize the full range of regime complexity that is typical to developed democracies, characterized by fundamentals such as the rule of law, various personal, social and political freedoms, and a nuanced view of human rights. To illustrate this notion, scholars often use the US case study, in which—despite upholding a developed and perfectly executed electoral system for centuries—vast portions of the electorate were disregarded and excluded, including the African American community (until the Fifteenth Amendment to the U.S. Constitution in 1870), and, until the Nineteenth Amendment to the constitution in 1920, the entire female population.[3] More generally, women's suffrage—the unconditional right of women to fully participate in the election process—was often granted at extraordinarily late stages in the history of modern democracies: Switzerland only allowed women to participate in federal elections in 1971, Lichtenstein introduced women's suffrage as a result of a 1984 referendum, and Portugal fully abolished various limitation on women's vote as late as 1976. While all these states were considered democracies according to the binary criterion of free and fair elections long before instating women's suffrage, today it seems practically unimaginable to concur with such unripe classification. Moreover, while various polities may all be characterized as democratic according to the binary classification, the quality and diversity in the manner that they exercise their sovereignty is surely different. This may include, among other things, the domestic interpretation for upholding standards that can be widely considered as part of the "democratic basket," such as the rule of law, uprooting public sector corruption, and the freedom to exercise numerous personal freedoms. The external conduct and foreign relations of various democracies also play a role, as some regimes that domestically uphold free and fair elections adopt different norms in their behavior abroad, a notion that necessarily effects the domestic development and assimilation of democratic norms. Several democratic countries are currently under a certain form of investigation or preliminary examination by the International Criminal Court (ICC)[4]: Israel's practices with regard to the Palestinian arena; alleged crimes against humanity and war crimes committed in Afghanistan since 2003, including by US forces; possible crimes against humanity committed in the Philippines between 2011 and 2019, during the domestic "war on drugs" campaign; and a new preliminary examination into alleged crimes against humanity committed in Bolivia in 2020. All these examples represent states that are widely considered democratic according to a majority of existing indices. This understanding of complexity and domestic diversity (even among electoral democracies) makes a binary definition somewhat unaccommodating and insufficient to conceptualize a wholesome democratic regime. In a general sense, the underlying principle of these approaches entails the existence of a certain form of social contract between the sovereign polity and its citizens, under which the former undertakes the responsibility to provide governance and deliver public goods that contribute to the overall well-being, in exchange for a free and willful grant of the legitimacy to rule. While the former represents the basic building blocks of democratic rule, the de facto execution of the social contract (in its democratic form) entails measures such as free and fair elections and the establishment of a certain form of representative government.

As noted in the previous section, holding free and fair elections effectively translates the preferences of the general public into political output, and generates popular accountability and responsiveness. It does not, however, constitute an exhaustive representation of the notion of democracy, which entails a myriad of other traits that comprise the term. A modern scholarly account of the conceptualization of democracy suggests that the core component that underlies most existing definitions concentrates on the presence of substantial personal political freedoms in a given polity. The notion of political freedoms was said to be divided between the freedom of choice (the autonomy to choose political representatives and influence policy outcomes), freedom from tyranny (regime protective checks and balances to avert oppression), and the principle of equality to all in exercising such freedoms.[5] Building on Dahl's account of democracy as consisting of two major attributes—contestation and participation—Munck moves on to identify several components that comprise the two attributes: the right to form political parties, freedom of the press, the right to vote, fairness of the voting process, access of parties to public financing, and the extent of suffrage.[6] It is also useful to reflect on the notions of policy responsiveness and accountability, as they are often considered key in a comprehensive conceptualization of the democratic process. Democratic responsiveness is the translation of civilian input into the governing process, and is usually defined according to four key attributes: the formation of policy preferences, followed by mobilization and aggregation, eventually leading up to the point of implementation.[7] In other words, effective policy responsiveness involves a successful interface between public preferences and real-world policy decisions, and generally requires a competitive environment that allows deliberation. Political competitiveness can become constrained in an environment that allocates vastly imbalanced resources to incumbents, or when the interests of powerful actors are protected with the help of specialized legislative/statutory mechanisms such as gerrymandering (manipulating the boundaries of electoral districts in a manner that benefits particular candidates or parties). Accountability advances this notion one step further, as it involves an actual obligation to be held responsible for various policy choices, eventually enabling the engaging voters to punish rogue politicians for escaping proper liability for their own policy output. A thinner definition of accountability entails a mere obligation by political actors to inform and justify their actions in the eyes of their constituents (i.e., the notion of "answerability").[8]

As for NATO's point of view, free and fair elections are indeed imperative in order to perceive a candidate state as democratic, but insufficient with regard to the broader interpretation implied by the Alliance as the depiction of its core values. Such an account calls for an effective institutional translation of the results of a given election into policies that actively promote various civil liberties and social and political rights, taking into account the Western post–World War II approach to the centrality of personal freedoms that underlies the sometimes abstract democratic "way of life" NATO frequently references. Additionally, NATO emphasizes the importance of civilian control over the military establishment—a core component that is little if at all affected directly by the character of national elections, but rather builds on a political culture that views the notion of oversight over the execution of power as a central domestic principle. This notion is also valid for the element of economic and financial freedoms—as the Alliance frequently harnessed the component of a competitive market economy to describe its perception of how the democratic dimension is ideally designed. While economic freedoms do not always go hand in hand with political freedoms, the execution of a modern market economy requires certain institutional arrangements that are more frequently found in functioning democracies. To attend to this theme, a more nuanced view of a state's legislative and executive functions must be taken into account when considering the notion of democracy, and a certain analysis of equal opportunity structures for citizens—including political equality before the law—is warranted. Another core component is the domestic form of government—for example, presidential, parliamentary, or other models of mixed regimes—all may hold equal democratic attributes, but the particular form of appointing and dismissing the head of state and exercising authority is an important facet in characterizing types of polities.

Considering the application of the regime features mentioned above with regard to NATO member states, several prevalent indexes do indeed aim for a broader conceptualization of democracy, providing a more suitable and nuanced representation of the values presented in the inaugural NATO texts and speeches surveyed in the previous chapter. A prominent example is the Varieties of Democracy (V-Dem) data set[9]—a renowned series of indicators coded by country experts to conceptualize and measure the various tenets of global democracy since the late 1800s. This conceptualization rests on five approaches to defining democracy—electoral, liberal, participatory, deliberative, and egalitarian.[10] This definition coincides with other renowned conceptualizations of democracy, that rely on four central avenues—constitutional democracy, substantive democracy, procedural democracy, and process-oriented democracy.[11] Indeed, a process-oriented approach to democracy is reflected in a conceptualization that sees effective and equal participation in voting, relying on an inclusive interpretation that emphasizes active civilian contribution to the agenda-setting, as the core mechanism that underlines democracy.[12] In practice, these attributes are translated into formal devices that include a comprehensive free and fair election process and institutions whose role is to preserve various personal and societal freedoms. Mukand and Rodrik distinguish between liberal democracies and electoral democracies based on the interface between three variations of rights—property rights (protection against state expropriation), political rights (ensuring the impartiality of the electoral process), and civil rights, which attend to the dimension of equality. Accordingly, states characterized as liberal democracies guarantee all three forms of rights, while those defined as electoral democracies concentrate on property and political rights.[13] This interpretation coincides with the view that liberal democracies must defend minority rights and safeguard personal liberties, typically under a widely accepted constitution and checks and balances on the execution of power.[14] A model of this sort has been said to represent a Western interpretation of democracy, realized by the basic principle of majority rule and coupled with a decisive fortification of individual rights, as well as a strong emphasis on the rule of law and the institutional designs derived from it.[15] Other conceptualizations in the literature also include the models of a majoritarian democracy, which places an emphasis on the notion of majority rule, reflecting this principle via dedicated institutional and legal structures. The electoral component traces the basic extent to which rulers compete for their roles via broad and periodic elections, while the liberal component implies respect for individual and minority rights against oppression, and the participatory element evaluates the extent of active contribution by ordinary citizens to the political arena. The deliberative component is concerned with the provision of information and enabling open dialogues on national matters, while the egalitarian tenet looks into the actual levels of inequality in the exercise of rights and the division of resources. All modes of democracy eventually merge to represent an integrative structure that takes into account the principles of electoral competition via participatory ideals (governed by the people), individual rights and liberties, and a centralized majority rule that makes rationalized and well-debated outcomes and takes into account the notion of political equality before the law. This wholesome conceptualization constitutes the final score in this index, attempting to offer an evidence-based blend for evaluating democratic attributes. This approach is particularly highly regarded, winning V-Dem points for academic integrity and balance. According to this index, the levels of democracy among NATO members have been constantly eroding in the last two decades (see figure 3.1).[16]

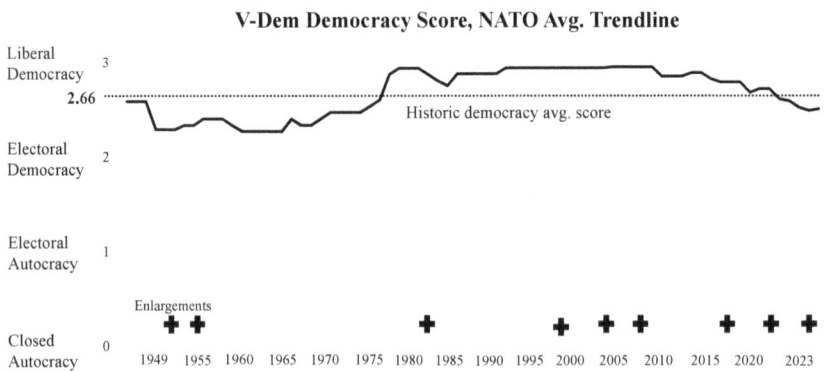

Figure 3.1. V-Dem Democracy Score, NATO Avg. Trendline. *Source*: V-Dem.

The trend line presented in figure 3.1 demonstrates the historic fluctuations in the average levels of democracy among the members of the Alliance, in light of its eight enlargement rounds. At its inception, the original group of NATO founding-states (Belgium, Canada, Denmark, France, Iceland, Italy, Luxembourg, Netherlands, Norway, Portugal, the UK, and the US) averaged at a democracy score of 2.58—slightly closer to the pole of liberal democracy (a score of 3.0). After the first round of enlargement, incorporating Greece and Turkey (1952), this score dropped to 2.28—closer to the pole of electoral democracy, which maintains free and fair elections but excludes the majority of attributes typical to liberal democracies: guaranteed access to justice, personal liberty, and sufficient levels of the rule of law. The average score slightly improved with the accession of West Germany in 1955, and peaked in the mid-1970s, reaching a nearly flawless score of 2.93 in 1977. With the inclusion of Spain (1982), and during the first Eastern European enlargement wave in 1999 (the integration of the Czech Republic, Hungary, and Poland), the average democracy scored steadily persevered above 2.9, highlighting the robustness of democracy in early post–Cold War enlargements. Indeed, while the 1999 enlargement round was relatively strong in terms of adherence to democracy, the large expansion of 2004 (Bulgaria, Estonia, Latvia, Lithuania, Romania, Slovakia, and Slovenia) moved the needle by 0.1 point toward an average of 2.84, dropping further to 2.78 after the accession of Albania and Croatia (2009), and to as low as 2.5 in the aftermath of the Alliance's inclusion of Montenegro (2017) and North Macedonia (2020). This concluded a striking drop of 0.5 points over the course of seventeen years, altering the democratic nature and composition of the entire Alliance. In the aftermath of the Russian invasion of Ukraine in February 2022, Finland and Sweden historically opted to abandon their longtime neutrality and military nonalignment and sought NATO membership. As of early 2024, Finland already gained full membership, while Sweden still attempts to overcome political skirmish with Turkey and Hungary. This turn of events had slightly enhanced NATO's overall democratic composition, rising from 2.43 to 2.45 on average. Another small increase is expected after Sweden's membership is finalized.

Table 3.1 offers more in-depth insight into this tectonic movement, integrating the separate rankings of four prominent democracy indices that cover the period since 2000—the Freedom House Political Rights Index;[17] the Polity IV index[17] the Economist Intelligence Unit Democracy Index,[18]

Table 3.1. Normalized democracy rankings at accession year

Candidate Country	Accession Year	Freedom House Index at Year	Polity IV Ranking at Year	Economist Democracy Index at Year	V-Dem Score at Year
Turkey	1952	n/a	0.90 (Democracy)	n/a	0.33 (Electoral Autocracy)
Greece	1952	n/a	0.40 (Open-Anocracy)	n/a	0.33 (Electoral Autocracy)
W. Germany	1955	n/a	1.00 (Full Democracy)	n/a	1.00 (Liberal Democracy)
Spain	1982	n/a	1.00 (Full Democracy)	n/a	0.66 (Electoral Democracy)
Czech Rep.	1999	0.92 (Free)	1.00 (Full Democracy)	n/a	1.00 (Liberal Democracy)
Hungary	1999	0.92 (Free)	1.00 (Full Democracy)	n/a	1.00 (Liberal Democracy)
Poland	1999	0.92 (Free)	0.95 (Democracy)	n/a	1.00 (Liberal Democracy)
Estonia	2004	1.00 (Free)	1.00 (Full Democracy)	0.77 (Flawed Democracy)	1.00 (Liberal Democracy)
Latvia	2004	1.00 (Free)	0.90 (Democracy)	0.74 (Flawed Democracy)	0.66 (Electoral Democracy)
Lithuania	2004	0.92 (Free)	1.00 (Full Democracy)	0.74 (Flawed Democracy)	1.00 (Liberal Democracy)
Romania	2004	0.75 (Free)	0.95 (Democracy)	0.71 (Flawed Democracy)	0.66 (Electoral Democracy)
Slovakia	2004	1.00 (Free)	0.95 (Democracy)	0.74 (Flawed Democracy)	1.00 (Liberal Democracy)
Slovenia	2004	1.00 (Free)	1.00 (Full Democracy)	0.80 (Full Democracy)	1.00 (Liberal Democracy)
Bulgaria	2004	0.92 (Free)	0.95 (Democracy)	0.71 (**Flawed Democracy**)	0.66 (Electoral Democracy)
Albania	2009	0.67 (**Partly Free**)	0.90 (Democracy)	0.59 (**Hybrid Regime**)	0.66 (Electoral Democracy)
Croatia	2009	0.83 (Free)	0.90 (Democracy)	0.68 (**Flawed Democracy**)	0.66 (Electoral Democracy)
Montenegro	2017	0.67 (**Partly Free**)	0.90 (Democracy)	0.57 (**Hybrid Regime**)	0.33 (**Electoral Autocracy**)
North Macedonia	2020	0.54 (**Partly Free**)	0.90 (Democracy)	0.60 (**Hybrid Regime**)	0.66 (Electoral Democracy)
Finland	2023	1.00 (Free)	1.00 (Full Democracy)	0.93 (Full Democracy)	1.00 (Liberal Democracy)

Source: Freedom House; Polity IV; The Economist; V-Dem.

and the V-Dem Index). The Freedom House Political Rights Index assesses the extent of political and civil liberties within states on a 1–7 scale, dividing political systems into three categories: free (1.0–2.5 points); partly free (3.0–5.0 points), and not free (5.5–7 points). Countries are awarded points for political rights (electoral processes, political pluralism, and functioning of government) and civil liberties indicators (freedom of expression, associational rights, rule of law, and personal liberties). Based on dedicated yearly surveys, constructed in accordance to the corresponding degree of freedoms, these are eventually combined to an overall score dividing various regimes between the said categories. The relevant scores for NATO enlargement countries under this index exemplify how three new member states were ranked partly free at their accession year (Albania, Montenegro, and North Macedonia). Another particularly prevalent democracy index, widely cited in the literature, is the Polity IV ranking—which classifies regimes according to a scale ranging from autocracy (a score of minus ten to minus six), anocracy (minus five to five), and democracy (six to ten). The final ranking relies on six measurement components that assess "the quality of executive recruitment; constraints on executive authority and political competition, and changes in the institutionalized qualities of governing authority."[19] According to this index, only three candidate states held the status of full democracy (i.e., a score of ten) at the year of accession, while the rest ranked within the minimal democratic range (six to nine). The Economist Intelligence Unit Democracy Index classifies regime levels of democracy based on civil liberties, political participation, electoral process, the functioning of government, and political culture. According to this index, only two enlargement states qualified as full democracies (Slovenia and Finland), that is, political systems with robust political cultures, functioning governmental arrays and independent media, judiciary and uninterrupted opposition forces. Six other NATO members were classified as flawed democracies (Estonia, Latvia, Lithuania, Romania, Slovakia, and Bulgaria)—countries with free and fair elections, that experience "significant weaknesses in some aspects of democracy, including problems in governance, an underdeveloped political culture and low levels of political participation."[20] Three other NATO states—Albania, Montenegro, and North Macedonia—were dubbed hybrid regimes. This category incorporates polities with "substantial election irregularities . . . government pressure on opposition parties and candidate . . . serious weaknesses in political culture and weak rule of law, civil society and political culture."[21] As of 2021, hybrid regimes represent around 20 percent of the world's regimes—thirty-five countries, that incorporate 15 percent of the global population. No NATO members were defined as authoritarian—where heavy restrictions on basic freedoms and basic respect for human rights is absent. Last, the Varieties of Democracy (V-Dem) dataset encompasses a series of indicators, coded by area specialists who aim to evaluate the robustness of a myriad of democratic sub-components in a wide array of independent states since 1800.[22] In assessing the vitality of democracy, the index ranks states based on their performance in such elements of democracy pertaining to its electoral, liberal, participatory, deliberative, and egalitarian characteristics. As explained above, NATO's overall level of democracy has been eroding since 2004, after maintaining a nearly perfect score of three out of three (liberal democracy) since the mid-1970s.

Despite their advantages and enhanced sensitivity, these indices too suffer from certain weaknesses, particularly over the consequences of aggregating scores in many separate components into an overall assessment.[23] This methodological practice hampers the reliability of these indexes and makes it harder to interpret the actual quality of democracy in a comparative manner, as countries with perfect Polity IV scores such as Denmark, Panama, and Uruguay are inherently different from each other, and their flawless scores rely on divergent conditions and preferences. Other limitations include enhanced reliance on secondary sources, especially to cover earlier years, increased dependence on survey and polling data (which can sometimes prove particularly problematic in areas with accessibility challenges and higher public suspicion rates), as well as cultural differences that may drive undesirable and artificial differences between countries. Finally, it has also been noted that several of these indexes tend to conflate personal and group freedoms, rights, or liberties with the notion of democracy, somewhat expanding the boundaries of this term to areas worthy of independent examination and evaluation, as the "democratic," family may seem more limited in nature. Nonetheless, these tools are still highly regarded as generally dependent, thoughtful and constantly improving measurements that provide a trustworthy assessment of the levels of democracy in domestic contexts, especially when compared to binary indices and other nonquantitative assessments. It is important to emphasize, however, that real-world dynamics tend not to stick to the script when considering building or managing democratic clubs or other groupings in global political. A highly relevant representation of this principle is the US-hosted "Summit for Democracy" (virtually hosted by President Biden in December 2021, followed with second session in

March 2023), aimed to convene leaders across government, civil society, and the private sector from more than 100 democratic countries invited by the US to take part in the event. While the Summit aimed to "set forth an affirmative agenda for democratic renewal and to tackle the greatest threats faced by democracies today through collective action,"[24] it is particularly thought-provoking to explore the criteria and various political considerations that drove the Biden administration to invite certain actors to the event and abandon others. According to the indexes surveyed above, many of the Summit's participants cannot be considered fully democratic, including European nations such as Albania, African countries like Angola and the Democratic Republic of Congo, and others whose democratic status is heavily debated (e.g., Armenia, Ecuador, and Iraq). Several participants are considered authoritarian regimes, most notably Pakistan. Surprisingly, among those uninvited states are core NATO Allies like Hungary and Turkey—where considerable democratic backsliding has taken place over the last decade—while other seemingly comparable nations in terms of democratic decline (e.g., Poland and Brazil) were in fact included among the participants. Overall, about 70 percent of all participant states are considered fully democratic according to Freedom House, while the remaining participants are either defined as partly free or not free. V-Dem rankings display similar conclusions, emphasizing entirely nondemocracies such as Iraq, Malaysia, Pakistan, and others. Overwhelmingly, the composition of the list of participants suggests that political and diplomatic considerations were essentially at play in constructing the concept of the Summit. Recent commentary of the US decision-making in this regard noted that regional dynamics played a major role in deciding on the participants (e.g., inviting Israel and Iraq as representatives from the Middle East), and US strategic interests vis-à-vis Pakistan, the Philippines, and Ukraine were also considered.[25]

Another core aspect of the wider notion of democracy and associated values and norms is the degree of domestic respect for human rights. While not directly related to the core conceptualization and interpretation of democracy, respect for human rights is deeply correlated with democracy and often constitutes an extension of it—as is also evident in the myriad references to human rights in NATO inaugural text and speeches. Data from two prominent indexes shed light on the human rights practices of those Allies that scored lower on democracy. First, the CIRI Human Rights Data Project, containing standards-based records on government respect for fifteen universally recognized human rights for 202 countries between 1981and 2011, as quoted in the Latent Human Rights Protection Scores project.[26] Another helpful resource is the human rights chapter of the Fragile State Index, measuring freedom of the press, civil liberties, political freedoms, human trafficking, political imprisonment, religious persecution, torture, and executions since 1999[27] (for an evaluation of NATO member states' human rights records—see table 3.2).

As table 3.2 exemplifies, Romania, Slovakia, Bulgaria, Albania, Montenegro, and North Macedonia are all characterized as "weak" in terms of human rights protection—an insufficient result, which gradually becomes the norm in recent decade expansions. This notion leaves much to be desired, as liberal democracies are typically particularly adamant on this key tenet. After laying out the various conceptualizations, scores, and complexities of the most prominent democracy indexes and evaluating NATO's position within this space, the next section attends to this reality from a theoretical perspective. In doing so, it offers original framework

Table 3.2. Normalized Human Rights performance indicators, Eastern European NATO members since 1999

Candidate Country	Accession Year	Human Rights Protection Score	Human Rights— Fragile States Index
Czech Republic	1999	0.69 (fair)	n/a
Hungary	1999	**0.65 (weak)**	n/a
Poland	1999	0.80 (fair)	n/a
Estonia	2004	0.69 (fair)	0.63 (fair)
Latvia	2004	0.69 (fair)	0.63 (fair)
Lithuania	2004	0.74 (fair)	0.63 (fair)
Romania	2004	**0.49 (weak)**	**0.52 (weak)**
Slovakia	2004	**0.65 (weak)**	**0.54 (weak)**
Slovenia	2004	0.76 (fair)	0.63 (fair)
Bulgaria	2004	**0.52 (weak)**	**0.51 (weak)**
Albania	2009	**0.58 (weak)**	**0.42 (weak)**
Croatia	2009	0.76 (fair)	**0.53 (weak)**
Montenegro	2017	**0.62 (weak)**	**0.55 (weak)**
North Macedonia	2020	**0.55 (weak)**	**0.58 (weak)**

Source: Human Rights Protection score; Human Rights—Fragile States Index.

to engage with the question of what drove NATO to willingly erode its stringent criteria for democratic conditionality for candidate states.

NATO's Decision-making on Enlargement as a "Normalization of Deviance": A New Theoretical Framework

What explains NATO's willingness to disregard the existing organizational democratic conditionality benchmarks in the process of considering potential members? To evaluate this theme, I argue that the relaxed enlargement standards result from a gradual process of organizational socialization. This process involves lowering the requirements for democracy as a condition for accession, ultimately establishing these reduced criteria as the new norm. This phenomenon builds on the notion of normalization of deviance—a term coined by Diane Vaughan as part of a sociological-cultural study of the US National Aeronautics and Space Administration during the period that led up to the 1986 *Challenger* crash.[28] Vaughan systematically studied the organizational environment, norms, and day-to-day practices that enabled the disaster, focusing on NASA's decision to maintain the regular operation of its space shuttle, in spite of a well-known manufacturing defect in a particular part (known as the O-ring), designed to seal the vessel's joints. Organizational patterns that encouraged NASA staff to move forward despite acknowledging the risks involved, normalizing negligent professional behavior in the name of advancement and fast technological evolution, eventually pushed a culture that standardized the practice of turning a blind eye on mischief in the name of the larger cause. In the process of normalization of deviance, over time the irregular behavior becomes typical and well accepted, until newer generations of practitioners are sometimes not even aware of the previous norm, and are entirely blind to the formerly deviant practice they inherited. While Vaughan's original conceptualization referred to NASA's practices leading up to the *Challenger* explosion, researchers have identified the same attributes and tendencies that drove the *Columbia* disaster in 2001—demonstrating how the exacerbation of widely acknowledged design defects drove deviant behavior in the context of both tragedies.[29] In addition to flawed organizational patterns in NASA, the concept of normalization of deviance has been applied to study numerous other issue areas, including management,[30] business,[31] medicine,[32] and economic decision-making.[33] As expected, these and other examples lucidly demonstrate how various organizational norms gradually and inadvertently weaken until they become standard practice in the field—which usually results in a certain form of damage, disruption, and in some cases, tragedy. In the helm of IOs, a well-known line of investigation studied the UN Secretariat and the UN Refugee Agency (UNHCR), vividly demonstrating the process of bureaucratic adjustment using seemingly small behavior alternations that eventually spill into deviant behavior with regard to the most important humanitarian efforts (e.g., practices concerning refugee repatriation).[34] According to this approach, normalization of deviance was only one of several "IO pathologies" that stem from IO organizational culture, while the others include the irrationality of rationalization, universalism, organizational insulation, and cultural contestation.[35] At the core of the notion of normalization lies the idea according to which entire generations of staffers and key position holders across various organizational disciplines become accustomed to certain behavioral shifts, until these become the norm. This implies an erosion of previously ironclad organizational principles, in a manner that is eventually objectively visible (e.g., the disregard of certain instructions in the production process). In the process of this gradual erosion, transpires a seemingly meaningless deviation that almost always occurs underneath the surface, leaving the various actors involved under the impression that no harm is caused and that the quality of the "product" remains unaffected. Deviant conduct can result from behavioral interactions to which actors respond negatively or perceive as undesirable[36]—a notion that can only materialize after the deviant norm has amounted to actual influence on events or damage to so-called products. Be this "product" space shuttles, industrial steel pipes or the day-to-day function of international organizations—it is vital that initially, the deviation remains unnoticed and does not inflict visible consequences, but eventually becomes visible and reflected on. This understanding entails a combination between the subjective-societal nature of interpreting deviations and a more realist idea of objective manifestation. Certain organizational characteristics are likely to enhance the likelihood for efficient trickling of deviant behavior. For instance, weak regulatory regimes and inherently frail organizational enforcement mechanisms can play a significant role in the ability of the norm in question to bypass the oversight system and gain a hold within the group.[37] This notion coincides with the lack of fitting oversight and governance structures in the form of internal auditors or an effective ombudsman position. The latter are particularly likely to constantly scrutinize within-organizational behavioral patterns and perform routine observations designed to prevent the formation of corrupt or inefficient habits. Alternatively, organizations may adopt various forms of incentive mechanisms to encourage reporting, or even awareness by low- and mid-level employees that become aware of faulty organizational norms.[38] These may include various "whistleblower" protection programs and other mechanisms designed to encourage responsible and change-oriented employees to actively notice and notify the organizational authorities of potentially harmful habits. In lieu of such mechanisms, it becomes more probable for professional and bureaucratic staff to develop organizational complacency, which entails a certain structural blindness. Organizational complacency may easily lead to other harmful behavioral norms taking hold, expanding the cycle of deviance. In an analysis of the 2003 Columbia shuttle explosion, NASA organizational complacency was said to be composed of several components—overconfidence in expert competences, unwarranted confidence placed in technological measures and excessive group thinking without proper diversity of opinion.[39] Among the possible strategies to manage organizational complacency are the provision of further autonomy to analysts and other core figures, introducing new approaches for risk management and the formation of mechanisms to mitigate professional dissent.

At the subjective level, the shared knowledge of deviation may remain concealed, as individuals are usually exposed to it at different time frames and act with a degree of uncertainty with regard to the validity of the norm in question. This is particularly applicable to new employees, who are more likely to feel uncomfortable to challenge existing organizational behavioral norms, even when presented with official guidelines that contradict the de facto work environment habits. Moreover, while deviant behavior is frequently met with some form of negative reaction, the normalization process frames deviant behavior as part of common-practice organizational culture—when offenders are rewarded rather than ostracized. This notion may prove particularly true when other parallel organizations also adopt a similar norm or behavior, embedding it into their own conduct, making the deviant conduct cross-sectional. For instance, as NATO decides to integrate an inspiring candidate state into the organization, this decision constitutes a valuable signal for other IOs that may consider the same states as candidates—most notably the EU. The expansion process of these two central IOs in post–World War II global order has frequently been intertwined: after the democratization of Spain and its integration into NATO in 1982, it became an EU member state in 1986; many Eastern and Central European states simultaneously became EU and NATO members in 2004, including Estonia, Latvia, Lithuania, Slovakia, and Slovenia, and Croatia's NATO membership in 2009 was followed by its accession to the EU in 2013. Finally, two of NATO's newest member states—North Macedonia and Albania are in the preliminary stages of EU membership negotiations, after the European Council provided a green light for the process in March 2020. In July 2022, the EU held its first intergovernmental conference with Albania and North Macedonia—a joint session between ministers and EU officials, meeting with the candidate's counterparts.

Other intertwined examples exist in additional issue areas across the IO universe, as bureaucratic and professional personnel in these organizations feed off each other and frequently share relevant insight and knowledge. This notion was seminally described as moral disengagement, as organizations become numb with regard to their responsibility for deviant behavior, simply because they rationalize the collective immoral behavior of their peers and other actors in their proximity as a justification for harmful conduct.[40]

At the organizational level, after the deviant behavioral norm has already become embedded in the structural and day-to-day practice, it is extremely difficult to uproot, as long-standing customs that remain unchecked over time are assimilated into the organization in a persistent manner.[41] However, normalization of a deviant norm is not irreversible, but denormalizing long-standing organizational behavior requires revised institutional framing—which may either be driven as a result of leadership reshuffles, or in a "bottom-up" manner, as an internal enterprise. The latter can be supported by institutional entrepreneurs—actors who actively identify the existing problem set and are able to grasp the hazardous potential it may inflict on the organization.[42] Under their leadership, newly injected motivations and senses of meaning are developed, driving a sluggish course of gradual correction, through raising awareness and mitigating alternative measures and practices. Such actors provide a clear alternative that if applied convincingly enough—can contribute to resist deviant habits, as demonstrated in an analysis of loan repayment practices among a large sample of Chinese business firms.[43] Alternatively, newly elected or appointed organizational leaders may also drive a process of denormalization, as it is uncommon for them to be bound by their predecessors' practices, and at times they are even required by the appointing authority to reinvigorate a seemingly stagnated organization. This notion could drive an internal review of organizational practices, leading up to the resurfacing of the corrupt norm. Then, denormalization may occur.

Leadership reshuffles often drive an internal organizational process of reappraisal of various internal practices, which may inadvertently flesh out the deviant norm and recommend technical amendments to mitigate it.

Vaughan identifies three core tenets that underpin the process of organizational normalization of deviance, all under the broader theme of "organizational culture." In the context of IR, the cultural aspects of international organizations are rooted in the tradition of the constructivist school of thought. Constructivists assert substantial roles to IOs in international politics, and often see them as reflections of social processes and ideas, maintaining interpretations that rely on norms, beliefs, and knowledge are best suited to explain IO behavior.[44] This perception builds on the assumption that for most actors in the international arena, breaking fundamental norms of behavior, especially in the field of human rights and essential freedoms, constitutes a costly move that infringes on their identity, and entails certain reputational consequences. According to constructivists, reputations in global politics comprise of audience beliefs about various actors (states, IOs, NGOs, and others), taking into accounts their history, perceived capabilities, and intentions. These are then gained or lost, and ultimately constitute an important component in international relations, particularly so with regard to IOs. Building on this departure point, constructivists ascribe IOs a central role in global politics, in contrast to the realist interpretation of IOs as sets of rules built to serve the interest of powerful actors. As part of this worldview, constructivists particularly stress the influence of organizational culture. This notion can be defined as a set of shared ideologies, norms, and routines that shape the expectations of the various organizational actors with regard to the manner in which agendas and responsibilities are determined, designated, and eventually implemented and evaluated.[45] A related conceptualization views organizational culture as an embedded system of rules, rituals, and beliefs.[46] Importantly, organizational culture—with IO cultural aspects in particular, given their highly heterogenous and diverse environments—is key to understanding decision-making machineries and overarching principles. Organizational culture also affects the bureaucratic composition of IOs, playing important roles in constructing an autonomous organizational identity. One of the most notable examples for the notion of autonomous organizational identity is the possibility for the development of organizational slack—when organizations autonomously initiate undesirable policy-making, contrary to the original preferences of the delegating member states, as thoroughly discussed in chapter 1.

To shed light on the practical mechanisms by which normalization of deviance takes place, Vaughan identified three devices that work simultaneously to manufacture this dynamic.[47] The first of those vehicles is the production of culture, according to which deviant behavioral patterns penetrate into the organizational culture (e.g., NASA's reluctance to consider considerable hazards in the process of preparation for the shuttle launch and beforehand). Second, Vaughan identified a factor called the culture of production, under which mounting pressures from within and outside the organization instigate incentives to turn a blind eye on various risks and cautionary procedures in order to enable faster delivery. Last, by a process of structural secrecy, limited access to undisclosed and privileged information is used to hamper due process and manipulated to create a "business as usual" atmosphere. As these mechanisms, taken separately or combined, enable the substantiation of an organizational normalization of deviance, it is particularly interesting to assess the internal process within NATO vis-à-vis enlargement with reference to the latter criteria. NATO is a complex organizational web of thousands of employees who originate from thirty member states, with headquarters, offices, regional bureaus, and various military and civilian agencies across myriad locations. This entails countless specializations, roles, and bureaucratic avenues—all extremely susceptible to possible normalization of deviance. The NATO organizational arrays involved in enlargement considerations and recommendations is quite vast. Most notable, however, is the role of the Political Affairs and Security Policy Division (PASP), whose mission is to examine and evaluate an aspiring state's overall compatibility for membership, focusing on the political, legal, administrative, and regulatory aspects of the candidacy, with the purpose of drafting a clear strategy and making policy recommendations to the NATO leadership. This evaluation will then be weighted against the military and operational assessment of capabilities and overall strategic advantage for the Alliance. Understandably, this process entails an extremely sensitive scenery for varying interpretations of the potential suitability of candidates, inevitably influenced by the organizational culture and the personal background and judgment of those individual professionals who make policy recommendations. This is further enhanced by a normative environment, which originated during an extremely hopeful moment in time after the collapse of the Soviet Union, placing a substantial emphasis on democratization and the central role of democracy in the future form of the Alliance. As these expectations formulate after the Cold War, in subsequent enlargement rounds it gradually became more challenging to uphold the same strict standards of democracy, generating a strategic dilemma between continuous growth and—on the other hand—maintaining the strong standard of democracy across the Alliance. The principle of the culture of production—according to which expectations for continued growth enhance production pressures—captures the essence of this dilemma, as it becomes practically impossible to deliver on the promise of democracy with a dwindling pool of candidates, characterized by increasingly lower democratic standards. As emphasized in a recent analysis of this topic, NATO was forced to slacken on its enlargement criteria in order to meet the demands for sustained enlargement.[48] Enlargement, in this case, represents the so-called product, driving organizational socialization of the lower standards of democracy as an inevitable reality, regardless of the original normative expectations reflected in the Alliance's robust democratic membership conditionality.

Elite Interviews with NATO Personnel: An Evaluation of the Prospects for Normalization of Deviance

To further substantiate the many manifestations of the principles of normalization of deviance and its three elements (the production of culture, the culture of production, and structural secrecy), this section lays out the results of a series of elite interviews with prominent NATO figures, carried out during and after my tenure as research fellow at the NATO Defense College in Rome in 2019 (for a full list of interviewees and communications, see Appendix). The conversations focused on professionals from the Political Affairs and Security Policy Division and other NATO figures, but also involved military personnel from various member states and national permanent representatives to the NATO headquarters in Brussels. The interviewees were either directly involved or witnessed from within the internal dynamics during the progression of accession negotiations and decision making over the recent two decades. The methodology of elite interviews is efficient for attaining firsthand accounts of strategic organizational intersections, and provides important context for complicated bureaucratic processes.[49] This approach allowed me to emphasize the role of those individuals likeliest to provide an intimate assessment of how the enlargement deliberations on the organizational level actually took place behind closed doors. It is, however—pursuant to the book's line of argumentation—concentrated on the IO perspective of the enlargement process, and hence not expected to fully convey a domestic standpoint.

All interviews carried out with NATO officials involved two lines of questioning. First, all face-to-face interviewees were presented with a nonstructured question that attended to the notion of the erosion of democracy in enlargement decisions. The wording for this question was as follows: *In your opinion, has the Alliance lowered its standards of adherence to democracy, as part of the enlargement process?* This wording was selected to allow the interviewee with the greatest amount of autonomy for interpreting the notion of democratic conditionality as a core pillar of the enlargement process. Along these lines, one respondent noted—in line with the concept of normalization—that over time the Alliance has become less adamant about matters related to democracy and human rights, acknowledging the limitations vested in this situation: "We are less strict about democracy and human rights than what we used to be. . . . NATO is not comprised of perfect democracies, but as long as the general democratic trend of a candidate is positive . . . we should give them a chance." This respondent opined that the organization was indeed more stringent on its democratic conditionality in the past, attributing the shift to the perceived inherent limitations of reality, apologetic about the current organization approach. This notion constitutes a good illustration of the concept of production of culture, since deviance in this case is rationalized, internalized, and actually presented as encouraging. Other respondents explained—in an attempt to rationalize the constantly eroding organizational admissibility standards—that NATO considers democracy indexes to be mechanisms aimed at future improvement, rather than real-time evaluation, and acknowledge the politicization of the decision-making: "Enlargement is eventually a political instrument to attain stability in the North Atlantic region . . . and therefore there's no clear line in the sand for firm political membership criteria. . . . We consider the indices to be more of a future roadmap." This constitutes another demonstration of the optimistic approach, rationalizing the poor results newcomers obtained in the various indices, distancing NATO from its original democratic conditionality. A different official, personally involved in past enlargement negotiations, offered a retrospect justification, suggesting that the political requirements set out under the framework of the MAP were too ambitious, substantiating the likelihood of a cognitive process that took place in the minds of decision-makers on enlargement: "The MAP was designed as an extremely ambitious framework . . . but over time there has been a general decrease in the attentiveness of particular criteria, and what became important was a more general sense that the candidate operates in an honest fashion and show a real desire for improvement." This notion was also echoed by a NATO military official, who attributed a central role to the political considerations of the largest NATO allies in the overall process of enlargement: "It (MAP—the author) started as a grand desire to democratize every country in the region . . . but very quickly the U.S. came to the realization that this approach was in the way of actual progress in the further integration of the North Atlantic region."

The underlying logic of these approaches is reparative: the respondents suggest that initial requirements—enshrined in NATO's fundamental texts and documents—were exaggerated and overstated, in need for readjustment. In other words, it is NATO's founders that originally overstepped in their assessment of the limits of democratic expansion, rather than the modern-day NATO organizational democratic flexibility. In the language of normalization of deviance, these statements express the logic of structural secrecy: the officials viewed conditionality mechanisms as void, purposely misinterpreting them, taking advantage of their privileged access to promote a narrative where they were actually overestimated. Another demonstration of the principle of structural secrecy lies in the view expressed by a civilian PASP Division analyst, voicing their distrust in existing indices as part of a construction of an alternative perception—in line with the constructivist school of thought that sees identities as formed by behavioral and social contexts: "Some of these so-called metrics portray only a partial picture, and that's why we examine every bit of information ourselves, whether open-sourced or confidential, our job is to assess the reality as we see it." This is complemented by a quote from a NATO military official, who downplayed the importance of regime types and the behavior of the political establishment, expressing an abstract, perhaps futile hope that in the so-called moment of truth these regimes can be expected to adhere to democratic standards: "I regularly meet with all kinds of colleagues from recent member states . . . and I know for a fact that what the regime does politically is separate from the reality of how they handle things where it really matters." One step further, a different respondent acknowledged that failure in advancing democratic standards does not necessarily disqualify an aspiring nation from gaining membership (expressing the idea of culture of production): "It's true that some of these countries made nice progress in the military requirements, with almost no evolvement in democratic standards. . . . While this is not ideal, we did think at the time that this should not stand as a sole obstacle to membership." This argument builds on imagined confidence, as today's hybrid and partly free regimes are in no way obligated to alter their governance standards after accession. Quite the contrary—after being integrated into the Alliance, NATO holds no powers over any member's domestic policy aspect or external decision-making. This further renders the hopeful expectation that Allies shall alter their behavior entirely void. On a similar note, a different NATO military official mentioned that the Alliance often views new members—mostly smaller states—as politically insignificant, and hence it might be more inclined to focus on their geostrategic positioning rather than dwell on their democratic shortcomings: "In terms of contribution to the Alliance, small countries like Montenegro or Albania provide invaluable access to the Adriatic and the Mediterranean . . . and their internal political and institutional practices are eventually not of much interest." A Brussels policy-maker reiterated this view, explaining that "while we do our best to check all the right boxes, NATO's ability to extensively vet the complex political system in the smaller enlargement states is finite, and it is the spirit of democratic intent that matters." This sentiment represents a somewhat realistic, cynical view of the prominence of democracy as a core part of the enlargement process, inadvertently normalizing borderline democratic features as a form of realist interpretation that accepts the inevitability of expansion. This approach was echoed by a different NATO military figure, involved in the various defense aspects of the early 2000s enlargement discussions: "The recent group of new Allies is militarily, financially and politically insignificant, and therefore these details [democracy and human rights—the author] are almost esoteric . . . some of the pivotal Allies that push for enlargement consider the bigger picture." The above quotes demonstrate an alienation process, in which democracy is viewed as an esoteric component compared to the bigger picture of sustaining the growth of the Alliance, and building its military edge. The mere understanding that NATO officials were aware of this phenomenon and made peace with it, could at first glance trigger a logic of "organized hypocrisy"—inconsistency between statements and practice on account of diverting interests, causing IOs to adopt certain symbolic measures to signal conformity with acceptable standards.[50] And indeed, thinking of NATO democratic conditionality as a form of "cheap talk"—placing accession criteria without sincere implementation intentions or feasibility[51]—is reasonable from a rationalist standpoint. However, this approach eventually falls short in explaining this reality, given the sincere belief among NATO officials in the dire importance of democracy as a fundamental tenet in enlargement decisions, as repeatedly demonstrated in myriad statements, communiqué, and documents.

To further flesh out this theme, all respondents (face-to-face interviewees and officials with whom communications took place via email conversations) were requested to answer a set of structured questions, with reference to the theoretical components for the development of normalization of deviance. This entailed ranking agreement on a one–five scale, where a score of one stands for *strongly disagree*, two means *disagree*, three equals *neutral*, four stands for *agree*, and five means *strongly agree*. This series of questions was phrased in the following manner:

On a scale of 1 to 5, please indicate to what extent you agree with the following statements:

1. In case of strong political will to incorporate a candidate state, the Alliance would be willing to overlook certain shortages in the democracy and human-rights adherence of a potential member.

2. In recent years, the role of political considerations is becoming more and more relevant in strategic decision-making.

3. A central driver of the readiness to overlook shortages in the democracy of a potential member is NATO's will to counter threats originating from Russia and curb its influence.

As table 3.3 illustrates, the respondents agreed (3.63 out of 5, on average) that NATO would be willing to overlook shortages in adherence to democracy in the process of enlargement, and were under the impression that this tendency only increased over time (3.87 out of 5, on average). This view was only faintly associated with the interpretation that relaxing democratic requirements was the result of the will to curb Russian aggression (2.45 out of 5, on average). However, as recent events on NATO's Eastern Flank demonstrate—most notably Russia's invasion of Ukraine in February 2022—it is entirely reasonable that the lingering Russian threat had contributed to the smoothness of the enlargement process, including NATO's flexibility on democratic criteria. Indeed, while the Russian threat may not have been the most prominent component in enlargement decision-making in the 1990s and early 2000s, it has certainty become more present since Russia's war with Georgia in 2008, its annexation of Crimea in 2014, and the events leading up to the February 2022 full-scale war in Ukraine.

Table 3.3. Structured interview with NATO personnel and permanent representatives to NATO, responses

Respondent #	Willing to Overlook Democratic Shortages	Increasing Politicization	Tackling Russian Influence
1	5 (strongly agree)	3 (neutral)	4 (agree)
2	2 (disagree)	4 (agree)	1 (strongly disagree)
3	4 (agree)	4 (agree)	2 (disagree)
4	4 (agree)	5 (strongly agree)	2 (disagree)
5	4 (agree)	3 (neutral)	3 (neutral)
6	5 (strongly agree)	4 (agree)	3 (neutral)
7	3 (neutral)	4 (agree)	2 (disagree)
8	3 (agree)	4 (neutral)	3 (neutral)
9	2 (disagree)	3 (neutral)	2 (disagree)
10	4 (agree)	4 (agree)	2 (disagree)
11	4 (agree)	4 (agree)	3 (neutral)
12–14	n/a	n/a	n/a
Avg.	**3.63**	**3.81**	**2.45**

Source: Created by the author.

Appendix—List of Interviewees

1. Mr. Petr Chalupecky—Head, NATO and Multilateral Affairs (NAMA) Section in the Political Affairs and Security Policy Division (interviewed May 23, 2019).

2. Dr. Benedetta Berti—Head, Policy Planning Unit, Office of NATO Secretary General (interviewed May 24, 2019).

3. Ms. Tanya Hartman—Analyst, NATO Political Affairs and Security Policy Division (interviewed May 24, 2019).

4. Mr. Steffen Elgersma—Analyst, NATO Political Affairs and Security Policy Division (interviewed May 24, 2019).

5. Mr. Nicola de Santis—Head, Middle East and North Africa Section, Political Affairs and Security Policy Division (interviewed May 24, 2019).

6. Colonel, Senior military adviser, NATO Defense College (interviewed May 28, 2019).

7. Colonel, Faculty adviser, NATO Defense College (interviewed May 30, 2019).

8. Dr. Stephen J. Mariano, Dean and deputy commandant, NATO Defense College (interviewed June 13, 2019).

9. Mr. Vesko Garčević—Former ambassador of Montenegro in Brussels (NATO) and Vienna (Organization for Security and Cooperation in Europe [OSCE]) (interviewed June 14, 2019).

10. Permanent representative (#1) of a NATO Member State to the Headquarters in Brussels (interviewed via email on December 16, 2019).

11. Permanent representative (#2) of a NATO Member State to the Headquarters in Brussels (interviewed via email on December 17, 2019).

12. Permanent representative (#3) of a NATO Member State to the Headquarters in Brussels (interviewed via email on December 17, 2019).

13. Permanent representative (#4) of a NATO Member State to the Headquarters in Brussels (interviewed via email on December 19, 2019).

14. Permanent representative (#5) of a NATO Member State to the Headquarters in Brussels (interviewed via email on December 29, 2019).

Chapter 4

NATO Enlargement during the Cold War Era

The Inaugural Enlargement: Greece and Turkey, 1952

As the newly formed Alliance celebrated its third anniversary, it was already preparing for an unprecedented enlargement, strategically planned to incorporate Greece and Turkey. These two actors were particularly valuable for the Alliance, on account of their geostrategic setting, which rendered them key in the Cold War battle for ideological influence between the West and the Soviet Union. Greece and Turkey are neighboring East Mediterranean nations whose bilateral relations have been characterized with significant animosity throughout the twentieth century. Having fought on opposite sides during several regional wars (in 1912–1913 and throughout World War I), and also experienced direct military confrontations and clashes (in 1897 and during 1919–1921), the decision to incorporate the two in the same accession basket was not an entirely natural development for the Alliance. As a result of these historical clashes, civilian populations in both countries experienced expulsions, destruction of religious symbols, and other hostilities that amount to dire conflicting narratives and bitterness that still looms large to this day.[1] Nevertheless, both Greece and Turkey rallied around the flag of NATO enlargement in the initial post–World War II years, as the prospects for communist involvement in the region were materializing in the early days of the Cold War. In the aftermath of World War II, Greece plunged into intense domestic confrontations between British and US-backed and Greek-monarchist forces and the Greek Pro-Communist camp, quickly deteriorating into a civil war. As the war ended in late 1949 with a Communist defeat, the country was torn apart by a death toll of approximately 100,000 and additional tens of thousands forcefully displaced and evacuated. The country then entered a lengthy period of political instability, with several election campaigns, resulting in frequent leadership rotations between Liberal/Center politicians (including Alexandros Diomidis of the Liberal Party, June 1949–January 1950; Ioannis Theotokis of the People's Party, January–March 1950; former General Nikolaos Plastiras of the National Progressive Center Union, April–August 1950 and October 1951–October 1952; and Sophoklis Venizelos of the Liberal Party, who served as Prime Minister between August 1950 and October 1951). Nevertheless, throughout the pre-NATO years, Greece's pro-Western orientation persisted, and the pro-Alliance forces were particularly dominant in shaping the country's foreign policy during that formative period. This sentiment was shared by postwar Turkish society, intellectual elites, and political and military circles. With the birth of the Republic in 1923 under Mustafa Kemal Atatürk, the country's compass heavily focused on democratization and modernization, and other Western-oriented reforms aimed to anchor Turkey as a modern-day success story. A central beneficiary of the Marshall Plan, Turkey's affiliation with the West persevered throughout the İnönü regime (who served as president between November 1938 and May 1950), and then under President Celâl Bayar and Prime Minister Adnan Menderes of the Democrat Party, who assumed his position after winning the country's first free election campaign in May 1950. Bayar and Menderes adopted significant domestic democratic restructurings, including further economic liberalization, encouraging privatization and entrepreneurship, while curbing excessive bureaucratic powers. At the same time, Turkey's foreign policy orientation toward the West intensified, with NATO as centerpiece for the country's regional security doctrine. As the political and military elites in Turkey and Greece alike pushed to side with NATO, forces from both countries participated (under the auspices of the UN) in a peacekeeping mission in the Republic of Korea (ROK), defending the country against North Korean infiltrations. As the ROK was formed in 1948 and recognized by the UN General Assembly, the organization filled an important role in monitoring local elections and various reconstruction programs, before unprecedently intervening in the war on the Korean peninsula with UN Security Council Resolution 82 in June 1950. Turkey and Greece took part in this campaign chiefly as an attempt to signal to the West their wholehearted intention to join NATO.[2] At this strategic juncture, the US (and other NATO founding nations, such as Italy) publicly supported a joint Turkish-Greek accession to the Alliance, with hopes to secure their position within the Western bloc and thereby mobilize their material resources in an event of a regional confrontation. Crucially for the Alliance, Greece and Turkey created a barrier for possible progression of the Soviet sphere to the vital Eastern Mediterranean region, rich with natural resources and crucial for the freedom of navigation in the Mediterranean Sea. While these advantages were deemed particularly attractive on the American side of the Atlantic, other founding NATO members (with the UK in the lead) expressed concerns over the likelihood for unwanted involvement in domestic and regional disputes in a theatre ravaged by worries of communist influence, only a few years after their great sacrifice during World War II. The UK was under the opinion that the regional defense of the Middle East should be organized under the auspices of a separate organization that shall bring together regional powers such as Egypt, and directly integrate them with Turkey and Greece.[3] Other key Allies were also worried that Greece and Turkey were not culturally and socially compatible with what they saw as the foundations of the Atlantic community, even though they were already associated with both the Council of Europe and the Organization for European Economic Cooperation.[4] At the time, political and military elites in both countries shared pro-Western ideology and a natural tendency for democratic values, so prominently represented by the Alliance. According to Spiros Lambridias, Greece's former permanent representative to NATO, Greece supported the basic ideas and principles that underlined the establishment of the Alliance, and hence became a natural candidate for accession.[5] The concern for the de facto consolidation of democracy in Greece and Turkey is compatible with the perception that NATO was chiefly a value-based community, designed to execute this vision via providing strategic stability and military deterrence to the North Atlantic region. In parallel, these early hesitations experienced by several Allies were somewhat overshadowed by the quickly increasing regional instability, which drove the US to push for the necessarily adjustments to beef up NATO's southern flank.[6] The simultaneous accession of Turkey and Greece to NATO was seen in Washington as a treasured "package deal" for the West at the height of the Cold War, a natural extension of Turkey's defense pact signed with the UK and France in 1939. As noted by Sayle, another reason that the US actively advocated to allow Greece and Turkey to join the Alliance is vested in its impression that these states were crucial to Eisenhower's military strategy, facing what was thought to be an actual risk that Turkey would opt for Cold War neutrality, or even side with the Soviets.[7] Greece, for its part, was ravaged by devastating fighting during World War II and a long-lasting civil war, which only comprehensively concluded in late 1949. As early as 1947, President Harry S. Truman pledge to Congress to provide extensive funding to Greece and Turkey, who were allegedly at the brink of deciding between allegiance to the two rival ideologies of the Cold War—a notion also supported by then Undersecretary of State Acheson.[8] As noted by Lord Ismay, NATO's first secretary general, in his account of the Alliance's first five years of existence—in 1947 Greece and Turkey hung in the balance, and it seemed certain that "without the continuance of the substantial military and financial aid . . . Greece would succumb to the Communists and be dragged behind the Iron Curtain, and Turkey would then be left to the mercy of the Soviet Union."[9] This approach prompted the swift US aid scheme that came to be known as the Truman Doctrine, under which President Truman decisively led an initiative to provide Greece and Turkey funding of nearly $400 million until mid-1948, and substantiate US presence in these countries to prevent Soviet interference. The UK's initial reservations were finally lifted in July 1951, clearing one of the most substantial obstacles in Turkey and Greece's road to membership.

A key aspect underpinning the 1952 enlargement was Turkey and Greece's strong relationship with NATO since its inception. The two countries were involved in various aspects of policy coordination with NATO, including exchanges of information, assessments, high-level coordination, and a strong working relationship between junior officers. In October 1950, after a first unsuccessful attempt to apply for full membership earlier that year, Turkey and Greece became integrated in consultations regarding security coordination mechanisms in the Eastern Mediterranean, and continued to push for unequivocal membership. However, NATO was not yet ready to grant full membership to both countries. An October 1950 meeting of the North Atlantic Defense Committee gave no particular reason for this verdict (after the question was considered by the North Atlantic Council a few weeks earlier), but made clear that the future integration of both countries shall be considered in tandem.

> The request of the Turkish Government for admission into the North Atlantic Treaty was carefully considered by the North Atlantic Council. Consideration was simultaneously given to the position of Greece, since it was felt that any arrangement

made in the case of Turkey should also be extended to cover Greece. It was the opinion of the Council that at the present stage of development of the North Atlantic Treaty Organization it would not be feasible to extend the Treaty to either country.[10]

As Leffler notes, during a visit by Assistant Secretary of State George McGhee to Turkey in February 1951, Turkish President Celal Bayar conveyed his dismay of NATO's rejection of Turkish membership, causing McGhee to adopt the view that the US was better inclined to provide Turkey with a solid commitment in the form of promise for future accession. The American stance was further shaped in May 1951, after a sequence of intense bilateral exchanges between US senior officials, including Admiral Robert B. Carney and US Secretary for Air Thomas K. Finletter, and their Greek and Turkish counterparts.[11] As for NATO's perspective, archival documents shed light on the manner in which the Alliance viewed the prospects of Greek and Turkish Accession. In a protocol of a meeting of the NATO Military Representatives Committee (June 22, 1951), which discussed the implications of such possible accession,[12] several concerns were raised. The Dutch representative, Rear Admiral Jonkheer H. A. van Foreest, expressed his alarm over the possible political influence vested in the inclusion of Greece and Turkey: "Close military and political cooperation with these countries might have disadvantages . . . the North Atlantic Treaty Organization as a whole becoming involved in Middle East rivalries such as the sovereignty of Cyprus, the possibility of the diversion of emphasis from Western Europe to the South and Southeast . . . and inevitable military and political arguments, which might result in loss of efficiency and team-spirit." Major General Marc H. Fouillien of Belgium agreed with this notion, but emphasized that the risk for leaving these states outside the Western sphere were greater than any other drawbacks: "Any such diversion would be completely overweighted by the advantage of having Greece and Turkey members of the North Atlantic Treaty Organization."

Like Fouillien, others too were eager to discard the fears of possible political interference in enlargement decision-making. Most notably, France's Lieutenant General Paul Ely was under the impression that van Foreest's comments were "purely political, and better left out of the paper." In July 1951, a meeting of the North Atlantic Military Committee was dedicated to examining the implications of Greek and Turkish membership. The Italian representative noted the strategic value of associating these two nations with the Alliance: "The Italian Government is of the opinion that . . . there is no doubt that the bastion represented by Asia Minor (Turkey) has the same value for the South Mediterranean sector of NATO as the Scandinavian bastion has for the Northern sector. The loss of the former bastion would drive Atlantic defense back to the Central Mediterranean . . . [and] the defense of the Continent would become extremely difficult."[13] Lord Ismay described in his book a similar concern raised by the Allies: "It was felt, on the one hand, that the addition of these countries to the coalition would carry obvious advantages; on the other hand, that it would involve extending NATO's strategical commitments as far east as the Caucasus. Moreover, some member governments feared that the admission of Turkey, which had a common frontier with Soviet Russia and Bulgaria, might aggravate international tension."[14]

An August 1951 meeting of the North Atlantic Military Committee determined that an extraordinary 1951 follow-up session of the NAC shall be devoted to discussing the political aspects of the participation of Greece and Turkey in NATO's Defense structure.[15] And indeed, at a subsequent meeting of the NAC in November 1951, the Alliance concluded that Greece and Turkey made a considerable service for the purpose of freedom and peace, and were in fact part of a mutual democratic way of life: "Greece and Turkey have already given courageous evidence of their devotion to the cause of freedom and of peace. It is easy to see what links us . . . the traditional inspiration of Western civilization, and the democratic way of life which we are pledged to preserve. That is why we are glad to see representatives of Greece and Turkey with us here today."[16] This has clearly indicated that the NAC found both states suitable in terms of the Alliance's democratic criteria, making a particular effort to decisively include Greece and Turkey in the so-called club of democracies that underpins the Alliance. However, as table 4.1 demonstrates, at the time of this statement, Greece held a Polity-IV democracy score of four out of ten (with its regime dubbed open anocracy), after a sharp decline from its 1948 score of eight (democracy). Simultaneously, V-Dem's regime classification defined Greece as an electoral autocracy (one out of three), hence struggling to meet the modern-day criteria for democracies. Turkey, on the other hand, attained a Polity-IV score of seven out of ten (meeting the threshold for democracy) in 1947, consistently preserving this status until 1953, after it had already joined the Alliance. Like Greece, its V-Dem regime classification defined the country as an electoral autocracy (one out of three), suggesting that the country's democratic regime was not entirely consolidated.

Table 4.1. Democracy rankings at NATO accession year

Candidate Country	Accession Year	Polity IV Ranking at Year	V-Dem Score at Year
Turkey	1952	7.00 (Democracy)	0.33 (Electoral Autocracy)
Greece	1952	4.00 (Open-Anocracy)	0.33 (Electoral Autocracy)

Source: Polity IV; V-Dem.

Nevertheless, at the NAC meeting in October 1951, the Alliance concluded that "the security of the North Atlantic area will be enhanced by the accession of Greece and Turkey," and recommended that the member states take the necessary measures to accommodate their formal membership invitation.[17] As the domestic deliberation process was taking place among the member states, representatives of both Greece and Turkey made an effort to include democratic signaling in their case for membership. For instance, at a February 1952 session of the North Atlantic Council, Mr. Sofocles Venizelos, Greek Deputy Prime Minister, reiterated the notion of NATO's democratic principles as part of Greece's membership bid: "Greece is extremely glad that in future she will also be a member of this Treaty, whose aims and principles correspond so closely to her own. We believe, like all of you, in the need for safeguarding democratic freedom and preserving the common civilization of our peoples."[18]

Ultimately, in February 1952, Greece and Turkey's membership was finalized, and the Alliance's first enlargement was complete. In the aftermath of this historic development, NATO accession closely integrated Greece and Turkey with the West, paving the way for what would become a central tenet in regional security and diplomacy even when bilateral ties between the two will have become more tense. Greece and Turkey's accession was also said to contribute to domestic democratic consolidation. Indeed, an opinion was voiced according to which NATO membership played a crucial role in stabilizing and solidifying the democratic regimes in these states, as fragile democracies are found in particular need to curb external and internal threats on the core pillars of democracy.[19] In 1999, then Turkish President Sulyeman Demirel reflected on his county's democratic orientation as the pivoting factor in Turkey's accession to the Alliance, and the founding principle connecting it with the West.

On 18 February 1952 Turkey became a member of NATO. Turkey was not only compelled by her anxieties emanating from Soviet claims, but also by her strong belief in the common values of the Alliance. By deciding to join NATO, the Turkish nation anchored its destiny in the West . . . basing her political and legal systems on modern, secular European models . . . committed to democracy, respect for human rights and the rule of law, and the free market economy.[20]

This narrative coincides with the view that NATO accession, in tandem with its 1949 affiliation with the Council of Europe, helped Turkey substantiate the notion that it was indeed a part of the West—a component of Turkish national identity that has been gradually eroding in recent decades.[21]

The Second Enlargement: Reintegrating the Federal Republic of Germany to the Family of Nations, 1955

At the inception of the Alliance in 1949, only a few years after the conclusion of World War II, the notion of West Germany's integration into the newly established military-political mechanism seemed almost abnormal. A defensive Alliance aimed to deter an external enemy from any aggression on European soil appeared nearly tantamount with the collective experience the world has seen over the first decades of the twentieth century, repeatedly battling German forces in devastating, endless wars that brought sheer destruction to the continent, and, indeed, the entire world. And yet, as the Communist threat already loomed large, redefining the basic assumptions of the global system toward an ideological clash as the underlying principle of the postwar period, a new Western security discourse and paradigm were being shaped. The Federal Republic was formed in May 1949 as a new political entity under the auspices of the Allied zones of control, divided between the US, UK, and France. The new Republic's founding Constitution (Grundgesetz, or basic law) of May 1949, approved by the occupying Allied forces, anchored democracy as one of the core values of the Republic, and stressed that its political parties must conform to democratic principles. The document also encouraged Germany's participation in a European Union committed to democracy, the rule of law, and basic rights, and ensured the freedom of movement, occupation and assembly.[22] The Federal Republic held its first democratic elections to the Bundestag in August 1949, bringing to power the Christian Democratic Union of Germany (CDU) candidate Konrad Adenauer as first chancellor. Among the various roots for the swift success of democratization in the Federal Republic, researchers noted the profound societal transformation in the post-Nazi period, coupled with an Allied-led vision to remake Germany's political culture and governance mind-set, and, importantly, the country's tremendous economic rehabilitation in the postwar years.[23] Indeed, as the prominent democracy indexes demonstrate, since its formation West Germany already ranked as a full democracy (ten out of ten) in the Polity IV index (consistently keeping its score in the following years), coupled with a score of three out of three (liberal democracy) in V-Dem's regime classification. This reality is particularly remarkable, taking into account the very short period of time since the end of World War II, and the enormous societal and political transformations that transpired in Germany, empowering its rebirth as a democracy. However, despite West Germany's newly instated democracy, not all member states viewed its NATO candidacy positively. As noted by Haftendorn, while some in the US sought to leverage Germany's manpower and vast resources to boost American defenses in Western Europe, the French resentment to the idea of German integration into the Alliance at such an early stage was too robust to translate these dilemmas into action.[24] Referring to this point, NATO Secretary General Ismay noted that in September 1950, all member states were willing to accept the principle of German participation in NATO, excluding French Foreign Minister Robert Schuman. Ismay also emphasized that US Secretary of State Acheson said that his government's involvement in the North Atlantic Treaty "should involve the participation of German units and the use of German productive resources for its supply."[25] The tide began to turn with the break of the Korean War in June 1950, when it became evident that the notion of a centralized European defense mechanism would have to be fashioned, and as France and other key Allies finally opted to lock in German power rather than see it resurge autonomously. According to historical accounts, Acheson was able to convince President Truman that West Germany had to become involved in European collective defense, in a manner that would not provide it with too much strength to play the kingmaker role.[26] While the question of Germany's integration into NATO was considered in the past, Lord Isamy notes that the anxiety caused by the Korean War had "brought the question to a head," and that defending Europe was inconceivable without the political and military participation of West Germany. Around that context, West Germany's accession was beginning to become seriously contemplated. At a meeting of the NAC in May 1950, Luxembourg's Minister for Foreign Affairs Joseph Bech stressed his will to see a free and democratic Germany integrated into the Alliance: "It is in this spirit of prompting and as vigorously as possible the aims of our Treaty that my country envisages the integration of a loyal and democratic Germany to the community of Western Europe."[27] Yet, as sensitivities were still extremely present, a September 1950 meeting of the three occupying powers in New York also alluded to the matter of Germany's future role in European security, maintaining that "the question raised by the problems of the participation of the German Federal Republic in the common defence of Europe was at present the subject of study and exchange of views."[28] In November 1950, the French representative to the meeting of the twenty-eight's Council of Deputies, stressed the importance of the eventual integration of Germany to the NATO system to render a reality of a peaceful Europe and avert another war: "Peace will not be established on a firm foundation if a democratic Germany is not an integral part of a strong and prosperous Western Europe, and if she is not attached to it by such ties that it becomes an impassibility, for her to make, a bargain with the East or to be tempted, to join with the East against us."[29]

In the following month, a joint report by the Council of Deputies and the Military Committee was able to advance as far as determining that "realistic defence of Western Europe . . . could not be contemplated without active and willing German participation,"[30] and a corresponding meeting of the NAC in late December 1950 invited the three Occupying Powers to explore the various proposals for German participation. Notably, these developments coincided with the declaration in April 1951 of the establishment of the European Coal and Steel Community (which comprised of France, Italy, Belgium, the Netherlands, Luxembourg, and West Germany), and provided further clarity and legitimacy for the future of inclusion of the Federal Republic under NATO's auspices. The reality in which West Germany was perceived as a full-pledged democracy, upholding the Alliance's values and norms, clearly underscored the benefits in its eventual inclusion, and indirectly soothed potential value-based objections (contrary to the case of Turkey and Greece's integration in 1952). A January 1952 memorandum on the German defense contribution in a future membership scenario emphasized this notion, as the Federal Minister of Finance Fritz Schäffer acknowledged the importance of the German transition to democracy in maintaining the peace in Europe: "On behalf of the Federal Government, the undersigned emphasize already at this stage that no effort to secure peace and to oppose Eastern aggression can be successful, unless internal social peace and adherence to the idea of democracy can be maintained."[31] After expressing a favorable opinion with regard to the possibility of German participation in a future European Defence Community (February 1952),[32] a major breakthrough was recorded at the December 1952 meeting of the NAC, when UK Deputy Prime Minister Anthony Eden noted Germany's crucial future role in the making of a free and secure Europe, encouraging the federal government to proceed with the reestablishment of its democratic institutions: "Bearing in mind the vital part which the German Federal Republic could play in the strengthening and development of a united, free and democratic Europe, it remained our policy . . . to foster the partnership of Western Germany with the free world. It was especially desirable that at the same time the Germans should . . . maintain the standing of their democratic institutions."[33]

Eden was also concerned with the fragility of the newly established Republic, with a particular attention on its ability to maintain a moderate political line while distancing itself from ex-Nazi figures. Referring to the uproar after ex-General Hermann-Bernhard Ramcke's criticism of the Allied actions against German war criminals, Eden noted: "The internal political situation in Western Germany had given rise to some uneasiness. While such incidents as the speech by ex-General Ramcke should not be ignored, it would be unwise to exaggerate their significance, taking into account such other compensating signs as the maintenance of public support in the German Federal Republic for the two major moderate Parties."

At that meeting, the foreign ministers also took note of the creation of the European Coal and Steel Community (ECSC), and the German participation under its auspices, as an indication for satisfactory progress toward European integration. While the ECSC was prima facie a regulatory mechanism for European industries, in practice it served as the first supranational European integration vessel, paving the way for what would be later known as the EU. Famously, the ECSC was proposed by French Foreign Minister Robert Schumann, who in his renowned May 1950 Declaration proclaimed that the creation of the ECSC "will make it plain that any war between France and Germany becomes not merely unthinkable, but materially impossible."[34]

In December 1953, the US, UK, France, and NATO Secretary General Ismay met in Bermuda to discuss the fate of Germany's future role in European security. At the time, the status of the French initiative to establish a European army, known as the European Defence Community

(EDC), introduced by French Prime Minister René Pleven, still hung in the balance. The realization of the EDC as a core strategic enterprise could pose an alternative to Germany's entry into NATO, and was initially supported by Washington and London, until ultimately rejected by the French Parliament in 1954—paving the way for Germany's future NATO membership.[35] At a meeting of the Military Committee in December 1953, the delegates stressed that "a free, united and democratic Germany was essential to the well-being of the Atlantic countries," and that the mere fate of the entire European civilization was dependent on the ability to manufacture a single community with an "indissolubly linked France and Germany."[36]

In the European arena, no substantial multinational integration project could take shape without the participation of both France and Germany—the core mainland pillars of European power. Historically, the grand desire to place Europe on a track of transnational integration was driven not by the Communist threat, but rather by a vivid understanding according to which deep, inseverable political, financial, and military ties between these two giants was vital to effectively restructure decades of destructive animosity. Speaking at a meeting of the NAC in May 1954, Greek Minister of Foreign Affairs Stephanos Stephanopoulos alluded to the imperativeness of German integration with the Alliance: "It is true to say that this association of the West would not be complete until Western Germany formed a part of it. The Council were all agreed on this point, though aware of the difficulties, based on reasons of history."[37] British Foreign Minister Eden agreed, further tying the matter of German accession to NATO with the Cold War, stressing the advancements of the German society and the Republic's success: "The Russians know . . . how greatly NATO's defence would be strengthened by a German contingent. All this emphasized the necessity for the earliest possible German contribution to the joint defence effort. . . . With every month that passed the need to add Western Germany to the association of free countries became more clearly evident: the Germans were prosperous and conscious of their economic strength." During an NAC meeting in April 1954, Italian minister of Foreign Affairs, Gaetano Martino, expressed strong confidence with the state of German democracy and the Republic's compatibility with the Alliance's values, signaling how important this notion has been in the overall decision-making process: "On the occasion of the entry of the Federal Republic into the defensive front of the Atlantic nations and into the Western European community he reaffirmed his government's firm confidence in the spirit of democracy of the German people. The free world had watched the recent rebirth of Germany with warm and friendly interest and was confident that under the leadership of a great European such as Chancellor Adenauer Germany would make a major contribution to peace and freedom."[38] At the same meeting, Greek Defense Minister Panagiotis Kanellopoulos concurred with the optimistic approach vis-à-vis the state of German democracy, expressing enthusiasm over what he perceived as history in the making: "This is a historic event marking the outcome of many international developments since the end of the Second World War. The division of the world into the two camps of freedom in the West and totalitarianism in the East called for the integration of Germany among the forces of the free world, where her contribution was needed and where she belonged by right." Approaching the decision to offer West Germany full membership, the Alliance sent another signal regarding the weight of democracy and the rule of law in making that judgment. In October 1954, NATO issued a declaration inviting Germany to accede to the Brussels Treaty, emphasizing the Alliance's satisfaction with the Federal Republic's democratic composition: "Noting with satisfaction that their devotion to peace and their allegiance to democratic institutions constitute common bonds between the countries of Western Europe."[39]

Ultimately, at the Nine-Power Conference that took place in London in late September 1954, Foreign Ministers representing the US, Canada, Italy, Belgium, France, Luxembourg, the Netherlands, and the UK, with participation of high-ranking West German officials, declared their intention to recommend the accession to NATO of the Federal Republic of Germany, and the integration of its forces into the NATO machinery.[40] With a particular emphasis on democracy, the representatives of France, the UK and the US made clear that they recognize that Germany "can no longer be deprived of the rights properly belonging to a free and democratic people." As the question of Germany's membership was settled, Allies were still inclined to stress the strictly defensive nature of Germany's participation in NATO, in what seemed to be merely a declaratory tool to gain a sense of security, less than a decade after the conclusion of World War II. In that spirit, as part of the October 1954 draft protocol for Germany's accession mechanism, Allies emphasized Germany's acceptance of article 2 of the UN Charter, which stresses that "All Members shall settle their international disputes by peaceful means and . . . refrain from the threat or use of force" as a necessarily precondition for its accession: "Being satisfied that the security of the North Atlantic area will be enhanced by the accession of the Federal Republic of Germany, and having noted that it has by a declaration dated 3 October, 1954, accepted the obligations set forth in Article 2 of the Charter of the United Nations and has undertaken upon its accession . . . to refrain from any action inconsistent with the strictly defensive character of that Treaty."[41] In the aftermath of German accession, US Secretary of State John Foster Dulles alluded to the question of the underlying purpose of its inclusion in NATO, making clear that its integration derived from the imperative to create a political order that could effectively prevent another war, and thwart the possibility of resurfacing domestic extremism: "Everyone knows that the post-war policy being followed by the Federal Republic of Germany in co-operation with its NATO allies is to bring about such an integration, military political and economic, of the Federal Republic with the countries of Europe, that there will never again be the possibility of a Federal Republic pursuing such a course as was pursued under Hitlerism."[42]

As an immediate response to West Germany's integration, the Soviet Union formed the Warsaw Pact in May 1955, with the German Democratic Republic (East Germany) as a full member. This signaled a new political reality in Europe, effectively lasting for more than three additional decades. With the fall of the Berlin wall in November 1989, and the eventual reunification of Germany in October 1990, the former territory of East Germany was inherited by the Federal Republic, and hence effectively extending NATO's territory to include the former Soviet protégé-state. Soon thereafter, the Warsaw Pact was formally dissolved, and the Soviet Union ceased to exist in its Cold War form. While the inclusion of East Germany does not constitute an enlargement per se, it is a central landmark in NATO expansion history, as it concluded the lengthy process of German postwar divide, anchoring the country in the West. On the day German unification became a reality, then NATO Secretary General Manfred Wörner issued a public congratulatory address, routinely referring to the entire territory of unified Germany as a member of NATO: "On behalf of our Atlantic Alliance, I congratulate the German nation on the achievement of its unity. I salute and welcome the united Germany as a loyal member of our Alliance and an active partner in the building of a Europe whole and free."[43]

Germany's postunification NATO status was dramatically debated over the formative period after the fall of the Berlin Wall in November 1989, when the security architecture in Europe was being shaped over a series of diplomatic channels between Bonn, Berlin, Moscow, and Washington, DC. This fascinating dynamic is masterfully unraveled in M. E. Sarotte's seminal book on the history of NATO's enlargement during the 1990s, told primarily from the major capitals' perspective.[44] As the author illustrates, the West attempted to "ascertain what Gorbachev would want in exchange for letting all regions of a unified Germany become part of NATO," and waged a careful diplomatic battle to expand the Alliance's reach into East Germany. One of the most defining events in this effort was a famous February 1990 meeting between then US Secretary of State James Baker and Soviet leader Mikhail Gorbachev, who was said to agree that Moscow would acknowledge Germany's unified status in NATO in exchange for a halt in additional NATO expansion eastward. This policy came to be known as *not one inch*, after Baker's assurance to Gorbachev, and brought about a series of contested narratives among academics and former diplomats, resonating to this day.[45] The next chapter, discussing post–Cold War expansion rounds, attends to this debate.

The Third Enlargement:
Reinstating Democracy in Spain, 1982

West Germany's accession to NATO in May 1955, marked a twenty-seven-year moratorium on further expansion, as the remaining potential of European democracies interested in joining the Alliance had practically been exhausted. With the Cold War looming large, Europe was divided between a NATO-bloc, a strategic Warsaw Pact adversary (including East Germany), and a group of nonaligned nations, including Ireland, Sweden, Finland, Switzerland, Austria, and Yugoslavia. With other viable options out of sight, the question of Spain's prospects for NATO membership was viewed somewhat differently in Brussels. From a NATO perspective, Spain was most likely to meet the military-structural accession criteria even at the inception of the Alliance in 1949, but was severely disadvantaged given its flagrantly autocratic regime, under the brutal leadership of General Franco. As noted by van Dijk and Sloan, value-based considerations were able to block Franco's dictatorship, despite the view among certain US politicians that the military advantages of integrating Spain should outweigh democratic ideals.[46] Indeed, some of the Alliance's founding members, most notably Portugal—frequently dubbed as autocratic during NATO inception—alleged that NATO should disregard this reality in favor of the clear interest to militarily and politically fortify the Alliance in the midst of the Cold War. A statement by Portuguese minister of Foreign Affairs, Prof. Paulo Cunha, at a February 1952 meeting of the NAC, reiterated the Portuguese stance according to which Spain's exclusion was unfortunate and should be overturned: "It is regrettable that it hasn't been possible yet . . . to complete the circle and put an end to the strategic nonsense of the absence of Spain in the system of Western defence. If we agree that we can't do without the effort of the Iberian Peninsula, we have got to face realities and find the best possible solution."[47] Despite the Portuguese interpretation, in practice NATO unequivocally refrained from weighing or discussing Spain's accession in its mutual high-profile organs, as internal opposition from within the Alliance was vast, most heavily influenced by the leadership of the Benelux countries and Norway.[48] As noted in a historical account created by NATO's Supreme Headquarters Allied Powers Europe (SHAPE) in 1951, Spain's accession to NATO was indeed operationally desirable, but extremely problematic with regard to its basic adherence to the Alliance's core values, and hence practically impossible at the time: "The entrance of Spain into NATO, which is obviously desirable militarily and would cause satisfaction in Portugal, depends on whether it is considered by the other nations that Spain safeguards the principles of democracy, individual liberty, and the rule of law."[49]

This bold and decisive statement speaks volumes to the place democratic considerations received in early-day Alliance decision-making. Albeit contentious, the accession of Greece and Turkey in February 1952 was nearly not as controversial as the possibility to integrate Spain—a full-fledged authoritarian regime—into the Alliance. By firmly rejecting this option, NATO sent a clear signal with regard to the Alliance's character and role in the early days of the Cold War. Still, during the following decades, NATO had maintained certain ties with Madrid, authorizing the release of NATO publications to Spain in May 1957,[50] August 1960,[51] and October 1962,[52] while some member states sustained a bilateral partnership with Madrid. Most prominent among the latter was Portugal—which during an annual NATO review defined its core security goal as "the defence of the Iberian Peninsula in cooperation with Spain,"[53] and the US, which repeatedly emphasized its bilateral defense ties with Madrid in several NATO forums.[54] Nevertheless, NATO refrained from discussing the possibility of Spanish membership throughout Spain's authoritarian period, and considering the standoff with Communism in Eastern Europe, the volume of debates on expansion had dramatically decreased.

Only nearly two decades later, in the late 1970s, as Spain's transition to democracy slowly manifested, the fierce opposition within NATO to forge closer ties with Madrid had gradually relaxed. As early as 1975, the Spanish transition government attempted to promote NATO accession with an implicit American backing, but the prospect for accession talks was rejected by the NAC in May 1975, on the grounds of insufficient democratic consolidation. Even though this early attempt was blocked, following Franco's death in January 1976, the Alliance began to seriously contemplate Spain's status. The underlying notion was vested in the view that Spain's inclusion in the Alliance is both important for the consolidation of the young Spanish democracy, but also imperative in order to move toward the vision of a Europe whole and free, standing united in managing the (still) towering challenge vested in the Soviet bloc and its efforts to counter the free world. As Spain's transition to democracy was still being realized, then Spanish Minister of Foreign Affairs, Marcelino Oreja, declared in June 1980 that Madrid intended to pursue NATO membership, with the purpose of completing the accession process by 1983—supporting Spain's European integration efforts.[55] According to Carothers, the prospects for strengthening Spain's fragile newly reinstated democracy through NATO accession were widely debated domestically between the ruling Union de Centro Democratico (UCD) bloc, and the Socialist party. While the former viewed NATO membership as a credible signal for the country's pro-Western and European identity, the latter expressed concerns over domestic support and over NATO's internal record of democracy (e.g., with regard to the original inclusion of Portugal among the Alliance's founding members). As noted by Tovias, the prospects for Spanish entry into NATO were particularly praised by the military establishment, which viewed the Alliance's integrated military structure as an opportunity to modernize the army, break its long-lasting international isolation and enhance its capabilities via modernized training, access to knowledge and equipment.[56] Moreover, pro-democratic officers among the ranks of the Spanish army praised NATO's promotion system, based on skill rather than political loyalty or seniority, signaling their desire to embrace this scheme. This ideological line was also evident in the Spanish view of the importance of the democratic component as prerequisite for NATO accession in the early stages of the accession negotiations. Spanish Minister Perez Llorca stated at a December 1981 meeting of the NAC that restoring democracy was particularly challenging and meaningful for Spain's reintegration into the West: "Spain, having regained, not without effort, a democratic system, with public freedoms and the respect for human rights, recovering in a definitive and irreversible way her history, her culture and her place in the world, is today beginning to join the efforts of this group of Western democracies, as expressed in the Treaty."[57] However challenging, this realization points to a well-established Spanish perception according to which the prospects for NATO (and EU) membership will be derived first and foremost from the functionality of its democratic organs, after decades of authoritarian rule. As NATO did not expand since the accession of West Germany in 1955, Spanish membership seemed fairly desirable, albeit requiring the Alliance to proceed with a great deal of caution. A ministerial session of the NAC in May 1982 emphasized the importance of the democratic component within the Alliance, as reflected by Spain's impending accession: "The Allies welcome the impending accession of Spain, which offers fresh evidence of the enduring vitality of the Alliance—a community of free countries inspired by the shared values of pluralistic democracy, individual liberty, human dignity, self-determination and the rule of law."[58] In the spirit of this statement, a special address by the president of Spain in June 1982 reiterated the notion of the primacy of the ideological component within the Alliance: "As opposed to those who tend to see in the Alliance only a military organization . . . my government's understanding of the Alliance is that of a community of free people's united in the defence of essential values . . . that are also those of the Spanish democracy."[59] And indeed, according to the Polity IV democracy index, Spain first regained its democratic status in 1978, with a score of nine out of ten (democracy), later upgraded to a score of perfect ten in 1982—the country's accession year. V-Dem's regime classification also dubbed Spain as an electoral democracy since 1979, before turning into a full-fledged liberal democracy in 1983—one year after its eventual accession to NATO (see table 4.2).

Table 4.2. Normalized democracy rankings at accession year

Candidate Country	Accession Year	Polity IV Ranking at Year	V-Dem Score at Year
W. Germany	1955	1.00 (Full Democracy)	1.00 (Liberal Democracy)
Spain	1982	1.00 (Full Democracy)	0.66 (Electoral Democracy)

Source: Polity IV; V-Dem.

As Spain's democratic transformation was complete in May 1982, NATO was a sixteen-member strong Alliance, gradually adding four new members to its ranks since the organization's inception in 1949, over the course of thirty-three years. In the next thirty years to come, with the end of the Cold War approaching, NATO will further grow its membership in an incomparable pace, reaching twenty-six members in the span of two significant enlargement rounds (1999 and 2004), before adding six other members until 2020. These massive expansion rounds will be the subject of the next chapter.

Chapter 5

NATO Enlargement after the Cold War

A New Era in NATO Enlargement:
Poland, Hungary, and the Czech Republic, 1999

As early as October 1989, at the annual session of the North Atlantic Assembly, NATO Secretary General Manfred Wörner alluded to the prospects of Poland and Hungary's swift democratic reform, and how these interact with their possible accession to the Alliance.

> We are concentrating the major part of our efforts on Poland and Hungary, the two countries that are taking the necessary political steps to move closer to democracy, and to create the political conditions that will give their reforms a fighting chance of success. Poland and Hungary are the two test cases for our Alliance strategy.[1]
>
> Democratic institutions must be allowed to take root; human rights and the undertakings of the Helsinki Final Act must be respected in full; only in this way will the Eastern governments persuade their populations to accept the sacrifices of reform, and to work to rebuild their nations.

The following month, Hungary formally applied to join the European Community (EC), in a burst of enthusiasm that soon attracted similar signals from Poland's leadership of their intention to join their peers.[2] These two states, teaming up with the Czech Republic, further signaled to the West their desire for integration by withdrawing from Warsaw Pact's military activities in October 1990, nearly six months before the

89

organization's dissolution. The three then proceeded to form the Visegrad partnership in early 1991, originally aimed to collectively promote their integration efforts. According to Gheciu, these signals were well received at the NATO headquarters (NATO HQ) in Brussels, promoting a series of socialization practices aimed to build democratic institutions from scratch, substantially contributing to the reconstruction of these post-Communist states around a framing of liberal democratic norms.[3] The Czech Republic, Hungary and Poland were among the first to become associated (in February–March 1994) with NATO's Partnership for Peace program, set in motion in January 1994 at the Brussels Summit meeting, designed as a mechanism to facilitate a direct route for future membership. Famously, then President Clinton declared that further NATO expansion "was no longer a question of whether . . . but how and when,"[4] pushing to finalize an enlargement round on the occasion of the Alliance's fiftieth anniversary in 1999. Goldgeier argues that the US hoped that further enlargement will help to consolidate democracy, expand the realm of market economies in Europe, and contribute to the establishment of more advanced human rights mechanisms in the region, while at the same time providing better protection against a possible reemergence of the Russian threat. As the three states were being considered for membership at the eve of the 1997 Madrid Summit, they consistently met the criteria for democratic regime characteristics, according to all prominent democracy indices: Freedom House Index (where all three were dubbed *free*); Polity IV Ranking (where they were considered full democracies); and the V-Dem Score (according to which they were defined as *liberal democracies*).[5] According to Barany, the 1999 round involved consensual support around states that enjoyed consolidated democratic regimes and well-functioning market economies—a club in which Poland was "clearly the front-runner."[6]

Poland saw its first post–Communist era multiparty elections in June 1989, after an exemplary process of liberalization and transition to democracy, widely known for the role played by the Independent Self-Governing Trade Union Solidarity (Solidarność) in the gradual demise of Eastern European Communist regimes. Solidarity was led by Lech Wałęsa, a Nobel Prize–winning activist and dissident, who led Poland's pro-democracy camp and eventually became the country's first democratically elected President since 1926, after a successful campaign in November 1990. Under Wałęsa, Poland has undergone a series of democratization and market liberalization reforms, including substantial privatization of former state assets and the redefinition of the country's foreign relations doctrine, for which NATO and EU accession were centerpieces. Early in his tenure, Wałęsa was said to appeal to then US President Bush, expressing Warsaw's strong desire to join the West in the form of its political, economic, and military institutions.[7] Poland's democratization process earned the country the status of liberal democracy (three out of three) in the V-Dem democracy index since 1990, maintained consecutively until the country's accession to NATO in 1999. The Polity-IV ranking similarly assessed Poland's record, placing it above the democratic threshold in 1991 (eight out of ten), raising its score to nine in 1995, finally settling for a perfect ten (full democracy) in 2002. Since 1992, Freedom House also defined Poland's regime status as free, praising it for its swift transition to a free-market economy and successful coping with a severe political crisis with a balanced and freedom-oriented approach. During the early 1990s, Poland saw significant improvement in the state of its rule of law and civil and political rights. The country's modern-day Constitution was adopted in 1997, reflecting the nature of Poland's modern democratic values, instating a complex system of institutional checks and balances and establishing a Western-model Judiciary.

Hungary too has seen a relatively rapid and successful post-Communist transition, after over forty-five years of as a Soviet satellite state. János Kádár, general secretary of the Hungarian Socialist Workers' Party (MSZMP) since 1956, has been removed from power in 1988 and died in 1989, as Moscow's grip in Central and Eastern Europe was quickly wearing away. MSZMP began a series of national consultations with pro-democracy opposition elements in March 1989 (including the Federation of Young Democrats [Fidesz], and the), known as the Round Table Talks, heralding in a series of mass demonstrations calling for Soviet withdrawal from the country. Hungary's first multiparty elections since 1945 took place in March 1990, won by the center-right Hungarian Democratic Forum (MDF), seeing its leader József Antall's rise to power as Prime Minister. Under Antall, Hungary adopted a modern Western-style market economy, and promoted substantial reforms in the rule of law and preliminary transformation to democracy. Antall's policy earned Hungary the status of liberal democracy (three out of three) in the V-Dem democracy index since 1991, maintained consecutively until its accession to NATO in 1999. The Polity-IV ranking similarly assessed Hungary's record, providing it with the perfect ten out of ten score (full democracy) as early as in 1990, also defined as free by Freedom House. Faced with an economic downturn, Antall oversaw a period of increased stagnation and enhanced domestic instability, until his death in office in December 1993. The Parliamentary elections held in May 1994 saw the Hungarian Socialist Party's return to power, with the appointment of Gyula Horn as the country's new Prime Minister. In a challenging step for Horn's party, the newly appointment government adopted severe austerity measures to cope with the looming crisis, and significantly promoted Hungary's membership bid in NATO and the EU.

The third member of the 1999 NATO enlargement club, the Czech Republic, experienced decades of oppression under Communist-led regimes, including the notorious 1968 Soviet invasion of the country after attempted domestic reforms aiming for economic and political liberalization. Toward the end of the 1980s, in a similar fashion to other prominent Central and Eastern European actors, mass public demonstrations implemented an intolerable amount of pressure on the Communist regime, driving its demise in what came to be known as the 1989 Velvet Revolution. This series of nonviolent demonstrations occurred during a consecutive month between November and December 1989, driving the collapse of the Communist regime in the country with the Politburo's resignation, and the eventual rise to power of prominent pro-democracy dissident leader Václav Havel—who became president of Czechoslovakia in December 1989. The country's first multiparty elections took place in June 1990, and under Havel's leadership (who remained in power consecutively until 2003), it adopted far-reaching reforms aimed to consolidate the democratic regime in the country, and strongly promote the prospects for EU and NATO membership. This effort earned the Czech Republic the status of liberal democracy (three out of three) in the V-Dem democracy index since 1990, maintained consecutively until the country's accession to NATO in 1999. The Polity-IV ranking placed the Czech Republic above the democratic threshold in 1990 (seven out of ten), raising its score to a perfect ten out of ten (full democracy) since 1993, while also being characterized as free by Freedom House all through its accession in 1999. Havel oversaw Czechoslovakia's peaceful dissolution in 1993, and the corresponding transition to an independent democratic Czech Republic, with a newly adopted constitutional document in January 1993, coupled with the country's Charter of Fundamental Rights and Freedoms. Throughout his tenure, Havel heavily campaigned for Czech membership in NATO, and is considered to be a key driver of the Alliance's decision to integrate three ex–Warsaw Pact members into NATO as early as 1999. A particularly noteworthy attempt, described by historian M. E. Sarotte, involved Havel's request from then US President Bush to consider an association agreement between the Czech Republic and NATO, to which Bush replied: "I assure you we don't want Poland, Hungary, or Czechoslovakia in a European no man's land."[8]

Following the initial invitation for accession talks during the NATO summit in Madrid (July 1997), membership negotiations with the Czech Republic, Hungary, and Poland were underway. The process lasted four consecutive rounds, covering a wide array of issues ranging from the topical military reform procedures to the political scope of democracy and rule of law. Eventually, the domestic ratification process among all NATO Allies was finalized in late 1998, and the three became full members in March 1999. NATO's statement that accompanied their final incorporation stressed that further enlargements are welcome, as long as they meet the requirement to further the reach of democracy, human rights and the rule of law.

> Today a new chapter opens in the history of the Atlantic Alliance and of Europe. The North Atlantic Council warmly welcomes three new Allies—the Czech Republic, Poland and Hungary. The Alliance will continue to welcome new members in a position to further the principles of the Treaty. . . . NATO's door will remain open to all those willing and able to contribute to our common vision of a lasting order of peace based on human rights, freedom and democracy.[9]

Charles Grant, founding director of the Centre for European Reform and veteran Europe correspondent, opined in a 2002 article that the 1999 enlargement wave expressed the importance of the Alliance's political role as a "pan-European security organization," and exemplified NATO's path of becoming more of a political club than a rather than a coherent military structure.[10]

NATO Reinvented: The Integration of Bulgaria, Estonia, Latvia, Lithuania, Romania, Slovakia, and Slovenia, 2004

With the accession of the Czech Republic, Hungary, and Poland in 1999, NATO sent a clear signal of its interest in continued expansion, repeatedly declaring that the Alliance's door will remain open to all those willing and able to contribute to the common vision of a lasting order of peace based on human rights, freedom, and democracy. This sentiment was formally stressed in NATO's 1999 Strategic Concept, and at the corresponding 1999 Washington Summit, which adopted the newly established Membership Action Plan (MAP). As noted by Goldgeier, while some observers were dissatisfied with NATO's decision not to immediately pursue further enlargement rounds, the mere introduction of MAP and the commitment to review other candidates as early as 2002 locked the Alliance into a vector of expansion.[11] One year after the Washington Summit Declaration and the accession of Poland, Hungary, and the Czech Republic, a Ministerial meeting of the NAC (May 2000) unequivocally assured that further enlargements were expected down the road: "We reaffirm the Alliance's commitment to remain open to new members. We are all the more convinced that our decision to enlarge was an important strategic choice. . . . The three countries which joined NATO in 1999 will not be the last. The Alliance expects to extend further invitations in coming years to nations willing and able to assume the responsibilities and obligations of membership.[12] A similar approach was voiced by NATO Secretary General Lord Robertson at a press conference in June 2001, clarifying that "there will be an enlargement at the Prague Summit next year . . . we believe [that] NATO enlargement will contribute to the security and stability of the Euro-Atlantic area as a whole. . . . The Heads of State and Government decided today that the zero option is off the table."[13]

However, key NATO members and decision makers were at odds over the question of democratic suitability and commitment to the Alliance's normative domain by other prospective members, referring to some of them as "anti-communist . . . but far from democratic."[14] Indeed, the seven new members that eventually acceded in the next enlargement wave in 2004 (Estonia, Latvia, Lithuania, Romania, Slovakia, Slovenia, and Bulgaria) were somewhat divergent in their democratic characteristics. While the Baltics (Estonia, Latvia, and Lithuania), and to a certain extent Slovenia and Slovakia, were considered relatively well suited in terms of their adherence to democracy and the rule of law, the two others—Romania and Bulgaria—scored lower in the various democracy indices. The next sections examine the domestic circumstances underpinning this reality, and NATO's policy in light of their democratic constellation.

Romania

Ever since the Romanian revolution in December 1989, and the subsequent demise of the Communist regime in the country, Romania has been on the path to build and consolidate its democratic institutions and adopt Western-inspired values with regard to its civil society and the structure of its economy. This multifaceted effort included various reforms in the governance process, together with the civilian control and oversight of

Romania's armed forces and intelligence apparatuses—a core requirement for future NATO membership.[15] This effort coincided with the institution and strengthening of Romania's freedom of the press—as well as the gradual solidification of other rule-of-law mechanisms in the country, which had been shaken by decades of Communist rule. As dozens of new political parties came into being, the country held its first democratic national elections in May 1990, resulting in the ascent to power of Ion Iliescu, leader of the governing National Salvation Front (FSN). A few years later, in October 1993, Romania achieved a significant landmark in the road toward democratization by joining the Council of Europe. As noted by Gheciu, NATO decision-makers had a positive view of the reform pace in Romania in the period leading up the 1997 Madrid Summit, yet they concluded that the actual progress achieved under Iliescu's socialist government and the short period after his electoral defeat in 1996 was still insufficient with regard to the Alliance's expectations for adequate democratic norms and mechanisms.[16] In line with this view, Barany argues that in late 1996, Romania was still struggling to exhibit a consolidated democracy, also lacking a properly functioning market economy, and that (somewhat compensating for rejecting Romanian membership in 1997), the US was willing to offer Romania a bilateral strategic partnership.[17] After Iliescu's successor—Emil Constantinescu of the Romanian Democratic Convention Party (CDR)—took office in November 1996, his government embarked on a series of reforms on democratization, privatization, and anticorruption legislation, despite several economic downturns that led to social unrest (known as *mineriads*). In 1999, NATO advisers were involved in drafting the country's national security principles under the Annual National Plan, subsequently endorsed by the Alliance, indicating its deep involvement in the Romania's reform progression.[18] This process coincided with the country's newly adopted National Security Strategy, which involved, among other things, the consolidation of democracy and the protection of civil freedoms and minority rights.[19] As Iliescu's Party of Social Democracy in Romania (PDSR) returned to power in 2000, the country experienced several consecutive years of economic growth, despite continuous political turbulence over alleged corruption accusations, and actively participated in the international coalition in Afghanistan, taking part in the NATO-led International Security Assistance Force (ISAF) mission. This effort helped cement Romania's candidacy status within NATO decision-makers and among the political circles in the US, as the country's membership aspirations were still being evaluated by the Alliance and remained undecided, in what then Romanian Foreign Minister Mircea

Geoana referred to as a shadowy area.[20] With the turn of the century, Romania first earned the status of *democracy* according to the Polity IV ranking, also characterized as free (Freedom House), while at the same time it was considered a flawed democracy according to the Economist index, and an electoral democracy (V-Dem score)—as opposed to the superior liberal democracy status.

BULGARIA

Emerging from nearly forty-five years under Communist rule with strongman Todor Zhivkov at the helm between 1954 and 1989, Bulgaria held its first multiparty free parliamentary elections in June 1990. The campaign resulted in a victory for the Bulgarian Socialist Party (BSP), the successors of the Communist Party, sidelining the reformist Union of Democratic Forces (UDF). Nevertheless, over the course of the following months, the country initiated a series of roundtable negotiations between the Socialist Party and members of the pro-reform opposition, eventually leading to up to the adoption of a new Bulgarian constitution in 1991. The drafting process was widely praised as a valuable mechanism for fostering democratic amendments in the country, allowing for a constructive dialogue between all stakeholders.[21] In October 1991, Bulgaria saw its first elections after the adoption of the new constitution, resulting with an unprecedented victory for the SDS Party, which led to a reformist government under SDS leader Philip Dimitrov. Under Dimitrov, Bulgaria had undergone some key democratic reforms, including instating human rights legislation, curbing domestic ethnic tensions, and beefing up democratic institutions, the rule of law and market economy. Bulgaria's first presidential elections, held in January 1992, saw the rise of Union of Democratic Forces leader Zhelyu Zhelev, having already served in the role since August 1990, after an internal election process in the Grand National Assembly. Bulgaria first earned the status of democracy in 1990, according to the Polity IV ranking (a score of seven out of ten), and gradually improved its standing until reaching an impressive score of nine in 2001. Freedom House also characterized the country as free since the early 1990s, citing its multiparty system, newly adopted constitution (1991), and first presidential elections (1992)—coupled with adequate freedom of expression, association, and assembly.[22] Finally, Bulgaria was dubbed an electoral democracy in 1991, according to the V-Dem democracy index. The county's path toward the West continued in 1992, as Bulgaria joined the Council of Europe, and forged stronger ties with the EU, but the pace of reform slowed with the appointment of a new Socialist government in late 1992, followed by another BSP government elected in 1994. In the following years, the country coped with a severe financial crisis, resulting in skyrocketing inflation and widespread protests and civil unrest across Bulgaria. A new pro-market government, led by UDF leader Ivan Kostov, took power in 1997, speeding up economic reforms and publicly supporting applying for NATO membership.[23] Under this political climate, which involved sustained efforts for democratization and market liberalization, Bulgaria received praise from key NATO Allies, and its status as a NATO aspiring nation has slowly cemented, making it a strong candidate leading up to the 2002 Prague Summit. Like its regional peers, it also took part in NATO-affiliated operations in the Balkans, and then Afghanistan, signaling its commitment to the Alliance's involvement in military campaigns.

The Slovak Republic (Slovakia)

Like other polities in Central and Eastern Europe, Slovakia (formally named the Slovak Republic) had undergone a substantial political transformation in the period between 1989 and1990, signaling the country's future transition to democracy. However, unlike adjacent states, the Slovak case for democratic shift entailed a more complex process of determining the faith of the Czechoslovak state—a sovereign nation first created in 1918, dissolved during World War II, and later reinstated as an Eastern-bloc protégé state. In November 1989, the country entered a phase of peaceful transition of power known as the Velvet Revolution, which eventually ended over forty years of Communist rule in Czechoslovakia, following mass demonstrations in Prague. This process of transition, which involved vast constitutional amendments, brought about the first democratic election in the (still) unified country (June 1990), followed with the creation of a caretaker government—that is, a national understanding government. While economic, social, and political reforms were being implemented, the political progression also drove debates over the future of Czechoslovakia that eventually developed into its dissolution and split into two separate entities: the Czech Republic and the Slovak Republic, as of January 1993. The initial period following Slovak independence (under the leadership of Vladimir Mečiar, head of the People's Party) saw deterioration in personal freedoms and the autonomy of the press, coupled with stagnation in economic reform. These semi-authoritarian measures prevented democratization and eventually destabilized Mečiar's government, leading to its breakdown in 1994. The new government, led by former Foreign

Minister Jozef Moravcik, was essentially unstable from its inception, allowing Mečiar's return to power. While Mečiar maintained that the Slovak Republic was aiming for NATO and EU membership, in practice his tenure was characterized by a further narrowing of political liberties. According to a European Parliament brief, Mečiar's government "became increasingly populist, nationalist and authoritarian in nature," eventually stepping down from power only after an unsuccessful 1998 election bid.[24] This state of affairs significantly decelerated the country's integration prospects with NATO and the EU. As noted by Gheciu, in the road leading to the 1997 Madrid Summit decision to extend an invitation to Poland, the Czech Republic, and Hungary, Slovakia's candidacy was disregarded given its antidemocratic practices under Mečiar's regime, suspension of economic liberalization, and a particularly poor human rights record.[25] A similar sentiment is shared by Barany, who defined Slovakia's regime in 1998 as quasi-authoritarian, under Mečiar's rule,[26] quoting repeated US and NATO warnings over the latter's lack of commitment to democracy and the rule of law. Mečiar's successor, Mikuláš Dzurinda, leader of the Slovak Democratic Coalition (SDK) Party, went on to serve as Prime Minister from October 1998 to July 2006. Under Dzurinda, the pace of domestic reform increased, bringing the country's EU and NATO membership campaign back on track, also securing a prestigious association with the OECD in September 2000. According to Barany, immediately after Dzurinda's rise to power in October 1998, his government sent an open letter to NATO Secretary General Jaiver Solana, promising to introduce political and economic reforms in line with democratic principles and respect for the rule of law.[27] In accordance with Dzurinda's democratic and market reforms, the Slovak Republic's Polity IV democracy score rose from a status of preliminary baseline democracy (seven out of ten), to a solid score of nine points in 1998 onward, eventually gaining a perfect score of ten in 2006, after its EU and NATO integration. Freedom House, which in its 1995–1996 report cited concerns over freedom of expression, freedom of the judiciary, and government pressure of the media, conveyed significant improvements since 1998 in Slovakia's civil and political rights.[28] Finally, the Slovak Republic was dubbed an electoral democracy since 1994, according to the V-Dem democracy index, gaining the status of a full-fledged liberal democracy in 1999. The regime's continued commitment to NATO and EU integration (including staging an October 2000 conference titled Slovakia Belongs in NATO) surpassed domestic political differences, as several political factions agreed to bolster the country's attempts to finalize the integration efforts.[29] This entailed, among other things, the deployment of local forces in tandem with NATO missions in Yugoslavia (1999) and Afghanistan (2002).

SLOVENIA

The winds of change toward the approaching end of the Cold War, and the burgeoning democratic awakening in Central and Eastern Europe, posed a special challenge for Slovenia—then still part of the Yugoslav Federation. The notorious lingering political instability in the region added complexity to its transition process, as it entailed domestic reforms as well as disengagement from the existing political order—a federation of six autonomous Socialist republics (Slovenia, Bosnia and Herzegovina, Croatia, Macedonia, Montenegro, and Serbia). Slovenia had benefited from several domestic reforms in previous decades, viewed as a relatively liberal polity compared to its Yugoslav peers,[30] and traditionally distanced itself from Moscow.[31] However, a real turning point in its political transition was only recorded toward the end of the 1980s, when new political parties began to form in the country. Among those, the first party founded as part of this new reality was the Slovenian Union of Peasants (SKZ), in May 1988. During the years of transition in Eastern and Central Europe, it became clear that Slovenia could not fully form a democratic, pro-Western society without breaking away from Yugoslavia and attaining full national independence. This task seemed feasible, as Slovenia was considered relatively economically developed and open to the West, with a strong civil society that could help sustain democratic consolidation.[32]

The country's presidential elections in April 1990 saw the rise to power of Milan Kučan—a vocal opponent to Slovenia's participation in the Yugoslav union, and a strong independence enthusiast, who—according to Barany—is one of the few Communists in the region to have made a complete personal transition and become a genuine social democrat.[33] The parliamentary elections, also held in April 1990, led to the appointment of Lojze Peterle—president of the newly founded Slovene Christian Democrats—as prime minister. Under the leadership of Kučan and Peterle, with the support of the parliament, Slovenia held a referendum in December 1990, resulting in overwhelming support for autonomy and eventual separation from the Yugoslav Federation in June 1991. However, as Bebler notes, the process of leaving Yugoslavia was met with armed resistance by the Belgrade regime, which left seventy people dead after ten days of hostilities.[34] In the aftermath of these dramatic events, Slovenia adopted a new constitution (December 1991), featuring the importance of democratic and human rights pillars, the formal separation of powers and the establishment of autonomous governance institutions. Kučan was reelected in 1992, holding on to power for another decade, over the course of which he led substantive reforms and actively pushed for EU and NATO membership. Throughout this period, Slovenia received a score of ten out of ten in the Polity IV democracy index (maintained flawlessly to this day), while also securing the status of liberal democracy in the V-Dem index as early as 1991. Freedom House reports for 1992–1993 praised the newly established state for its freedom of speech, freedom of assembly and association, and freedom of religion.[35] After an acute domestic political crisis, Kučan was replaced in late 2002 by Janez Drnovšek, a renowned financial expert, leading a fiscally responsible line focusing on recovering the economy and adopting Western-inspired free market principles. Drnovšek continued his predecessor's pro-European line, and actively campaigned for EU and NATO membership throughout his multiple tenures as Prime Ministers until 2002. As of the mid-1990s, Slovenia swiftly adopted legislation and structural reforms to meet EU and NATO standards in issue areas such as policy making, political institutions reorganization public administration traditions, and improving rule of law standards.[36] Indeed, Slovenia has quickly emerged as a multilateral actor, signing a Cooperation Agreement with the EU in April 1993, applying for a NATO Partnership for Peace membership as early as March 1994, and in 1995 concluding a comprehensive Agreement with the EU. According to Hendrickson, Slovenia was a strong candidate for full membership in NATO's 1997 Madrid Summit, supported among others by Canada, Germany, France, and Italy. Similarly, Barany maintains that since the inception of its campaign for NATO membership, "NATO leaders recognized Slovenia's prominent position in post-communist democratization and market reform."[37] However, the US approach at the time favored a narrower expansion in 1999,[38] a view that according to several observers was derived from Slovenia's reluctance to become entangled in NATO's campaign in Bosnia. Nonetheless, several key US senators did back Slovenia's candidacy, including future-president Joe Biden, supporting Slovenia's accession on account of its consolidated democracy and market economy, coupled with a reputable record of minority rights.[39] Slovenia's NATO campaign continued in the aftermath of its exclusion from the 1999 enlargement, expanding its representation in NATO organs (e.g., forming a national mission to NATO HQ and to the Supreme Headquarters Allied Powers Europe in Mons). This effort was widely acknowledged by NATO decision-makers, who deemed Slovenia part of the Alliance's next expansion round at any possible scenario.

The Baltics: Estonia, Latvia, and Lithuania

Emerging from nearly half a century under Soviet rule, Estonia, Latvia, and Lithuania were among the first and most prominent ex–Soviet republics to experience mass pro-independence and liberalization demonstrations toward the end of the 1980s. During those years, vast crowds in Riga, Tallinn, and Vilnius gathered to protest against the Soviet Union, demanding reforms, as friction behind the Iron Curtain began to accumulate, exposing Moscow's increased weakness and erosion of regional power. The most prominent demonstrations took place in August 1989, as the Baltic Way two-million protesters joined forces to create a human chain between the three capitals. These events were also accompanied with an increased adoption of national characteristics (e.g., shifting the formal language to their local language, as an alternative to Russian). By September 1991, Estonia, Latvia, and Lithuania will have become fully independent, recognized by the Soviet Union, despite its forcible attempts to thwart this development (most notably during the January 1991 events in Lithuania, during which fourteen civilians were killed by Soviet forces). While the Baltic states are widely considered similar in their democratic traits and quality of transition compared to their 1999 enlargement round peers (I Czech Republic, Poland, and Hungary)— the concern over Russia's response to the early incorporation of the Baltics eventually managed to postpone their integration until the next enlargement wave in 2004. At first, the mere idea of a Baltic accession to NATO seemed unthinkable, as these states once comprised formal Soviet Republics and were subsequently famously viewed by the Russians as their *near abroad* area, in which NATO presence would remain implausible. As famously noted by former US Secretary of State Warren Christopher in early 1994, "A swift expansion of NATO eastward could make a neo-imperialist Russia a self-fulfilling prophecy. . . . Premature expansion could lead to the inclusion of states that are not ready, politically or militarily, for the responsibilities of membership."[40] Moreover, according to Katchanovski, the analysis of survey data demonstrates that public opinion in major NATO member states was less supportive of admitting former Soviet republics, compared to their Eastern European post-Communist counterparts.[41] One particular explanation, quoted by Gheciu, was the possibility that allowing the Baltics to prematurely join the Alliance would hamper Russia's prospects for democratization under Boris Yeltsin, curbing the slow emergence of political freedoms in the country and even conceivably overturning the regime in Moscow.[42]

This view was reiterated by Yeltsin, who stated that "I'm against NATO enlargement. . . . When NATO approaches the borders of the Russian Federation, you can say that there will be two military blocs, and this will be a restoration of what we already had"[43]—thus exclaiming that NATO expansion would constitute a major political error. Nonetheless, the relationship between NATO and the Baltic states steadily strengthened during the 1990s, with a starting point as early as November 1990, before the formal recognition of the states' independence was finalized, when the Baltic Information Bureau opened in Brussels. In May 1991, a Lithuanian delegation visited NATO headquarters in Brussels on Denmark's invitation, and later that year all three states jointly became members of the North Atlantic Cooperation Council (NACC). The following year (June 1992), the three Baltic states expressed their willingness to participate in multilateral peacekeeping mission, in an attempt to credibly signal their commitment to the Alliance's regional endeavors (though NATO did not directly take part in such missions at the time).[44] However, as noted by Poast and Urpelainen, this gesture too was met with hesitation at NATO HQ, citing concerns over sending aggressive messages to Russia. In September 1993, another similar attempt was made to formalize the Baltics' role in regional defense and peacekeeping, when the three states signed a Trilateral Declaration for Cooperation in the Field of Security and Defence, finalized the following year, establishing the trilateral Baltic battalion (BALTBAT). Poast and Urpelainen further explain that while the force eventually never deployed a peacekeeping unit, "the core mission of BALTBAT was to assist the Baltic states in Westernizing their military personnel," and, hence, better prepare them for future NATO candidacy, and more generally demonstrate the democratization achieved by their armed forces.[45] However, the real watershed moment was recorded in January 1994, when then Lithuanian President Algirdas Brazauskas sent a letter to NATO Secretary General Wörner, expressing Lithuania's wish to officially join NATO.[46] Shortly afterward, Lithuania became part of the Partnership for Peace program, and established a formal mission to NATO in August 1997. In 1996, the US finalized a roadmap for Baltic integration and anchoring in Europe, known as the Baltic Action Plan, which eventually fell short of full-pledged NATO membership, received with certain dissatisfaction by the Baltics.[47] In another attempt on the bilateral front, in January 1998 the US signed a Charter of Partnership with the Baltic states, cementing their geopolitical integration with the European and North Atlantic region, emphasizing the mutual commitment to democracy.

The Partners affirm their commitment to the rule of law as a foundation for a transatlantic community of free and democratic nations, and to the responsibility . . . to protect and respect the human rights and civil liberties of all individuals. As part of a common vision of a Europe whole and free, the Partners declare that their shared goal is the full integration of Estonia, Latvia, and Lithuania into European and transatlantic political, economic, security, and defense institutions.[48]

Indeed, not all Baltic states were able to fully meet the Alliance's democracy criteria in the mid-1990s, somewhat falling behind the first wave of NATO enlargement states—Poland, Hungary, and the Czech Republic. According to the Polity IV democracy index, while Lithuania achieved a perfect score of ten out of ten since its independence in 1991, Estonia was ranked below the democracy threshold until 1999, whereas Latvia was able to secure a score of eight out of ten since 1991 onward. Similarly, Estonia reached the status of liberal democracy in V-Dem's index in 1996, and Estonia as early as 1993, while Latvia was dubbed an electoral democracy (two out of three) throughout the 1990s. Likewise, the Freedom in the World report for 1997—the year in which NATO's Madrid Summit deliberated the first wave of enlargement—expressed several disturbing concerns over the state of democracy in the Baltics. Particularly, the report exclaimed that "The long-term stability and successful democratic development of the Baltic states is by no means assured."[49] Taking into account the most central critique, that is, the concerns over the delicate strategic balance with Russia and its possible reaction to the inclusion of the Baltics in the 1999 enlargement round, the certain glitches in the (relatively successful) democratic consolidation in some of the states in this region did not contribute to NATO's overall calculations. In April 1999, NATO's Washington Summit Declaration noted the achievements made by the Baltics in their reform process toward NATO membership, inviting them to take part (together with other aspiring members) in the newly established Membership Action Plan (MAP): "Today we recognise and welcome continuing efforts and progress in Estonia, Latvia and Lithuania. . . . We welcome the efforts and progress aspiring members have made, to advance political, military and economic reforms. We appreciate the results achieved, and look forward to further progress by these countries in strengthening their democratic institutions and in restructuring their economies and militaries."[50]

The newly incorporated MAP participants met in Vilnius in May 2000, issuing a statement (known as the Vilnius Statement) expressing commitment to NATO's core values, with an emphasis on the creation of a free and secure Europe. Eventually, the Prague Summit declaration in November 2002 emphasized the achievement reached by Bulgaria, Estonia, Latvia, Lithuania, Romania, Slovakia, and Slovenia in the path for accession, and was followed by a formal invitation to start accession negotiations: "Admitting Bulgaria, Estonia, Latvia, Lithuania, Romania, Slovakia and Slovenia will enhance NATO's ability to face the challenges of today and tomorrow. They have demonstrated their commitment to the basic principles and values set out in the Washington Treaty."[51]

The Age of Hybrid Regime Membership: Croatia, Albania, Montenegro, and North Macedonia, 2009–2020

Albania

Albania is widely considered to be among the last Eastern European pro-Communist states to enter a process of political transition toward a democratic regime with a market economy.[52] After over four decades of Communist rule under Albania's strongman Enver Hoxha—who single-handedly ruled the country from 1941 until his death in 1985—Albania entered a period of mild diplomatic openness and preliminary economic reforms, ending a period of extreme isolationism imposed by Hoxha. Indeed, while Hoxha's successor as first secretary of the Party of Labour of Albania, Ramiz Alia introduced preliminary steps to achieve certain liberalization, the country's Communist-led one-party system persisted into the 1990s, as the first instances of social unrest unfolded. This chain of events led the regime to announce further openness measures (e.g., the autonomy to travel abroad and formally committing to the pro-human rights Helsinki Final Act), eventually succumbing to widespread students' demonstration by agreeing to hold the country's first election since the 1940s, taking place in March 1991. As noted by Pano, between 1991 and 1996, Albania generally succeeded in its democratic transformation process, owing to strong public support for democratic reform, coupled with material backing from the West and a period of economic recovery since 1993.[53] This path was accompanied with the country's accession to the North Atlantic Cooperation Council, and membership in NATO's Partnership for Peace. According to Tafili, in the early 1990s, the notion of democracy in Albania was perceived merely as anticommunism, with a complete abolition of Communist-era governance norms and mechanisms, coupled with a vast and swift drive for privatization. This cultural aspect brought about legitimacy concerns over various democratic pillars, including a deep contestation of the election results in March 1992, won by the newly established Democratic Party of Albania. The Party's charismatic leader, Sali Berisha, became president of Albania, and attempted to advance a set of new reforms; eventually he failed to meet the public's expectations for fast-paced change, though he was criticized for his semi-authoritarian leadership style, citing, among other things, lack of restrictions on executive powers. Berisha enjoyed a close relationship with the American political establishment, and under his directive, Albania unprecedentedly allowed NATO naval and aerial forces to take advantage of the country's ports and runways.[54] Barisha visited NATO headquarters in December 1992, preceding a corresponding visit by then NATO Secretary General Manfred Wörner in Tirana in March 1993. After a series of corruption scandals, accusation of manipulation in the 1996 elections, and widespread public outrage, Berisha was forced to step down in 1997, leading to the eventual rise to power of the Socialist Party. At the time, Albania's prospects of joining NATO seemed particularly slim, and it was not considered a serious candidate at the 1997 Madrid Summit, which decided on the accession of Poland, Hungary, and the Czech Republic. In late 1998, Albania adopted a new Constitution, formally securing its democratic regime, rule of law and respect for human rights. As NATO's military campaign against Yugoslavia during the Kosovo War became imminent in March 1999, Albania managed to distance itself from the ongoing war, while in practice providing a back channel of assistance to NATO and Kosovo Liberation Army (KLA) forces.[55] These events coincided with Albania's association with the Alliance's Membership Action Plan in November 1999—a major landmark in the country's road toward future accession. In the parliamentary elections held in June 2001, the Socialist Party was able to preserve its power, with Prime Minister Ilir Meta at the helm. During his tenure between 1999 and 2002, Meta advanced a series of democratic reforms, including Albania's accession to the EU's Stabilization and Association Process (SAP)—signalizing its potential EU membership aspirations. These developments did not escape NATO's attention, and at the 2002 Prague Summit declaration, the Alliance charted a path for future membership for Albania (together with Croatia and North Macedonia), highlighting their progress in democracy and the rule of law: "We commend Albania for its significant reform progress . . . [and] the former Yugoslav Republic of Macedonia for the significant progress it has achieved in its reform process and . . . overcoming its internal challenges and advancing democracy. . . . Croatia, which has made encouraging progress on reform, will also be under consideration for future membership."[56]

One year later, a NAC ministerial meeting that took place in Brussels in December 2003, reaffirmed that Albania, Croatia, and North Macedonia were on course to join the Alliance, citing their successful reform efforts: "We encourage Albania, Croatia and the former Yugoslav Republic of Macedonia to continue pursuing the reforms necessary to advance their candidacies for NATO membership. We want them to succeed and will continue to support their reform efforts."[57] After a period of political turbulence in Albania, Fatos Nano returned to power as prime minister in July 2002, and went on to further reinforce Albania's Western reorientation, with an emphasis on enhancing the country's ties with EU institutions, but also on taking part in NATO-affiliated military campaigns in Afghanistan (August 2002) and Iraq (2003). During this period, Albania first achieved the status of democracy, according to the Polity IV democracy index (with a score of 7 of out of 10), further improving its score to a solid nine in 2005—several years before its eventual NATO accession. Similarly, only in 2005 did Albania surpass V-Dem's electoral autocracy status (a score of 1 out of 3), and become an electoral democracy (with a score of two). According to the Economist Intelligence Unit Democracy Index, Albania's regime status remained hybrid (short of the democracy threshold) all the way to its accession in 2009, with an average score of 0.55 out of 1, and still remains below 0.6 to this day. Freedom House defined Albania as partly free in its 2005 *Freedom in the World* report, citing significant concerns over the country's corruption, weak institutional design, and political interference among its professional ranks.[58] The country remained partly free according to Freedom House on its accession year in 2009, and still maintains that status in the latest 2021 report. Nano's successor, former President Sali Berisha of the Democratic Party (PD), continued pushing Albania's NATO candidacy, including during an unprecedented visit by then US President George W. Bush in June 2007. According to the Albanian Ministry of Defense, during 2004–2008, Albania "continued the process of consultation with NATO during the annual meetings that are held in the framework of MAP, PARP, and the Ministerial of NATO/EAPC committed to meet the objectives of the partnership."[59] Eventually, Albania was invited to start accession talks with the Alliance in April 2008 (at the Bucharest Summit), finalizing its accession in April 2009. Shortly afterward, a report by the US Bureau of Democracy, Human Rights, and Labor, noted that despite the progress achieved, in Albania there are still "problems including widespread corruption, poor prison and pretrial detention conditions, security force abuse of prisoners, human trafficking."[60] This assessment coincides with previous US views of Albania's insufficient democratic consolidation. A prominent example involved the view voiced by Daniel Fried, US assistant secretary of State for European and Eurasian Affairs, who told the Senate in September 2008 that "Albania has made significant progress in democratic reforms . . . [but] it has more work to do, and we expect reforms to continue."[61] Fried relied on hopes for postmembership improvement, noting that "more reform is still needed . . . [but] fortunately, the history of NATO enlargement suggests that countries continue reforms rather than abandon them, when they join the alliance." During the signing ceremony for Albania's accession (October 2008), President Bush reiterated this notion, stressing that "the road of reforms does not end with acceptance in NATO."[62]

CROATIA

As the domestic and external shocks of liberalization spread across the continent, Croatia's growing pressure for regime reforms came about in December 1989, when internal grievances in the ruling League of Communists of Croatia (SKH) Party brought about the country's first free elections. The inaugural multiparty elections in April 1990 resulted in the rise to power of the Croatian Democratic Union (HDZ) party—a conservative political party founded in June 1989. According to Finn, HDZ's rhetoric portrayed nationalistic messaging, in a manner that can be considered populist and even authoritarian, dominantly aimed at winning the elections and holding on to power.[63] Under the country's first president, Franjo Tuđman, Croatia adopted a new Constitution in December 1990, following a May 1991 independence referendum and a June 1991 declaration of independence from the Socialist Federal Republic of Yugoslavia. The new Constitution laid the foundations Croatia's democracy, emphasizing personal freedoms, the rule of law, equality, and respect for human rights. Given Croatia's complex multiethnic background, the country then deteriorated into violent clashes between the newly establishment regime forces and the Serb militant faction known as the Yugoslav People's Army (JNA). While an initial ceasefire was achieved in 1992, the hostilities continued with Croatia's involvement in the confrontation in Bosnia and Herzegovina, until the war's eventual conclusion with the General Framework Agreement for Peace in Bosnia and Herzegovina (the Dayton Accords, December 1995). Tuđman was reelected twice during the 1990s, and remained in office until his death in 1999. Throughout his postwar presidency, Croatia experienced a period of significant economic growth as part of the country's transformation into a market economy, albeit concerns over corruption in the process of privatization grew significantly, and Freedom House reports even indicate incidents of political intimidation. As NATO's military campaign in Kosovo instigated, Tuđman supported the Alliance's operations by providing access to Croatia's airspace, and other forms of logistical support to the NATO-led Kosovo Force (KFOR). After Tuđman's death, amid concerns over autocratic and illiberal practices, the Croatian Constitution was amended to transfer additional powers to the parliament and to the cabinet, curbing presidential dominance. Tuđman's successor, Stjepan Mesić, viewed his predecessor as authoritarian, strongly pushed for EU and NATO membership, and is frequently credited for Croatia's democratic turn in the 2000s. According to Zakošek, during this period, Croatia transformed into a moderate pluralist system, with a significant decrease in nationalistic and antidemocratic tendencies, which was moving politically toward the center.[64] As part of this process, Croatia joined NATO's Partnership for Peace program in May 2000 (after senior diplomats already signaled the country's intention to do so as early as 1994), and in 2002 it became part of the Membership Action Plan. According to formal NATO accounts, the key domestic reform areas encompassed political restructurings, aimed at supporting its democracy, reducing corruption and improving Croatia's public sector.[65] In 2000, Croatia also first achieved the status of democracy, according to the Polity IV democracy index (with a score of eight of out of ten), further improving its score to nine in 2005—several years before its eventual NATO accession. Similarly, only in 2000 Croatia was able to achieve a status of electoral democracy, with a score of two out of three in V-Dem's democracy index. According to the Economist Intelligence Unit Democracy Index, Croatia was defined as a hybrid regime in the early 2000s, before achieving the status of flawed democracy in 2006—a position maintained to this day. Finally, Freedom House defined Croatia as Free in its 2005 Freedom in the World report, positively evaluating its process of democratic consolidating.

Since 2003, Croatia supported NATO's International Security Assistance Force (ISAF) in Afghanistan, and participated in several Alliance-led programs aimed to prepare the country for membership. These efforts came to fruition as NATO sought to deepen its focus on Eastern and Southeastern Europe, formally labeling these regions *priority areas*. This was particularly evident in a high-level statement titled Euro-Atlantic Partnership—Refocusing and Renewal, issued in June 2004: "NATO will continue to engage, and promote democratic transformation in, and regional co-operation between, Partner countries in Eastern and South-East Europe . . . [and] where possible and appropriate, NATO will refocus existing resources toward these two regions, consistent with NATO's long-term strategy."[66]

A December 2004 NAC ministerial meeting acknowledged the progress made by all three aspiring members in the region (Croatia, Albania, and North Macedonia), calling for further reform before eventual NATO membership.[67] This steady line of careful monitoring, followed with a public recognition of these countries' achievements, continued in the following years. A December 2007 NAC ministerial council reinforced NATO's commitment to democratic values in the Western Balkans, commending Albania, Croatia, and North Macedonia; recognizing their progress in exercising reforms; and expressing an intention to extend a membership invitation: "We recognise the strong reform efforts being made by . . . Albania, Croatia and the former Yugoslav Republic of Macedonia and urge them to intensify their respective efforts. At the Bucharest Summit, our Heads of State and Government intend to invite those countries who meet NATO's performance-based standards and are able and willing to contribute to Euro-Atlantic security and stability."[68] As planned, the Bucharest Summit Declaration in April 2008 echoed the perceived success of the process of NATO enlargement in promoting the vision of a free, democratic, and peaceful Europe based on the Alliance's common values, issuing an invitation to Albania and Croatia to begin accession talks (North Macedonia was left out, as it was yet to resolve the name dispute with Greece): "Our invitation to Albania and Croatia . . . marks the beginning of a new chapter for the Western Balkans. . . . We recognise the hard work and the commitment demonstrated by the former Yugoslav Republic of Macedonia. . . . Albania and Croatia . . . have demonstrated a solid commitment to the basic principles set out in the Washington Treaty as well as their ability, and readiness, to protect freedom and our shared values."[69]

MONTENEGRO, 2017

As the Balkan region was undergoing tectonic political shifts with the dissolution of the Socialist Federal Republic of Yugoslavia into several separate entities, political elites in Montenegro decided to opt for the preservation of a dual federation with Serbia, jointly called the Federal Republic of Yugoslavia. This policy was pushed by the successor of the long-timed ruling League of Communists—the Democratic Party of Socialists (DPS). Under the party's leadership, the support for the union with Serbia was significantly reinforced in March 1992, when over 62 percent of Montenegrins opted to remain tied to Serbia—a vote that was severely contested and hence boycotted by several groups supporting autonomy. During the Bosnian and Croatian wars in the early 1990s, Montenegrin forces supported the Serbian military efforts (including the infamous siege of Dubrovnik), which involved wide accusations of human rights violations. However, as noted by Darmanović, the country's transition toward independence and eventual democracy began with Prime Minister's Milo Đukanović disenchantment with Slobodan Milošević in the mid-1990s— after years of close political alliance between the two.[70] Acting as president since January 1998, Đukanović opted to limit Montenegro's involvement in NATO's military campaign against Serbia, adopting further legislative measures to substantiate Montenegro's autonomous institutional structure, in preparation for another independence referendum. These measures involved liberalization of the country's economy, including adoption of the deutsche mark as its new currency in 1999. In the following years, Đukanović apologized for Montenegro's role in the siege of Dubrovnik, and led the negotiations to replace the Federal Republic of Yugoslavia (FRY) with a union of states they named Serbia and Montenegro, with the involvement of the EU's High Representative Javier Solana—paving the way for a future referendum on independence. The independence referendum eventually took place in May 2006, passing with a small margin of slightly over the 55 percent necessary to support the resolution. In 2006, the Polity IV democracy index defined Montenegro as a democracy, with an impressive score of nine out of ten. However, the V-Dem democracy index repeatedly questioned Montenegro's democratic strength, inconclusively rotating its ranking between electoral autocracy (2001–2003, 2006–2009, 2013, and onward) and electoral democracy (2004–2005 and 2010–2012). This vagueness also appeared in the Economist Intelligence Unit Democracy Index, where Montenegro ranked as a flawed democracy from 2006 to 2009, before falling to the hybrid regime zone (below 0.6 points out of 1) since 2010. Finally, Freedom House defined Montenegro as partly free in 2009, free in 2012, falling back to partly free in its NATO accession year.

In October 2007, Montenegro adopted a new Constitution, replacing the 1992 document, formally identifying the country as democratic, emphasizing civil rights, social equality, and environmentalism. According to Darmanović, Montenegro's peaceful transition to democracy can be explained by its gradual pace—slowly adopting a pro-independence public stance since the early 1990s, with an active encouragement provided by the EU—and by the lack of extremist factions in the country. During his fifth term in office starting early 2008, Đukanović bolstered Montenegro's relationship with NATO and the EU, formally applying for EU membership in December 2008, and securing a NATO Membership Action Plan in December 2009 (after becoming part of the PfP in November 2006). Yet the long years of Đukanović's rule drove harsh criticism with regard to the regime's use of autocratic tactics and abuse of power, which consistently translated to various assessments classifying the country as a hybrid regime. This reality did not preclude, however, the Montenegro's path toward NATO membership, and at the Strasbourg/Kehl NATO summit in April 2009, the Alliance specifically commended Montenegro's progress in domestic reforms. At the Lisbon Summit in 2010, Montenegro received yet another honorable mention in the race for NATO membership, as Alliance leaders praised the country's evolution in implementing its tailored MAP reform mechanism: "We welcome the considerable progress that Montenegro has made on its road to Euro-Atlantic integration. . . . Its active engagement in the Membership Action Plan demonstrates firm commitment to join the Alliance."[71]

In December 2015, NATO Foreign Ministers had issued a special statement on the Alliance's open-door policy, officially inviting Montenegro to begin accession talks with NATO. The foreign ministers still expected further progress on reform, particularly in rule of law, but the decision to include Montenegro at that point was already settled—formally finalized in June 2017.

North Macedonia

The latest country to join the Alliance in March 2020 was North Macedonia. Previously known as the Former Yugoslav Republic of Macedonia (FYROM) until February 2019—the country gained its independence in September 1991, as a result of the dissolution of the Socialist Federal Republic of Yugoslavia. FYROM's decision to declare independence became undisputable after holding a national referendum on its sovereignty, supported by roughly 95 percent of participants. North Macedonia's first president, Kiro Gligorov, started his first tenure in January 1991, before the county's independence, and remained in office until the end of his second term in 1999, surviving an assassination attempt in October 1995. Under Gligorov, FYROM adopted a new constitution in November 1992, proclaiming the essentials for its newly established democratic system, including such foundations as equal civil rights and the rule of law. In 1995, North Macedonia joined NATO's Partnership for Peace program, forming a preliminary forum for consultations and mutual dialogue with the Alliance. One of Gligorov's most notable achievements was the normalization of the country's relations with Greece. As North Macedonian sovereignty did not involve resistance by the Yugoslav regime, international recognition was fairly swift, excluding the approach expressed by Greece. The Greeks viewed certain aspects of Macedonian history and symbols (including its originally adopted flag) as ancient representations of Greece's history and early heritage. Gligorov played an instrumental role in supervising the delicate ties with Greece, most notably by achieving a September 1995 bilateral agreement and introducing constitutional amendments to remove stalemates (e.g., agreeing to change the country's flag, lifting a Greek trade embargo). This enabled FYROM to attain full UN membership in 1993, bolstering its diplomatic status, despite the necessary to maintain the FYROM caveat. While Gligorov repeatedly expressed his desire that the country should aspire to EU and NATO membership, in 1999 FYROM hosted NATO-affiliated forces during the Alliance's military campaign in Serbia. At the same year, FYROM became part of NATO's Membership Action Plan, along with eight other future members, also taking part in the Vilnius Group—an informal club of NATO aspirant states, formed in May 2001. Under Gligorov's successor, Boris Trajkovski, FYROM adopted (August 2001) constitutional amendments designed to provide legal rights to the country's Albanian minority, as part of the Ohrid Agreement—a NATO-brokered settlement ending armed hostilities between FYROM armed forces and the separatist National Liberation Army. Trajkovski was credited with improving the country's intra-ethnic relations, thereby enhancing its democratic resilience, before tragically losing his life in a plane crash in February 2004, succeeded by Social Democratic Union of Macedonia acting Prime Minister Branko Crvenkovski. Trajkovski's tenure also brought FYROM above the threshold of democracy, according to the Polity IV democracy index, with an impressive score of nine out of ten since 2002. At the same year, FYROM achieved a status of electoral democracy, according to the V-Dem democracy index, before falling back to the status of electoral autocracy in 2012–2016. As for the Economist Intelligence Unit Democracy Index, FYROM consistently ranked just below the flawed democracy benchmark, failing to rise above the inferior definition of hybrid regime (six out of ten). Finally, Freedom

House defined FYROM as partly free in all years prior to its eventual accession in 2020.

Trajkovski's successor, Branko Crvenkovski, prioritized NATO and EU membership, a stance also shared by Gjorge Ivanov, who was elected president in April 2009. Despite Greece's veto on FYROM's NATO membership at the 2008 Bucharest Summit, Ivanov famously appealed to then US President Barack Obama for support, requesting assistance in resolving the long-standing name dispute with Greece, aiming to push the country's prospects for integration. On the day after his inauguration, Ivanov traveled to Brussels to meet with NATO and EU officials, signaling the intensity of the country's intentions. After the Bucharest Summit, then Macedonian Foreign Minister Antonio Milošoski said that "it is very regretful for the principles of democracy that Macedonia's bid for NATO membership was punished, not because of what we have done but because of who we are." Nevertheless, throughout the first decade of the 2000s, FYROM participated in several NATO programs, including the Operational Capabilities Concept, the Defence Education Enhancement program, the Science for Peace and Security program, and the Building Integrity program, aimed at fostering good governance, reducing the risks for corruption and strengthening transparency. Additionally, the country supported the NATO-led coalition in Afghanistan, and played a significant role in the Alliance's operations in Kosovo.[72] Although at the 2008 Bucharest Summit NATO declared that FYROM would join the Alliance only after the resolution of the name issue, the debate with Greece would only be resolved in 2018 with the Prespa Agreement. Under the agreement, FYROM agreed to formally change its name to North Macedonia, allowing the commencement of accession talks with the EU (following the removal of Greece's veto). In July 2019, North Macedonia began its accession talks with NATO as well, finalizing as early as March 2020. In the interim period before finalizing its membership, NATO kept pushing for democratic reforms in the country: "The Allies continued to encourage and support the continuation of reform efforts within the country, particularly with a view to ensuring effective democratic dialogue, media freedom, judicial independence and a fully functioning multi-ethnic society."[73]

In summary, the most recent enlargement instances (which preceded the war in Ukraine in 2022)—incorporating Albania, Croatia, Montenegro, and North Macedonia—can be considered notoriously weak in their adherence to democracy, according to four prominent rankings (see table 5.1), demonstrating the notion of NATO's democratic erosion.

Table 5.1. Normalized democracy rankings at accession year

Candidate Country	Accession Year	Freedom House Index at Year	Polity IV Ranking at Year	Economist Democracy Index at Year	V-Dem Score at Year
Albania	2009	0.67 (**Partly Free**)	0.90 (Democracy)	0.59 (**Hybrid Regime**)	0.66 (Electoral Democracy)
Croatia	2009	0.83 (Free)	0.90 (Democracy)	0.68 (**Flawed Regime**)	0.66 (Electoral Democracy)
Montenegro	2017	0.67 (**Partly Free**)	0.90 (Democracy)	0.57 (**Hybrid Regime**)	0.33 (**Electoral Autocracy**)
North Macedonia	2020	0.54 (**Partly Free**)	0.90 (Democracy)	0.60 (**Hybrid Regime**)	0.66 (Electoral Democracy)

Source: Freedom House; Polity IV; V-Dem.

THE WILDCARDS OF NATO ENLARGEMENT: FINLAND AND SWEDEN

Historically, Finland's territory was part of Sweden until the Finnish War of 1809, when it became part of the Russian Empire, before eventually gaining its independence in 1917. Ever since, the defining factor of Finland's defense and security policy is vested in its relations with Russia—with whom the Nordic country fought a vicious war in 1939–1940 (known as the Winter War), followed with further World War II fighting (the Continuation War), lasting until 1944. These grand confrontations eventually resulted in the Soviet annexation of substantial border-adjacent territories (encompassing over 10 percent of Finland's territory), with the vast 1,350-kilometer international border separating the West from the Iron Curtain. The Cold War–era Finnish approach to NATO is rooted in its long-standing military nonalignment doctrine, anchored in traditional domestic agreement. According to this school of thought, which has attained the status of national consensus over the second half of the twentieth century—while Russia constitutes the country's foremost national security threat, Finland should not fully align itself with NATO, and abstain from formal membership. During the Cold War, Helsinki often sought to maintain relative neutrality while preserving a maximum degree of national autonomy in its foreign relations, in an attempt to prevent further confrontations with Moscow, seeking to maintain decent diplomatic ties. This approach was anchored by the Finnish-Soviet Agreement of Friendship, Cooperation, and Mutual Assistance of 1948, formalizing the relationship between the two neighbors. Subsequently, the Soviet Union retained significant influence in Finland's politics, as exemplified during Finland's 1958 parliamentary elections, when domestic political hardships strained the relations with the Soviet Union, eventually leading up to then President Kekkonen's high-level visit to Moscow to ease tensions and restore regional order.

Nevertheless, since the end of the Cold War, Finland's cooperation with NATO has encompassed several noteworthy spheres, including the Alliance's Partnership for Peace program and the Euro-Atlantic Partnership Council—in which it takes part since the 1990s.[74] More recently, Finland was defined as one of NATO's Enhanced Opportunity Partners, taking part in political consultations, intelligence sharing, and consistently contributing to NATO-led missions (including in Afghanistan and Iraq). In 2017, Finland signed a Political Framework Arrangement with NATO, according to which the parties will enhance their cooperation in cyberdefense. Finland's strategic importance grew significantly as a result of NATO's shift toward Arctic security over the recent decade, and in the aftermath of Russia's 2014 war with Ukraine. With these developments, Finland's coordination with NATO has intensified, positioning the intimate ties with the Alliance as a hallmark of Finnish national modern security policy, while maintaining its nonmembership doctrine. Indeed, since 2014, Finland also bolstered its military coordination with neighboring Sweden (another historically Western non-NATO ally), with both countries significantly playing an increasing role in the Alliance's collective security posture in Northern Europe (most notably through the Alliance's Enhanced Opportunities Partnership). With these developments in mind, the nonalignment approach prevalent in Helsinki and Stockholm has significantly eroded in recent years, de facto integrating the two Nordic states into NATO's operational umbrella, with strong EU backing. This also manifested in greater bilateral military ties with the US, who recently provided Finland with modem F-35 fighter jets, and maintains a close bilateral partnership with the two. Before 2021, Finland's national defense doctrine could have been described as maintaining extremely close relations with NATO, sharing a common threat perception, but falling short of full membership. Nevertheless, the February 2022 Russian war in Ukraine tilted the delicate balance in the country's stance toward NATO, as Moscow's aggression pushed Finnish public opinion closer than ever before to support NATO membership. According to a late February 2022 statement by Prime Minister Sanna Marin, "it is very understandable that many Finns have changed or are changing their minds after Russia's war on Ukraine."[75] Public support for NATO membership bolstered in recent surveys, demonstrating over 50 percent, sometimes even reaching 70 percent, of public support NATO membership. As the war in Ukraine unfolded, Finland unprecedentedly pledged weapon shipments to Ukraine, and held parliamentary debates over the future of the country's NATO policy, helped by a renewed national security review process. This state of affairs has brought effective public support for NATO membership to new levels, as the country had been preparing to make a final decision on membership before the NATO Summit in Madrid in June 2022, with significant parliamentary backing. In October 2021, as Russia was building its forces on Ukraine's borders, NATO Secretary General Stoltenberg met with Finnish President Niinistö, praising the Alliance's cooperation with Finland, and clarifying that NATO's door remains open for Finland: "The Secretary General welcomed the close cooperation between NATO and Finland, . . . including through NATO's enhanced forward presence in the Baltic region, our air policing mission and of course Finland's commitment to its national defence. . . . The Secretary General and President Niinistö also discussed NATO's Open-Door policy and the Secretary General reiterated that the Alliance's door remains open."[76]

As Stoltenberg also met with Finland's prime minister and foreign minister, NATO's communiqué noted that "NATO has deepened its cooperation with Sweden and Finland in recent years. . . . Allied leaders also pledged to bolster political dialogue and cooperation between NATO, Sweden and Finland in support of our common security, including by crisis management preparation, exercises, and exchanging information and analysis."[77] With tensions growing further on the Ukrainian front, Secretary General Stoltenberg met with Foreign Minister Pekka Haavisto of Finland and Foreign Minister Ann Linde of Sweden in January 2022, pointing out that "The worsening security situation in Europe makes NATO's cooperation and dialogue with Finland and Sweden even more important," stressing that it is for Finland and Sweden to sovereignly decide on their membership status. As the war in Ukraine became a staggering reality, Russian Foreign Ministry threatened Finland and Sweden, aggressively suggesting that their possible accession to NATO could carry grave consequences: "Finland and Sweden should not base their security on damaging the security of other countries and their accession to NATO can have detrimental consequences and face some military and political consequences."[78]

Later, the Russian MFA also stressed that it "regarded the Finnish commitment to a military non-alignment policy as an important factor in ensuring security and stability in northern Europe," further signaling the potential costs of such decision. Finnish President Niinistö unequivocally rejected Russian demands, stating that Finland reserved national sovereignty on its foreign and security policy. Finnish official documents had repeatedly underscored that the country's potential accession to NATO would have an unforeseeable effect on regional security and Finland's standing. A prominent example is found in an April 2016 report by the Finnish Ministry of Foreign Affairs, titled *The Effects of Finland's Possible NATO Membership*, offering the view that a decision to formally accede to NATO would transform the country's security posturing: "A decision to join the Atlantic Alliance and its Article 5 collective defence commitment would represent a sea change, transforming Finland's security policy overall, and its relationship with Russia in particular. Paradoxically, the deepest effects would not be in the sphere of military policy and dispositions. . . . The shift would be geopolitical and strategic in nature."[79] This approach seems to have sustained a momentous shift in the aftermath of Russia's invasion of Ukraine, as an April 2022 government report on changes in the security environment exemplifies.[80] The report stresses that the invasion demonstrates the necessity to reconsider Finnish longtime pillars of neutrality, and reassess its NATO policy: "Following Russia's invasion of Ukraine, a fundamental change has taken place in the security environment of Finland. This report assesses changes in the operating and security environment and the effects of the changed security situation. Maintaining national room to maneuver and freedom of choice remain integral parts of Finland's policy, . . . retaining the option of applying for NATO membership." More specifically, the report considers the main implications of Finland's possible application to join NATO, while maintaining that Helsinki meets all accession criteria, and bearing in mind the obligations that full membership may entail (including the placement of NATO forces and military facilities on Finnish soil),

> From NATO's perspective, Finland has a strong defence capability and resilient society. Finland is a country that provides security, is interoperable with NATO and meets the membership criteria. Should Finland become a NATO member, the threshold for using military force in the region would rise. . . . Finland would be prepared to support other NATO member countries in a possible Article 5 situation. The expected level of Finland's contribution to collective defence would be negotiated between Finland and NATO. . . . One of the questions raised in the accession talks would be NATO's possible military presence in Finland. Membership would not oblige Finland to accept nuclear weapons, permanent bases or troops in its territory.

The dramatic events in Ukraine also drove unprecedented parliamentary support for Finland's NATO option, as a vast majority of the country's political forces publicly expressed support for membership since the invasion of Ukraine. And indeed, in early May 2022, Finland had made a historic leap toward NATO membership, when President Niinistö and Prime Minister Marin jointly announced their intention to apply for membership, vowing that the step would shall bolster Finland's national security. Following parliamentary approval, Finland submitted its formal membership application to NATO, while also securing bilateral support for the country's interim ratification period from both the US and the UK.

Like Finland, Sweden had also maintained a long-standing policy of military nonalignment, seeking to promote its national security interests by remaining neutral with regard to the Cold War grand confrontations between the US and the Soviet Union. While neighboring Norway and Denmark sought to secure their defense interests by fully aligning with NATO, Sweden remained exterior to the Alliance's orbit, but simultaneously agreed to hold intelligence exchange with NATO during the Cold War, in tandem with receiving significant Western aid. Unlike Finland, Sweden does not directly border Russia, and hence could more easily maneuver during the Cold War in maintaining the delicate balance between its Western orientation and willingness for normalized diplomatic ties with Moscow. This position had also enabled it to maintain close collaboration with Washington and its regional NATO Allies, without prompting a direct threat against the Soviet Union. With the end of the Cold War, Sweden (jointly with Finland) became part of the EU in 1995, and initiated a wide array of cooperation schemes with NATO across several programs. In that regard, suffice it to mention Sweden's participation in the Partnership for Peace program since 1994, its membership in the Euro-Atlantic Partnership Council since 1997, along with the country's contribution to NATO's Kosovo Force (KFOR), NATO Mission Iraq (NMI), and its involvement in Afghanistan (2003–2014), Bosnia and Herzegovina (1995), and Libya (2011). More recently, Sweden has become associated with the Alliance's Partnership Interoperability Initiative as an Enhanced Opportunities Partner, along with Finland, Australia, Georgia, Jordan, and Ukraine.[81] Nevertheless, Sweden's modern defense policy watershed moment took place in 2014, as Russia's invasion and annexation of parts of Ukraine drove the country to ramp up its defense spending, reinstate its mandatory conscription in 2017, and boost its bilateral ties with NATO. In September 2020, NATO Secretary General Stoltenberg met with Swedish Foreign Minister Ann Linde to discuss bilateral cooperation, followed with Sweden's participation in a meeting of the NAC.[82] As tensions on the Ukrainian border were mounting, Stoltenberg visited Stockholm in October 2021, to meet with Carl XVI Gustaf, King of Sweden, and with Swedish Prime Minister Stefan Löfven, discussing greater information exchanges, joint exercises, and political dialogue.[83] Shortly thereafter, he also visited a joint Swedish-Finnish Naval Exercise, stressing the importance of the military ties with the Alliance in the wake of "Russia's aggressive posturing and its military build-up."[84] In the context of the February 2022 war in Ukraine, Sweden has already ramped up its ties and coordination with NATO, encompassing a wide range of political consultations. It also took steps to enhance its participation in the Alliance's Response Force (NRF), playing a role as a Host Nation Support partner, providing valuable logistical backing for NATO nations. Secretary General Stoltenberg met with Swedish Foreign Minister Ann Linde and Finnish Foreign Minister Pekka Haavisto in Brussels in January 2022, emphasizing the importance of bilateral ties with the two in the wake of the crisis, as well as NATO's respect for sovereign decision-making on possible membership:

"The worsening security situation in Europe makes NATO's cooperation and dialogue with Finland and Sweden even more important. . . . Finland and Sweden are NATO's closest partners; we share the same values and we face the same challenge. While NATO cooperates closely with Finland and Sweden, we fully respect your strong and independent security policies. It is for you alone to decide on your path. Not Russia. Not anyone else."[85] And indeed, the devastating events resulting from Russia's invasion of Ukraine contributed to Swedish public favorability vis-à-vis the possibility of joining the Alliance, as an Aftonbladet poll released in March 2022 demonstrated that over 50 percent of Swedes supported the country's NATO-option—a 10 percent rise compared to January 2022.[86] A Finnish HS-Gallup poll conducted in March 2022 showed similar numbers, climbing up to 48 percent,[87] reaching a tremendous support of 57 percent in April 2022. In April 2022, Swedish Social-Democrat Prime Minister Magdalena Andersson alluded to Sweden's ongoing security review, declaring that Sweden was ready to discuss its nonalignment policy in light of Moscow's aggression.[88] The Social Democratic Party statement also made it clear that "when Russia invaded Ukraine, Sweden's security position changed fundamentally." Soon thereafter, Swedish Prime Minister Andersson and Finnish Prime Minister Marin held a bilateral discussion in Stockholm to weigh their common transatlantic strategy, paving the way for a parliamentary discussion of the implications of NATO membership. Finally, in May 2022, Stockholm made an historic announcement of its intention to pursue full NATO membership, in tandem with the Finnish bid. As Russia's invasion of Ukraine stretched on, Moscow's initial response to the Nordic dramatic policy shift has been rhetorically powerful, given the Kremlin's traditional view of nonalignment as a pillar of regional stability. Accordingly, Moscow voiced its discontent with Finland and Sweden's decision to pursue NATO membership in an array of public statements and explicit threats. One of the most prominent speakers in this regard has been Russia's former President Dmitry Medvedev, who said that in a scenario of Finnish-Swedish accession, all Russia's forces in the Baltic region would be bolstered, including its nuclear capabilities,[89] and threatened that this development "makes the risk of a full-fledged nuclear war with the west rifer than ever."

As both Nordic states were on course toward full membership, Finland and Sweden rightfully expected swift vetting procedures in the Alliance's internal consultations, eyeing a possible integration as early as June 2022, as NATO was set to hold its Summit Meeting in Madrid. As both states demonstrate exemplary levels of democracy (see table 5.2), widely considered to hold significant military strength and enjoy tremen-

Table 5.2. Normalized democracy rankings

Candidate Country	Freedom House Index, 2022	Polity 5 Ranking, 2019	Economist Democracy Index, 2022	V-Dem Score, 2022
Finland	1.00 (Free)	1.00 (Full Democracy)	0.93 (Full Democracy)	1.00 (Liberal Democracy)
Sweden	1.00 (Free)	1.00 (Full Democracy)	0.94 (Full Democracy)	1.00 (Liberal Democracy)

Source: Freedom House; Polity IV; The Economist; V-Dem.

dous legitimacy and diplomatic support, the perception in Helsinki and Stockholm indeed seemed quite likely.

And indeed, the accession-talks stage was announced as being fully complete after NATO's Madrid Summit in July 2022, followed by signing the Accession Protocols, setting in motion the domestic ratification process by all NATO member states. Nevertheless, this step, in which thirty Allies ratify Finland and Sweden's accession to the Alliance, turned out to be quite lengthy and tedious, contrary to the preliminary optimistic expectations. While a vast majority of NATO member states completed the ratification process within six to eight weeks, a rather resolute opposition was expressed by Turkey, demanding Finland and Sweden to comprehensively halt their alleged support of Kurdish elements deemed terrorist organizations by Turkey. This request involved extradition of several individuals to Turkey, and other measured seen as infringing on the Nordic states' autonomous foreign and security policy. Although Turkey's demands were said to touch more on Sweden rather than on Finland, President Niinistö of Finland promised in June 2022 that Helsinki won't go forward without Stockholm in its accession process, in a step demonstrating the unity in their NATO bid. Alongside Turkey, Hungary remained the only NATO Ally to delay domestic ratification. While Budapest hadn't declared any specific conflicts of interest with regard Finland and Sweden's accession, various observers expressed concern that Hungary wished to refrain from displeasing Russian President Putin by ratifying quickly, as Hungary had been less vocal and decisive compared to other NATO members on Russia's invasion of Ukraine. As Turkey, Sweden, and Finland seemed to have reached an agreement to allow the accession process to move forward in June 2022, addressing Turkey's concerns, the parties held a trilateral meeting of the new Permanent Joint Mechanism in August 2022 in Finland, with hopes to drive Turkish ratification. Nevertheless, over the course of the following months, Turkey signaled its unwillingness to finalize Sweden's accession, while increasingly expressing political flexibility on Finland's membership. While initially aiming to join the Alliance simultaneously, Finland came to realize that Ankara was planning on further delaying Swedish membership until a major political breakthrough, and agreed to pursue a unilateral membership path. Ultimately, Turkey further withheld the vote over Finland's membership until March 30, 2023, when its Parliament formally approved the bill to integrate Finland into the Alliance (several days after the Parliament in Budapest took the same path), clearing the way for Helsinki to become NATO's thirty-first member state in April 2023. In one of its first acts as a formal Ally, Finland's Foreign Minister Pekka Haavisto participated in an informal meeting of NATO ministers of foreign affairs (May 2023), advocating for a swift completion of Sweden's membership ratification before the Alliance's summit in July 2023. Nonetheless, despite further efforts under the framework of the Permanent Joint Mechanism between Finland, Sweden, and Turkey, which convened in June, no substantial progress has been achieved concerning Sweden's accession.

Indeed, tensions between Ankara and Stockholm steadily grew over the recent year, after a demonstration in central Stockholm (January 2023) during which a far-right politician had burned the Quran, infuriating Turkish leadership. Hungary also maintains political grievances toward Stockholm, blocking its membership path, citing Swedish condensation over Hungary's democracy and rule of law standards, and accusing it of playing an active role in initiating EU sanctions over Hungary. The country's stance on Sweden is also believed to be influenced by Turkey's position, as Budapest increasingly views Ankara as an ally in an era of declining democratic order, and seeks to take advantage of its veto power to unfreeze EU funding and reboot its relations with Brussels from a position of power.

Nevertheless, in a July 2023 statement following a meeting between Turkey, Sweden, and the NATO secretary general, Turkey has agreed to transmit Sweden's accession protocol to the Grand National Assembly[90]—a step that is expected to finalize Stockholm's membership. The Alliance's Vilnius Summit Communiqué expressed the same sentiment: "We look forward to welcoming Sweden as a full member . . . and welcome the agreement reached between the NATO Secretary General, the President of Türkiye, and the Prime Minister of Sweden."[91]

Postaccession, Finland and Sweden are expected to occupy an imperative role within the Alliance's eastern flank, providing robust defense and national security capabilities on NATO's new and expanded border with Russia. Militarily, as noted by Ojanen, Finland and Sweden bring to the table their advanced proficiencies in the Baltic Sea region, with modern vessels and strong antiship capabilities (including a shallow-water submarine fleet), while also contributing to air domination and strong intelligence capabilities.[92] As Elgin and Lanoszka point out, their operational and strategic ties with the Alliance had already been extremely deep, even compared to existing Allies, thus making their formal accession important particularly in the realms of identity and strategic culture.[93] Sweden and Finland's vibrant democracy, rich historic tradition, and substantial military capabilities will undoubtedly make the Nordic states prominent members of the Alliance in the decades to come.

Chapter 6

The Prospects for Future Expansion

UKRAINE

Ukraine's relations with NATO date back to the early years of the post-Soviet period. The newly independent Ukraine joined the North Atlantic Cooperation Council (NACC) in 1991, and became part of the Partnership for Peace program in 1994. As the country's ties with the Alliance deepened, in 1997 NATO formed the NATO-Ukraine Commission (NUC), as part of the bilateral Charter on a Distinctive Partnership—built to enhance cooperation and consultations between the parties, often at the level of heads of state and government.[1] As part of this development, the Alliance's Madrid Declaration on Euro-Atlantic Security and Cooperation (July 1997) emphasized Ukraine's role in European security: "We attach great importance to the NATO-Ukraine Charter. . . . It will move NATO-Ukraine cooperation onto a more substantive level, offer new potential for strengthening our relationship, and enhance security in the region more widely. We are convinced that Ukraine's independence, territorial integrity and sovereignty are a key factor for ensuring stability in Europe. We continue to support the reform process in Ukraine as it develops as a democratic nation with a market economy."[2]

In the Alliance's 1999 Strategic Concept, Ukraine was recognized as a valuable partner to promote European stability and democracy, expressing support for further democratizations and reforms: "Ukraine occupies a special place in the Euro-Atlantic security environment and is an important and valuable partner in promoting stability and common democratic values. NATO is committed to further strengthening its distinctive partnership with Ukraine on the basis of the NATO-Ukraine Charter, including political consultations. The Alliance continues to support Ukrainian sovereignty and independence, territorial integrity, democratic development and economic prosperity as key factors of stability and security in central and eastern Europe."[3] This chain of events was accompanied with a record in Ukraine's democracy rankings, as the country first achieved a score of seven out of ten (minimum democracy threshold) in the Polity IV index between 1994 and 1999, coupled with a score of two out of three (electoral democracy) in V-Dem's regime classification, while also dubbed partly free by Freedom House. Ukraine's ability to secure such prominent democracy scores early on was particularly remarkable, and set the country on the fast track for stronger ties with the West. Further bilateral mechanisms between Ukraine and the Alliance, such as the NATO Information and Documentation Centre and the NATO Liaison Office (established in 1997 and 1999, respectively), were put in place to facilitate the public diplomacy aspects of this partnership. The NATO-Ukraine Commission hosted an array of meetings and consultation, generally adopting a favorable approach toward Ukrainian efforts to meet key Alliance requirements. In 2002, Ukraine publicly announced its intention to become a full member of the Alliance, although this declaration was not accompanied by concrete legal or policy-focused steps. NATO did, however, create the NATO-Ukraine Action Plan during its November 2002 Prague Summit, with the goal of strengthening the country's democratic composition, fighting corruption, and securing various personal freedoms.[4] Correspondingly, at a meeting of the NATO-Ukraine Commission in November 2003, NATO ambassadors made clear the Alliance's expectation from Ukraine in the field of democratic reform, hinting that much further progress was necessary: "Allied Ambassadors . . . emphasized the importance of free and fair elections, guaranteed media freedoms and rule of law, political reform, the strengthening of civil society and judiciary, and of improving defence-related export controls."[5]

Over the following year, the Commission accompanied Ukraine's advancement in reforms, often suggesting that the country's efforts left much to be desired. After the November 2004 mass demonstrations contesting the results of the presidential election (known as the Orange Revolution, resulting in the rise to power of Western-oriented President Viktor Yushchenko), the Ukrainian leadership became more invested in obtaining a MAP status. As the political establishment in the country grew increasingly divided over the character of relations with NATO (with Prime Minister Victor Yanukovych as chief opposition against integration), the bilateral ties became strained. Yet, in early 2008, Yushchenko (with backing from then Prime Minister Yulia Tymoshenko) formally applied to receive a MAP status, with the support of then US President George W. Bush. While Ukraine was eventually unable to secure MAP status, and despite the democracy and rule of law challenges to Ukraine's membership aspirations, NATO's Bucharest Summit Declaration (April 2008) included a direct commitment for the future accession of Ukraine and Georgia, praising them for the reforms already achieved.

> NATO welcomes Ukraine's and Georgia's Euro-Atlantic aspi-
> rations for membership in NATO. We agreed today that these
> countries will become members of NATO. Both nations have
> made valuable contributions to Alliance operations. We wel-
> come the democratic reforms in Ukraine and Georgia and look
> forward to free and fair parliamentary elections in Georgia in
> May. MAP is the next step for Ukraine and Georgia on their
> direct way to membership. . . . We will now begin a period
> of intensive engagement with both at a high political level.

This optimistic view of the prospects for future enlargement was promoted by the George W. Bush administration, which supported the notion of Ukraine's integration. During a press conference with Ukrainian President Yushchenko in April 2008, approaching the Bucharest Summit, Bush expressed support for MAP status for Ukraine: "Ukraine now seeks to deepens its cooperation with the NATO alliance through a Membership Action Plan. Your nation has made a bold decision, and the United States strongly supports your request. In Bucharest this week I will continue to make America's position clear: We support MAP for Ukraine and Georgia. Helping Ukraine move toward NATO membership is in the interest of every member in the Alliance."[6]

Despite President Bush's ambition, other member states opposed the inclusion of Ukraine within MAP, most prominently France, Germany, Italy, and Hungary. Hence, the wording of the Bucharest statement was vague enough to allow a future membership path for Ukraine, without making a credible commitment. Soon thereafter, in August 2008, Moscow launched a miliary offensive against Georgian forces, resulting with the Russian occupation of two Georgian regions bordering Russia. Despite the geopolitical complexity, subsequent NATO documents and declarations undertook a very confident tone in fortifying the commitment to inte-grate Ukraine into the Alliance. The Strasbourg/Kehl Summit Declaration of April 2009 powerfully reiterated the Bucharest pledge to Georgia and Ukraine, emphasizing the democratic component in the process toward building membership capacity: "In Bucharest we agreed that Ukraine and Georgia will become members of NATO and we reaffirm all elements of that decision. . . . We strongly encourage Georgia to continue implementing all necessary reforms, particularly democratic, electoral, and judicial reforms, in order to achieve its Euro-Atlantic aspirations."[7]

With an eye on the aftermath of the military escalation between Georgia and Russia, Ukraine's then President-elect Viktor Yanukovych decided in early 2010 to put a temporary lid on the country's membership prospects. Faced with his predecessor's Yushchenko's unpopular push for NATO and EU membership, Yanukovych opted a smoother relationship with Russia, embarking on a postelection effort to improve ties between both countries.[8] During the Chicago Summit meeting in May 2012, NATO alluded to the prospects for Ukrainian membership, highlighting substantial shortcomings in the country's democratic nature and state of its rule of law, which were clearly framed as a leading obstacle for its future integration: "We are concerned by the selective application of justice and what appear to be politically motivated prosecutions, including of leading members of the opposition, and the conditions of their detention. We encourage Ukraine to address the existing shortcomings of its judicial system to ensure full compliance with the rule of law and the international agreements. . . . We also encourage Ukraine to ensure free, fair and inclusive Parliamentary elections this autumn." In a similar fashion, as mass demonstrations in Ukraine (known as Euromaidan) broke in November 2013, protesting the regime's decision (under President Viktor Yanukovych) to suspend the EU-Ukraine Association Agreement, NATO condemned the government's excessive use of force: "We condemn the use of excessive force against peaceful demonstrators in Ukraine. We call on all parties to refrain from provocations and violence. We urge Ukraine . . . to fully abide by its international commitments and to uphold the freedom of expression and assembly. We urge the government and the opposition to engage in dialogue and launch a reform process."[9]

As events in Ukraine escalated further, with the persistence of mass demonstrations in the country and severe clashes between regime security forces and protesters in Kyiv, President Yanukovych was eventually ousted, and the Ukrainian government dissolved. Shortly thereafter, Ukrainian membership in NATO became even more unattainable, after a Russian military intervention in Eastern Ukraine, which resulted in the annexation of the Crimean Peninsula in March 2014. The Russian campaign came as a response to the ousting of pro-Russian Yanukovych in what came to be known as the Revolution of Dignity. As the Russians considered Yanukovych's ousting an illegal coup, pressures in the Russian-speaking Eastern Ukraine regions mounted, eventually resulting in a controversial Russian invasion. In September 2014, NATO heads of state and government held a summit in Wales to discuss the events in Ukraine, condemning the Russian acts in the strongest possible terms, calling on Moscow to "immediately withdraw its forces from inside Ukraine and cease the violation of its sovereignty."[10] Undoubtedly, the Russian acts made the scenario of Ukrainian NATO membership extremely difficult, as—similarly to the situation in Georgia—pro-Russian separatists now occupied parts of the country's territory. As things stood, NATO Allies would be extremely reluctant to admit a new member that is engaged in an active territorial dispute with Russia. The events also drove down Ukraine's democracy scores, because since 2014 it attained a ranking of four out of ten (below the democracy threshold) in the Polity IV index, coupled with a score of one out of three (electoral autocracy) in V-Dem's regime classification. While the country was still dubbed partly free by Freedom House, the 2014 Freedom in the World report noted Ukraine's downgrading of democracy, citing violence against journalists and media manipulation as part of President Yanukovych's "decision to forego an EU agreement and accept financial assistance from Russia without public consultation and against the wishes of a large portion of the Ukrainian people."[11] The Economist Democracy Index also consistently places Ukraine in the hybrid regime category (0.54 out of 1 in 2022, without significant variation in recent years). With this in mind, at the 2014 Wales Summit NATO could primarily release strong statements in support of democracy in Ukraine, but Allies were not in a position to discuss the prospects of membership: "Allies commend the Ukrainian people's commitment to freedom and democracy. . . . They welcome the holding of free and fair Presidential elections under difficult conditions, which testify to the consolidation of Ukraine's democracy and its European aspiration. Ukraine remains committed to the implementation of wide-ranging reforms, to combat corruption and promote an inclusive political process, based on democratic values, respect for human rights, minorities and the rule of law."

After the presidential election in May 2014 brought to power pro-EU Petro Poroshenko, followed with a relatively free and fair parliamentary election in October 2014, the NATO-Ukraine Commission issued an encouraging statement, yet still refrained from explicitly referring to the path toward full membership—highlighting the necessity for further reform.

> Allies welcome the free and fair conduct of the extraordinary parliamentary elections . . . despite challenging circumstances. The elections are a testimony to the Ukrainian people's commitment to freedom and democracy. Allies will continue to support Ukraine as it embarks on comprehensive reforms. The prompt implementation of such wide-ranging reforms to combat corruption and promote an inclusive political process, based on democratic values, respect for human rights, minorities and the rule of law, remains crucial for the consolidation of Ukrainian democracy.[12]

In lieu of a feasible political solution to the crisis in Ukraine, NATO offered further support in the process of reform implementation in a joint statement in May 2015, highlighting that "Allies welcome the steps undertaken by Ukraine to promote key constitutional reforms. . . . Allies strongly encourage the Government of Ukraine to continue reform efforts and wherever possible, accelerate them."[13] In 2016, NATO put in place a Comprehensive Assistance Package to Ukraine, providing further support and resources to the country, accompanied with several Trust Fund projects formed in direct response to the Russia-Ukraine conflict (including in the field of cyberdefense, military training, and command and control capabilities).[14]

In February 2019, under President Poroshenko, Ukraine adopted a constitutional amendment aimed to enhance the country's commitment toward NATO and EU membership, with the stated goal of applying for EU membership and a NATO MAP status in 2023. The amendment states in article 5 that Ukraine is committed to the "realization of the strategic course of the state on acquiring full-fledged membership in the European Union and in the North Atlantic Treaty Organization," and entrusts the president and the cabinet with the implementation of this mission.[15] This development was favorably received by NATO, implicitly alluding to its 2008 Bucharest Summit statement promising to integrate Ukraine into the Alliance, albeit refraining from directly reaffirming this commitment: "In light of Ukraine's restated aspirations for NATO membership, we stand by our decisions taken at the Bucharest Summit and subsequent Summits. We will work together to enhance and adapt our distinctive partnership. . . . An independent, sovereign and stable Ukraine, firmly committed to democracy, and the rule of law, is key for Euro-Atlantic security."[16]

Since the constitutional amendment, Ukraine's ties with the Alliance grew somewhat closer, as under Ukraine's newly elected President Volodymyr Zelensky the rhetoric on NATO membership became increasingly prominent. In particular, this shift was evident in the country's restructured national security strategy (2020), emphasizing its objective of obtaining full-fledged membership as key in the defensive doctrine against Russia. At the same time, NATO recognized Ukraine as an Enhanced Opportunities Partner in June 2020—part of the Alliance's Partnership Interoperability Initiative, designed to boost bilateral cooperation with partners that have made significant contributions to NATO-led operations and missions.[17] NATO did clarify, on the same occasion, that Ukraine's new status was not expected to prejudice membership decisions, emphasizing that the country is required to promote further reforms in security and defense, democratic oversight, and in the fight against corruption. As geopolitical pressures were mounting between Ukraine and Russia, Moscow embarked on a massive force buildup on Ukraine's eastern borders in March 2021, descending into continuous fear of escalation. In June 2021, the NATO Summit in Brussels emphasized the Alliance's support for Ukraine's sovereignty and territorial integrity, strongly condemning Russian acts: "We reiterate our support for the territorial integrity and sovereignty of Ukraine. . . . We call on Russia to withdraw the forces it has stationed. . . . We strongly condemn and will not recognise Russia's illegal and illegitimate annexation of Crimea. Russia's recent massive military build-up and destabilizing activities in and around Ukraine have further escalated tensions and undermined security."[18]

At Brussels, the Alliance also reiterated the 2008 Bucharest declaration committing to future Ukrainian (and Georgian) membership, while once more emphasizing the need for further reform.

> We reiterate the decision made at the 2008 Bucharest Summit that Ukraine will become a member of the Alliance. . . . We stand firm in our support for Ukraine's right to decide its own future and foreign policy course free from outside interference. . . . The success of wide-ranging, sustainable, and irreversible reforms, including combating corruption, promoting an inclusive political process, based on democratic values, respect for human rights, minorities, and the rule of law, will be crucial in laying the groundwork.

This declarative support for Ukrainian membership, albeit intertwined with demands for further reform, were rightly perceived by Kyiv as valuable backing during a time of increased potential for escalation, complicating even further the country's realistic prospects for membership. This inherently multifaceted political constellation tragically deteriorated in

February 2022, as Russia lunched a full-fledged war against Ukraine, citing—among other justifications—Moscow's concerns over Ukraine's possible NATO membership. What came about was a devastating megascale war, generating a massive refugee crisis, with millions of Ukrainians fleeing their country chiefly toward NATO-member territory, most prominently Poland. The invasion followed a Russian recognition of two self-proclaimed pro-Russian enclaves in Eastern Ukraine's Donbass area, with the alleged purpose of defending these districts from what the Russian proclaimed as Ukrainian aggression. In a later stage of the war, in October 2022, Russia had formally annexed the Luhansk, Donetsk, Zaporizhzhia, and Kherson regions, even though significant military setbacks prevented full Russian control over these territories. On the most shocking violence outbreak on European soil since the 1990s, Russia mobilized over 300,000 multipurpose military forces in several waves (including reserves recruited as a result of an emergency legislation), backed with indiscriminate fire power against civilians, most prominently in Ukraine's eastern regions. While facing a fierce Ukrainian resistance, the Russian destructive tactics brought about massive devastation of entire cities, threatening to tear apart the very statehood and mere existence of Ukraine. Before the end of 2022, Ukraine reported an official number of nearly 20,000 civilian casualties, including over 7,000 deaths. While Ukraine's military had exhibited persisted rigor and efficacy—outperforming all expectations and pushing back Russia's advancement—the humanitarian situation in Ukraine's combat adjacent regions remains dire, in need of urgent relief. According to OHCHR data, by June 2023, the number of nonarmed civilian deaths had reached nearly 9,000,[19] although it is probably more likely to be significantly higher.

Since Russia's full-scale invasion, NATO had ruled out any direct military involvement in the conflict, seeking to preserve the Alliance outside the hostilities. In line with this approach, the Alliance rejected Kyiv's early request to impose a no-fly zone over Ukraine, and avoided other strategic military measures that could create an undesirable miscalculation with Moscow. Responding to this policy, Ukrainian President Zelensky acknowledged the challenges for Ukraine's possible NATO membership: "For years we have been hearing about how the door is supposedly open, . . . but now we hear that we cannot enter. And it is true, and it must be acknowledged."[20] Shortly afterward, the Alliance issued a statement by NATO heads of state and government, which promised that NATO "reaffirms [its] commitment to the Open Door Policy under Article 10 of the Washington Treaty,"[21] but failed to repeat the pledge to offer Ukraine (and Georgia) membership in the future. Eventually, after nearly six months of devastating war, Ukraine formally submitted an application for NATO membership, requesting an "accelerated ascension" into the Alliance, later backed by (mostly) NATO's Eastern Flank countries—Poland, Romania, Slovakia, Czech Republic, Estonia, Latvia, Lithuania, Montenegro, and North Macedonia. But despite the considerable lifeline of military and financial support, NATO had very little to offer Ukraine concerning Kyiv's full membership aspirations. Approaching the NATO Summit in Vilnius in July 2023, Ukraine's minister of Defense, Oleksii Reznikov, expressed hopes that a new mechanism for NATO-Ukraine relations—the Ukraine-NATO Council—can restart their bilateral partnership and ramp up the level of cooperation: "[Under the Council] . . . Ukraine will not yet be a member of NATO, but will already be on an equal footing in all committees, in all representative meetings with the right to raise issues that are particularly spelled out in their agreements."[22] And indeed, at a meeting of NATO Defense Ministers in June 2023, Secretary General Stoltenberg alluded to the creation of the Council, where Ukraine and NATO could discuss security issues on an equal basis. He also pledged a substantial multiyear assistance package to Ukraine, while stopping short of promising an actual path for membership.[23] The inaugural meeting of the newly established Council took place during the Vilnius summit in July 2023,[24] where Allies agreed on a three-part package of support for Ukraine. In addition to the Council, this package is composed of a multiyear program of financial and military assistance, and a vague renewed affirmation of the original Bucharest 2008 commitment that Ukraine will become a member of NATO ("when Allies agree and conditions are met").[25] The Vilnius concluding communiqué also directly addresses the need for further democratic reforms in Ukraine, while recognizing significant progress in this realm: "Ukraine has become increasingly interoperable and politically integrated with the Alliance, and has made substantial progress on its reform path. . . . Allies will continue to support and review Ukraine's progress on . . . additional democratic and security sector reforms that are required."

To conclude, recent events teach a valuable lesson in the sometimes-mystical process of nation-building: if there was ever any doubt about Ukraine's society cohesion, or the willingness to vigorously stand up to protect its core perceived values, the 2022 war speaks volumes about Kyiv's watershed moment of acquiring a common defining sovereign narrative. Ironically, this defining moment in time encapsulates Ukraine's hopes to build a democratic pro-European nation—the mere scenario Moscow was aiming to thwart. The war over Ukraine had already entirely altered the regional, European, and international security architecture and diplomatic state of affairs, and its aftermath and implications on the domestic constellation in Russia and Ukraine are still to be determined. Under these circumstances, it seems almost inconceivable for Ukraine to enter NATO in the foreseeable future, while a longer-range outlook (a decade or more) entails a cautious, lingering hope for Ukraine's political ambitions.

GEORGIA: THE LAND OF UNFULFILLED POTENTIAL

A country of rich historic and sovereign heritage, modern-day Georgia was annexed to the Soviet Union in 1922, in the aftermath of the Red Army's invasion of the country in 1921. As the Soviet Union was rapidly losing grip in Eastern and Central Europe, Georgia also started experiencing a series of protests, strikes, and demonstrations, which grew more frequent and prominent at the beginning of 1989. During a series of mass rallies in April 1989, the Soviet Army violently clashed with protesters, resulting in the death of twenty-one activists, in what came to be known as the Tbilisi Massacre. As the road toward independence unfolded, Georgia's first multiparty Parliamentary elections took place in October 1990, with the pro-independence Round Table–Free Georgia Party claiming a substantial victory, securing nearly 54 percent of the votes. Following the election, Round Table–Free Georgia leader, Zviad Gamsakhurdia, was appointed chairman of the Presidium of the Supreme Council—a governing body later dissolved in January 1992, with the start of the Tbilisi War. Shortly after the parliamentary elections, in March 1991 Georgia held a national referendum on its independence—approved with an overwhelming 99 percent of the votes, with residents of the Abkhazia and South Ossetia districts boycotting the vote. This optimistic vector suffered a massive blow with a violent attempt to topple the Gamsakhurdia regime in late December 1991. After two weeks of fierce clashes, involving a siege of the Parliament building, President Gamsakhurdia was ousted, ceding power to a Military Council—supported by Russia. These dramatic developments signaled the return of Eduard Shevardnadze—former Soviet Foreign Minister and Communist leader of Georgia—who resurfaced in Tbilisi in March 1992. Shevardnadze's comeback marked the beginning of a lengthy civil war, as local clashes in South Ossetia and Abkhazia spread and turned into brutal fighting between the breakaway provinces and regime forces. The confrontations further escalated in 1993, as former President Gamsakhurdia's return to the country sparked a Russian-backed military intervention against Gamsakhurdia loyalists in western Georgia, resulting in extensive casualties and political instability. In 1995, shortly after the country joined NATO's

Partnership for Peace program, Shevardnadze became president of Georgia, after effectively controlling the country since 1992 (also opting for a North Atlantic Cooperation Council membership that year), winning nearly 70 percent of the votes in a November 1995 election. His first five-year term was characterized by significant domestic hardships, following sustained economic instability, flagrant corruption, and high crime rates, coupled with domestic and political challenges (including several attempted assassinations against Shevardnadze). His tenure did, however, involve the strengthening of bilateral ties with the US, as he adopted a declaratively pro-Western foreign policy, including openly defying Russia during its war in Chechnya in 1995–1996. At the same time, Shevardnadze declared his country's interest in EU and NATO membership, and actively contributed military forces to NATO's Kosovo Force (KFOR) beginning in 1999.[26] Shevardnadze was reelected in April 2000 by a large majority, but faced a severe political crisis after the November 2003 parliamentary elections were widely considered fraudulent, sparking mass demonstrations calling for his resignation. These large-scale protests, led by opposition leader Mikheil Saakashvili, exerted heavy pressure on Shevardnadze's regime, until his final resignation in what came to be known as the Rose Revolution in late November. Following a snap presidential election in January 2004, Saakashvili became a predominantly pro-EU and NATO president, leading a strong anticorruption campaign and significantly improving Georgia's economy. Saakashvili's resolute pro-Western line of foreign policy had increased tensions with Russia, wary of its neighbor's orientation and the possibility it could bring NATO and the EU closer to its borders, encouraging Moscow to provide material and political support to the separatist Abkhazia and South Ossetia provinces. Nevertheless, the North Atlantic Council recognized Georgia's advancement in state building efforts and continued reforms, and approved in October 2004 the country's Individual Partnership Action Plan. This chain of events was accompanied with a record in Georgia's democracy rankings, as the country first achieved a score of seven out of ten (minimum democracy threshold) in the Polity IV index in 2005, coupled with a score of two out of three (electoral democracy) in V-Dem's regime classification. The country was also dubbed partly free by Freedom House, due to the free and fair presidential and parliamentary elections. In the following years, Saakashvili's regime was under steady Western and domestic pressure to implement further reforms, while coping with repeated civil unrest and political instability, coupled with growing criticism of corruption. Nevertheless, Saakashvili managed to win the January 2008 presidential elections, with OSCE observers concluding that the vote was relatively free and fair.

A watershed moment for Georgia took place in April 2008, as NATO's Bucharest Summit Declaration pledged to grant the country full membership in the future, under the framework of the MAP mechanism. This seemingly resolute promise had cornered Russia, whose tensions with Georgia were already on the rise after Georgian President Saakashvili repeatedly announced his country's desire for NATO membership, and after a series of bilateral frictions—including a September 2006 exposure of a Russian spy network. In the aftermath of the Bucharest Summit, the situation quickly deteriorated into a twelve-day regional war between Russia and Georgia in early August 2008, that ended with effective Russian control and occupation of two self-proclaimed enclaves—South Ossetia and Abkhazia. The war lasted for twelve days, with several hundreds of casualties on both sides, and nearly two-hundred thousand displaced Georgian residents, expelled from South Ossetia and Abkhazia. Against this backdrop, Georgia's eventual membership became tremendously uncertain, given the vast geopolitical consequences of a potential member state with parts of its territory effectually occupied by Russia. Several months afterward, NATO formed the NATO-Georgia Commission (NGC), aimed to provide a forum for political consultation to assist Georgia in reaching eventual membership—set in motion by NATO Secretary General Jaap de Hoop Scheffer andGeorgian Prime Minister Lado Gurgenidze in Tbilisi. One of the NGC's stated goals was also to support the country's recovery in the aftershock of the war, with regular meetings on the Ambassadorial and military levels.[27] With the establishment of the NGC, the NAC had gone on a visible official visit to Georgia in September 2008, on the occasion of the inaugural meeting of the forum. The joint press statement emphasized Georgia's ambitions to obtain a MAP status, while NATO mostly stressed the continued support for Georgia's democratization and reform process as part of its Individual Partnership Action Plan: "Allied Ambassadors stressed NATO's determination to continue to assist Georgia in its democratic development and the program of reform. . . . They welcomed Georgia's efforts in the fields of democratic, judicial, economic, and defence reforms, and stressed the need to continue, even under the difficult circumstances it currently faces, to make every effort to deepen reforms and make them irreversible."[28]

The Alliance did, however, also emphasize the commitments made at the Bucharest Summit earlier that year, reiterating the promise to integrate Georgia into the Alliance and advance its MAP status: "Allied Ambassadors recalled the Bucharest Summit Declaration, in which NATO Heads of State and Government agreed that Georgia will become a member of NATO, agreed that MAP is the next step for Georgia on its direct way to membership and made clear their support for Georgia's application for MAP." NATO foreign ministers decided on an Annual National Program (ANP) for Georgia, replacing the previous framework of Individual Partnership Action Plan. With that in mind, NATO's Lisbon Summit Declaration in November 2010 continued the relatively confident tone with regard to Georgia's future membership prospects. The statement reaffirmed the commitment set forth in Bucharest in 2008, and reiterated the importance of the democratic factor in the journey toward membership: "At the 2008 Bucharest Summit we agreed that Georgia will become a member of NATO and we reaffirm all elements of that decision. . . . We will foster political dialogue and practical cooperation with Georgia. . . . We strongly encourage and actively support Georgia's continued implementation of all necessary reforms, particularly democratic, electoral and judicial reforms."[29]

At a meeting of the NGC in November 2011, with the participation of the prime minister of Georgia, the Alliance recognized the country's progress in democratic reforms during the 2011 Annual National Program, but noted that the depth and scope of these measures should increase: "Allied Ambassadors welcomed the concrete achievements in Georgia's democratic reform process. They stressed the importance of maintaining the momentum in electoral reform and upholding democratic principles to ensure free, fair and inclusive elections. They encouraged Georgia to continue to strengthen the rule of law and the role of the civil society and media, as well as to deepen reforms regarding the judiciary and the right of assembly."[30] The strong language referencing the commitment to grant membership to Georgia was sustained at NATO's Chicago Summit in May 2012, as leaders once again reiterated their decision at the 2008 Bucharest Summit. Seemingly, this notion became a rather permanent assertion in subsequent key events as well, with the role of the democratic component occupying an important factor for progress: "We continue to encourage and actively support Georgia's ongoing implementation of all necessary reforms, including democratic, electoral, and judicial reforms. . . . We stress the importance of conducting free, fair, and inclusive elections."[31]

As part of the Wales Summit in 2014, NATO provided Georgia with a new integration instrument, called the Substantial NATO-Georgia Package (SNGP), supporting various aspects of membership capacity building. A joint statement of the NATO-Georgia Commission in February 2015 assessed Georgia's performance under this scheme: "NATO Ministers welcomed the steady progress Georgia has shown. . . . They noted the positive trends in Georgia's democratic development, and encouraged

Georgia to continue implementation of reforms, including consolidating democratic institutions, taking forward judicial reforms, and ensuring full respect for the rule of law."[32] In parallel, since 2014 Georgia's democracy ranking slightly improved, as the country achieved a score of seven out of ten (minimum democracy threshold) in the Polity IV index, maintaining its partly free status in the Freedom House index, with a positive mention for its fair and honest presidential election. However, the Economist Democracy Index from 2014 onward places Georgia as a hybrid regime (0.57 of 1 in 2014), without visible improvement. As the stalemate on the Georgian front persisted, in December 2015 NATO Foreign Ministers offered a soothing statement, reassuring that "Georgia's relationship with the Alliance contains all the practical tools to prepare for eventual membership."[33] It did not, however, address in further detail the continued Russian occupation of South Ossetia and Abkhazia, and hence failed to offer a sustainable way forward for the country. This stalemate is also expressed in domestic public opinion toward NATO, as the Caucasus Research Resource Centers (CRRC) time-series survey demonstrated a plunge in support for NATO from a record high of 67 percent in 2012, to as little at 37 percent in 2015.[34] The Warsaw Summit in July 2016 repeated the commitment for the inclusion of Georgia—under the usual caveat that membership is obtainable for European democracies that share the values of our Alliance, and are willing and able to assume the responsibilities and obligations of membership. Nonetheless, Georgia was still in no position to advance toward membership, regardless of the pace of its domestic reforms, given the continued Russian occupation. Still, Georgia was encouraged to pursue the tedious process of reform-making, with a clear warning over the crucial importance NATO sees in its core principles—democracy, the rule of law and human rights: "NATO is an Alliance of values, including individual liberty, human rights, democracy, and the rule of law. These values are essential to what NATO is and what it does. Corruption and poor governance are security challenges which undermine democracy, the rule of law and economic development. The importance of implementing measures to improve integrity building, anti-corruption and good governance applies to NATO, Allies, and partners alike."[35]

At a session of the NGC at the level of foreign ministers, in parallel to the Warsaw Summit, the Alliance voiced its anticipation for democratic consolidation in Georgia, particularly emphasizing its expectation for a free and fair parliamentary election process that was due to take place soon thereafter: "NATO Ministers commended the steady progress made by Georgia towards stronger democracy. . . . Allied Ministers encouraged Georgia to sustain the momentum in its overall reforms . . . looking forward to the October 2016 Parliamentary elections being conducted in accordance with the highest democratic standards." The July 2018 Summit meeting in Brussels was sobering and realistic with regard to the future of NATO enlargement. With the approaching end of the second decade of the millennium, the Alliance was focused on the complex security environment it has been facing, which the Summit Declaration grimly framed in the following manner: "We face a dangerous, unpredictable, and fluid environment, . . . with enduring challenges and threats from all strategic directions, from state and non-state actors; from military forces; and from terrorist, cyber, and hybrid attacks. Russia's aggressive actions . . . challenge the Alliance and are undermining Euro-Atlantic security."[36]

In lieu of a meaningful way forward for Georgia, the Alliance could only offer general support, recognize the progress already made, and back additional reforms. A meeting of the NGC that took place in parallel with the Brussels Summit adopted this reasoning: "Allies recognize the significant progress on reforms which Georgia has made and must continue to do, which are helping Georgia progress in its preparations towards membership, strengthening its defence and interoperability capabilities with the Alliance."[37] A similar sentiment was expressed during the meeting of the NGC in October 2019, where the Alliance welcomed Georgia's progress in consolidating democracy, reiterating the decisions made at the 2008 Bucharest Summit, but once again noted that further progress must continue in order to etch closer to membership. At the June 2021 NATO Summit Meeting in Brussels, Allies called on Russia to "reverse its recognition of the Abkhazia and South Ossetia regions of Georgia as independent states," while repeating the reference to the 2008 Bucharest Summit, and emphasizing the pace of domestic reforms must increase. In a March 2022 interview, Georgian President Salome Zourabichvili acknowledged that Georgia's path to membership while some of its regions are still occupied by Russia is unlikely: "Georgia, having part of the territory occupied, being on the frontline, does not exactly behave as a country that is a member of NATO"[38]. Nevertheless, Georgia opted to submit a formal application to join the EU in May 2022. At NATO's 2022 Madrid Summit in June, the Alliance offered additional support measures for Georgia, helping its modernization and transition from Soviet-era equipment and enhancing its capabilities in the field of chemical, biological, radiological, and nuclear (CBRN) protection. Yet, in the aftermath of Russia's invasion of Ukraine, no particular statement was issued with regard to Georgia potential membership status, although the Alliance's new Strategic Concept (adopted in June 2022) vaguely promised to "reaffirm the decisions taken at the 2008 Bucharest Summit and all subsequent decisions with respect to Georgia and Ukraine." Indeed, as the war in Ukraine had been approaching its one-year anniversary, the NATO Military Committee held a discussion regarding the military cooperation between NATO and Georgia, alluding to the intensified operational relationship between both sides, for example, through Georgia's potential participation in NATO's Mediterranean maritime security scheme ("Operation Sea Guardian"),[39] but without a feasible political path toward membership. The Alliance's July 2023 Vilnius summit communiqué emphasized NATO's commitment to integrate Georgia, while clarifying that "to advance its Euro-Atlantic aspirations, Georgia must make progress on reforms, including key democratic reforms."[40] Hence, the way forward for Georgia toward full membership seems almost implausible, as its long-lasting territorial dispute with Russia—turned into an active military occupation—coupled with its familiar domestic democratic deficiencies, make the country's candidacy status a mere formality.

Bosnia and Herzegovina: Leaving Much to Be Desired

An integral part of the Socialist Federal Republic of Yugoslavia since 1945, the Socialist Republic of Bosnia and Herzegovina was shaped by its deeply rooted interethnic structure, comprising of three main groups: Bosnians of Muslim origin, Bosnian Serbs, and Bosnian Croats. Under Yugoslavia's rule, the federal state ensured multiethnic representation according to a designated ethnic key, without prominence for a specific group, thereby preserving relative domestic stability and avoiding national separatism. This approach began to erode with the destabilization of Communist regimes across Central and Eastern Europe, and the weakening of the Yugoslav Union. Bosnia and Herzegovina's first multiparty parliamentary elections took place in November 1990, resulting in an arrangement securing equal ethnically based representation for the country's national groups. More specifically, in the aftermath of the elections, each group retained dominance of a different domestic powerhouse (A Bosnian Muslim president of the Republic; a Serb president of the Parliament and a Serb prime minister), somewhat similar to the constellation in Lebanon. However, this delicate political pattern quickly became destabilized, as Croatia and Slovenia declared independence from Yugoslavia, creating friction among the ruling elements in the newly established government. Eventually, in January 1992, the Bosnian Serbs formed a separate entity, later known as Republika Srpska, aimed to ensure the domestic interests of the Serb community in Bosnia and Herzegovina. Against this backdrop, Bosnia and Herzegovina's referendum for independence in February 1992 became seriously contested, boycotted by the Bosnian Serb elements. Nonetheless, in the aftermath of the referendum, which resulted in an overwhelming support of over 99 percent of the voters, the Republic of Bosnia and Herzegovina declared its independence in early March 1992, and this was widely and rapidly recognized by the international community. Shortly afterward, the Bosnian War started in April 1992, lasting for nearly three and a half years until its final conclusion with the General Framework Agreement for Peace in Bosnia and Herzegovina (the Dayton Agreement), in December 1995. The war quickly became one of the continent's utmost tragedies since World War II, with over 100,000 casualties and multiple events of ethnic cleansing and war crimes, later investigated by the tailor-made International Criminal Tribunal for the former Yugoslavia. As Bosnian Serbs, supported by the Serbian government, attempted to secure the integrity of ethnic Serb territories, tragic events such as the siege of Sarajevo, the Srebrenica, and Markale massacres became part of the global heritage of wartime tragedies and atrocities. In the aftermath of the Dayton Agreement, Bosnia and Herzegovina integrated the semi-autonomous Republika Srpska, which preserved attributes of self-rule while remaining subordinate to Bosnia and Herzegovina's sovereignty. NATO played a key role in the implementation of the Dayton Agreement by providing peacekeeping forces for nearly ten years, until late 2004, when the EU took over its responsibilities.[41] In the postwar period, the country was engaged in consolidating its fragile domestic stability, helped by the constitutional instrument adopted as part of the Dayton Plan. The document defines the country's commitment to basic freedoms, equality, human rights, and the democratic nature of its regime—with the most prominent multilateral human rights treaties included as annexes to the Constitution. These developments placed Bosnia and Herzegovina in the category of electoral democracy in V-Dem's regime classification (a score of two out of three) since 1997; it was also dubbed partly free by Freedom House, while remotely classified as a hybrid regime by the Economist Democracy Index since 2006 (Polity IV rankings unavailable). Against this backdrop, Bosnia and Herzegovina fares worse than Ukraine and Georgia in adherence to democracy (see table 6.1), with Sarajevo lagging behind other NATO-aspiring states and recent members.

Table 6.1. Normalized democracy rankings

Candidate Country	Freedom House Index, 2022	Polity 5 Ranking, 2019	Economist Democracy Index, 2022	V-Dem Score, 2022
Georgia	0.58 (Partly Free)	0.85 (Democracy)	0.52 (Hybird Regime)	0.66 (Electoral Democracy)
Ukraine	0.61 (Partly Free)	0.70 (Open Anocracy)	0.54 (Hybird Regime)	0.66 (Electoral Democracy)
Bosnia and Herzegovina	0.53 (Partly Free)	n/a	0.50 (Hybird Regime)	0.66 (Electoral Democracy)

Source: Freedom House; Polity IV; The Economist; V-Dem.

Bosnia and Herzegovina has continuously experienced sustained intercommunal tensions, struggling with political corruption and substantial economic hardships. According to the country's constitution, the presidency of Bosnia and Herzegovina is shared among three equal members—Bosniaks, Serbs, and Croats, who serve collectively for a joint four-year term (on a rotating basis). Prime ministers are nominated by the president, then formally appointed by the Parliament. This newly gained relative stability enabled Bosnia and Herzegovina to forge closer ties with NATO. The country became part of NATO's Partnership for Peace program in 2006, and was invited to join the Alliance's Membership Action Plan in April 2010 (in a Ministerial meeting in Tallinn[42])—and currently remains the only state in this program after the accession of North Macedonia in March 2020. At the Lisbon Summit in November 2010, the Alliance noted Bosnia and Herzegovina's improvement and recognized its membership ambitions: "We fully support the membership aspiration of Bosnia and Herzegovina. . . . We reaffirm the decision taken by NATO foreign ministers in Tallinn in April 2010 to invite Bosnia and Herzegovina to join the Membership Action Plan, authorizing the Council to accept Bosnia and Herzegovina's first Annual National Program."

The Chicago Summit Meeting in May 2012 identified four partner states that were working to join NATO, whose progress had been substantial enough to sustain membership. Among those states was Bosnia and Herzegovina, which received further positive feedback for its reform process and other steps in the direction of possible membership, but remained clearly distant from its end goal of reaching full membership. This trend had persisted in the following years as well. While during a December 2015 NATO Foreign Ministers session, the Alliance expressed general support for Bosnia and Herzegovina's membership aspirations, significant concerns over the state of democracy and the rule of law persisted: "We call upon all of the country's leaders to undertake the political, economic, and defence reforms necessary for the country to realize its Euro-Atlantic aspirations. . . . We encourage the leadership of Bosnia and Herzegovina to continue pursuing reforms related to those aspirations."[43]

Under the framework of building its relationship with the Alliance, Bosnia and Herzegovina has committed to a structured reform mechanism, known as the Bosnia and Herzegovina Reform Program, with its first report submitted in December 2019.[44] As part of the country's participation in the PfP, it dissolved the armed forces of Republika Srpska, and merged other defense-related bodies to a centralized state-level. Bosnia and Herzegovina also took part in the Alliance's Building Integrity (BI) program, and over the years provided support to NATO-led operations, including the International Security Assistance Force (ISAF) in Afghanistan. Recently, in early 2021, the country formed a Commission for Cooperation with NATO, in order to enhance its coordination and improve bilateral synchronization with the Alliance. Bosnia and Herzegovina's current (and longest-serving) prime minister, Fadil Novalić, who has been in power since March 2015, is considered an ardent supporter of the country's ambitions to join NATO. During a joint military exercise with NATO, Novalić stated the following:

> In this small but proud country of Bosnia and Herzegovina . . . we can accept and present on the field the highest military standards set by our intention to become a member of NATO one day. . . . We have started the final path towards membership, we will be submitting a new Reform Program every year, working diligently to meet all standards, until NATO assesses that BiH has met all the required criteria and standards, and invites BiH to NATO membership.[45]

At the Brussels Summit in July 2018, Bosnia and Herzegovina was invited to submit its first Annual National Program under the MAP, in which the country took part since 2010. While this may have seemed promising, at a meeting of NATO heads of state in Bucharest in May 2020, the Alliance also sent a signal to Bosnia and Herzegovina on the required pace of reform: "We remain fully committed to the integration of those countries that aspire to join the Alliance, judging each on its own merits. We encourage those partners who aspire to join the Alliance to continue to implement the necessary reforms and decisions to prepare for membership. We will continue to offer support to their efforts and look to them to take the steps necessary to advance their aspirations."

NATO's 2021 Summit Meeting in Brussels marked the Alliance's seventy-first anniversary, a thirty-strong Alliance after North Macedonia's accession in March 2020. At the meeting, Allies were displeased with the slow progress in Bosnia and Herzegovina's political reform, with an emphasis on democracy, making clear that there remains much to be desired in that regard: "We are committed to maintaining strong political dialogue with Bosnia and Herzegovina, and offer our continued support to the implementation of all reform efforts. . . . Allies urge political leaders to work constructively and to demonstrate political will for the benefit of all in Bosnia and Herzegovina in advancing Euro-Atlantic aspirations by implementing the much needed political, electoral, rule of law, economic, and defence reforms."[46]

And yet, the war in Ukraine seems to have had a certain impact on NATO's approach toward the country, as the Alliance vowed to "increase its support for partners, including Bosnia and Herzegovina, to help them build their capabilities and strengthen their resilience."[47] One of these steps was the participation of the Defence minister of Bosnia and Herzegovina at the 2022 NATO Summit in Madrid, where the country was promised a new defense capacity building package. In response, the Russian embassy in Sarajevo accused NATO of pushing Bosnia and Herzegovina closer to the Alliance—"It seems that certain Western states, primarily the United States and Great Britain, are preparing the ground for creeping NATOisation."[48] During the Summit in Madrid, then UK Prime Minister Boris Johnson referred to that situation in Bosnia and Herzegovina, stating the Britain's goal was to "bolster Bosnia's ability to resist malign influences and block the attempts to undermine democracy in Bosnia and Herzegovina and the region," explicitly emphasizing that "we cannot allow the Western Balkans to become another playground for Vladimir Putin's pernicious pursuits."[49] Other NATO leaders, including the prime minister of Slovenia Robert Golob and Croatian president Zoran Milanović, expressed their support for Sarajevo, calling on NATO to enhance its posture and strengthen its presence in the region. In November 2022, as Bosnia and Herzegovina's new Presidency assumed office, Mr. Željko Komšić (representing Bosnian Croats) said that he aims to make NATO membership his first priority.[50] Shortly afterward, NATO deputy assistant secretary general for Political Affairs and Security Policy Javier Colomina visited the country, welcoming the adoption of political reforms, emphasizing NATO's willingness to "finalize a package of enhanced support aimed at enhancing Bosnia and Herzegovina's resilience and the modernization of its defence and security structures."[51] Secretary General Stoltenberg, in a meeting with the chair of the tri-presidency of Bosnia and Herzegovina Sefik Džaferović, promised to maintain NATO's role in Operation ALTHEA—the EU-led military deployment in the country, supervising the implementation of the Dayton Agreement,[52] and in a January 2023 meeting with Denis Bećirović, member of the tripartite presidency, vowed support for Bosnia and Herzegovina's Euro-Atlantic aspirations.[53] In an opinion piece published in April 2023, Bećirović called on NATO to expedite Bosnia and Herzegovina's membership path: "A NATO fast track for Bosnia and Herzegovina would justify the Alliance's value-based purpose. It is a moral obligation to do everything to prevent history from repeating itself in the Balkans. At the crossroads of history, of course with Ukraine in mind, personal and collective experience compel us to stand up and take bold actions."[54]

Looking forward, it seems likely that the aftermath of Russia's invasion of Ukraine could enhance (and soften) Bosnia and Herzegovina's path toward membership, as the Alliance's interest in fortifying its ranks seems more urgent. NATO Secretary General Jens Stoltenberg has recently tied the two together, stating in a press conference in November 2022 that the Alliance's meeting of foreign ministers in Bucharest presented a chance to "review [NATO's—the author] support for Ukraine, as well as other partners facing Russian aggression and pressure, [including] Bosnia and Herzegovina."[55] The Alliance's Vilnius summit in July 2023 reiterated a general commitment to the country's Euro-Atlantic aspirations, while emphasizing that substantial reforms are still in order, including on democracy and the rule of law: "We encourage Bosnia and Herzegovina to take advantage of NATO's support and intensify efforts to make progress on reforms in key areas, including the much-needed political, electoral, rule of law, economic, and defence reforms."[56] Clinched between NATO members Croatia and Montenegro, encompassing an area of 51,200 square kilometers in the Western Balkans and the Adriatic Sea, NATO cannot allow Sarajevo to become the next victim in its struggle with Russia over regional influence on its eastern flank. This goal is expected to prove increasingly difficult, as Russia ramps up its support for rebel factions in Republika Srpska, providing these paramilitary groups with advanced capabilities, with Russian presence on the ground.[57] Russia has acted in support of the Serb leader of the country, Milorad Dodik, who in November 2022 took the position of the president of Republika, and previously speculated a possible secession of Republika Srpska from Bosnia and Herzegovina. Without effective NATO involvement, Russia's hopes of destabilizing the country may lead to its disintegration, thwarting the possibility of its NATO (and EU) membership.

Imagining Further Enlargements: The Glass Ceiling of Expansion

Reflecting on the quickly-changing NATO membership landscape since Russia's invasion of Ukraine, it is conceivable that the Finnish and the forthcoming Swedish accession could drive more historically neutral EU members to reassess their NATO strategy. One possible candidate could be Austria, which adopted its neutrality in 1955, inspired by the classical Swiss model of neutrality, inscribing this policy into its postwar constitution. According to the formula reached between Vienna, Moscow, and Washington, Austria was banned from joining NATO and hosting foreign military forces, bases, and armaments on its soil. The country's State Treaty of 1955 explicitly prohibited all sorts of military engagement or intervention, including placing foreign forces on Austrian soil and association with military alliances.[58] And indeed, under Chancellor Bruno Kreisky, Vienna was able to position itself as a bridge between both sides of the iron curtain during the Cold War, and famously play host for East-West spy games. Nevertheless, the historic policy shift in Stockholm and Helsinki may have encouraged second thoughts in Vienna as well. In the first months after Russia's invasion, then Austrian Chancellor Karl Nehammer stated that Austria intended to maintain its neutrality, in response to an open letter by a group of prominent Austrian figures calling Federal President Alexander van der Bellen to reexamine the merit of the country's neutrality, which still gained the approval of a vast majority of Austrians.[59] In a July 2022 newspaper column, Austrian diplomat Thomas Mayr-Harting wrote that while Austrians still support neutrality, the country must invest further in its cooperation with NATO through the Partnership for Peace framework (in which Austria participates since 1995), and aim to modernize its Federal Armed Forces.[60] Another possible path could be deepening Vienna's ties with other militarily neutral states, such as Ireland and Malta, as suggested in October 2022 by Austrian Defense Minister Klaudia Tanner.[61] Werner Fasslabend, Austria's former minister of Defense, said in a February 2023 interview that Vienna's neutrality has lost its function, and that under NATO's umbrella, the country would be "in a better position to shape European security policy and will gain greater security."[62] Despite several isolated references, the lack of significant public debate on neutrality in Austria exemplifies how deep this principle is entrenched in the country's identity—a component extremely difficult to shift, after nearly seventy years of adherence. Correspondingly, a major public opinion poll carried out in May 2022 demonstrates this notion, concluding that only 14 percent of Austrians were in favor of pursuing NATO membership, while 75 percent opposed.[63] A May 2023 poll preserved this trajectory, with 60 percent opposition to the notion of Austrian NATO membership.[64] Additionally, while Austria takes an active part in the EU's post-2022 sanctions regime against Russia, the country has opposed providing Ukraine weapons or military aid, despite several calls from public interest groups, including a recent petition in February 2023.[65] As purported by Austrian Foreign Minister Alexander Schallenberg in an August 2023 interview, "We are funding more on the humanitarian side. . . . But to be clear, we may be militarily neutral, but Austria has never been neutral when it comes to values."[66] However, while reluctant to offer Ukraine military assistance, Austria (along with neutral Switzerland) has been recently contemplating joining the European air defense initiative ("Sky Shield")—potentially bolstering its own defense capabilities.[67]

The Austrian logic may apply in the case of Ireland—another historically military neutral state, also a long-standing member of the EU. Traditionally, the public sentiment in Ireland favored nonalignment, particularly as the island-state is geographically distant from the continent's East-West power struggles. It does, however, take part in NATO's Partnership for Peace program and participates in the Alliance's Euro-Atlantic Partnership Council. As part of the bilateral partnership, Ireland deployed military forces in support of NATO's operations in Bosnia and Herzegovina, and the Kosovo Force since 1999. Since 2014, Dublin took part in NATO's Partnership Interoperability Initiative, and contributed to NATO's Resolute Support Mission (RSM) in Afghanistan until 2016.[68] With a suboptimal domestic defense spending, and in lieu of full NATO membership, Ireland may now reconsider its traditional stance. Provided its close partnership with NATO, and the change of heart in Helsinki and Stockholm toward membership, it should not be entirely surprising if Ireland opts to recalculate its future membership path as well. The long-standing Irish nonalignment policy has been put to test shortly before the beginning of the war, when Russia announced its intention to hold a massive military exercise near the Irish coast (nearly 200 miles southwest of the city of Cork). This intention raised significant concerns in Dublin over its inability to cope with a possible emerging Russian threat, particularly considering its traditionally very low spending on defense. Shortly afterward, a *Report of the Commission on the Defence Forces* has suggested a significant boost in Ireland's defense spending, noting that "should the Government decide to accept the vision and recommendations proposed in this report, it will result in the Defence Forces of 2030+ being a more modern, diverse organization, with a coherent structure. . . . It will also have enhanced capabilities to defend the State and its people, serve on demanding overseas missions and support national resilience."[69] The report also directly identified Russia as the main threat to Ireland national security within the Western sphere, condemning Moscow's actions in Ukraine and expressing heightened concern over the "hybrid threats [it poses] to Western democracies." In parallel, public opinion polls carried out since the Russian invasion of Ukraine in February 2022 demonstrate that the Irish general public has become more favorable than before toward possible NATO membership, with support numbers reaching 48 percent in March 2022,[70] and a record-high 52 percent in August 2022.[71] The surveys also demonstrated that the core support for abandoning neutrality mostly originates with those who support the incumbent government (Fianna Fáil, Fine Gael, and the Green Party), while those who support the Sinn Féin Party were generally unfavorable. Another strong signal for Ireland's genuine soul-searching in the current era came at a meeting of the European Political Community in June 2023, when Prime Minister Leo Varadkar contemplated joining the EU's Permanent Structure Cooperation initiative (PESCO), and possibly taking part in NATO's Partnership for Peace program. This stems from Ireland's complex security landscape, and its increasing difficulty in sustaining the island's defense needs: "We are an island nation; our seas are seven times greater than our land area. Going through those seas are a lot of really important infrastructure, communications cables that connect Ireland to the world and Europe to North America. . . . I don't think we can protect these on our own."[72] Correspondingly, in June 2023 the country launched a "Consultative Forum on International Security Policy"—a four-day discussion designed, according to the Irish Foreign Ministry, to "build a deeper understanding of the threats faced by the State, and the links to, and between, [Ireland's] foreign, security and defence policy."[73]

Another long-term nonaligned European actor is Malta, which takes part in NATO's PfP program (reactivated in 2008) and participates in the EAPC, while maintaining its commitment to the policy of neutrality. Article 3 in Malta's Constitution stipulates that "Malta is a neutral state actively pursuing peace, security and social progress among all nations by adhering to a policy of non-alignment and refusing to participate in any military alliance."[74] And indeed, a February 2022 public opinion survey commissioned by the Foreign Affairs Ministry concluded that 63 percent of Maltese are strongly in favor of maintaining the country's long-standing position of international neutrality, while only 6 percent supported canceling this policy.[75] An editorial in *Malta Today*, published in April 2022, called for public debate on the notion of neutrality, while claiming that "NATO membership would entail further erosion of sovereignty," and that instead,

Malta should pursue a review of its defense policy.[76] Considering the war in Ukraine, Malta's role concentrated on humanitarian aid and medical support to Ukrainian refugees, while refraining from any sort of military support of defense funding. Malta was also criticized by the EU for failing to freeze Russian assets, in tandem with the EU scheme targeting Russia's economy. All in all, it seems that Malta is highly unlikely to forego its neutrality at this stage. And indeed, in a January 2023 interview, Maltese Minister of Foreign Affairs Ian Borg rejected any prospect for NATO membership (although, in June 2023, his party expressed support in renewing Malta's PfP membership[77])—"My answer is a straight no. . . . The concept of neutrality is enshrined in the Maltese Constitution, and Malta's foreign policy has been guided by this principle ever since it was introduced in our constitution in the late 1980s."[78]

Switzerland, whose long-standing military neutrality dates back hundreds of years, has historically engaged with NATO through several mechanisms, including the Partnership for Peace (since 1996) and the Euro-Atlantic Partnership Council (since 1997), and most recently—the Individual Partnership and Cooperation Programme (IPCP). Provided that Swiss legislation bans any active participation in combat, it chiefly participates in UN and PSCE missions, including the NATO-led Kosovo Force (KFOR), and even under the auspices of the International Security Assistance Force (ISAF) in Afghanistan. The country also takes part in various educational and training schemes with the Alliance, and provides support for a myriad of NATO projects and funds, such as the NATO Science for Peace and Security (SPS) Programme. Triggered by the Russian invasion of Ukraine in February 2022, Switzerland has taken an extraordinary step in adopting some of the EU sanctions against Russia (such as freezing assets of several Russian banks), citing grave violations of international law by Moscow. A poll conducted in January 2023 has even shown that the majority if the Swiss public (around 55 percent) supported reexporting Swiss arms combat equipment to Ukraine.[79] In July 2023, the country also announced its intention to take part in the European "Sky Shield" air defense project.[80]

And yet, the prospects for NATO membership remain vastly unpopular in the country, as demonstrated by a series of polls conducted in mid-2022, which revealed between 27 and 33 percent support for membership, and between 56 and 67 percent opposition to it. Nonetheless, a March 2023 survey conducted by the Swiss Federal Technology Institute (ETH Zürich) revealed that 55 percent of the Swiss public supported closer ties with NATO, 10 percent more than in a previous 2021 survey.[81] At the same time, the support for maintaining the strategic notion of Swiss neutrality remained particularly high.

Several small states in the heart of Europe—Andorra, Monaco, and San Marino—that are not formally members of NATO, but closely associated with its core Allies, may also opt to further validate their relationship with the Alliance, and follow Luxembourg's example of a Lilliput NATO Ally. Andorra, Europe's smallest state, does not possess its own armed forces, but maintains a ceremonial body of equipped volunteers. Instead, the microstate relies on its foreign relations with Spain and France, most prominently stipulated by the trilateral 1993 Treaty of Good Neighborliness, Friendship, and Cooperation, promising the protection of these key NATO and EU Allies in case of acute threats to Andorra's national security. The Principality of Monaco constitutes a similar example. According to Monaco's 1919 treaty establishing its relationship with France, the latter shall "assure the Principality of Monaco of the defense of its independence and sovereignty and guarantee the integrity of its territory as if this territory were part of France," while Monaco agrees to act "in full compliance with the political, military, naval and economic interests of France."[82] Given these circumstances, Monaco only maintains a small sovereign protection force, formed in 1817, which also operates several patrol boats around its coast. Another prominent example for a Lilliput state with core reliance on a NATO Ally is San Marino, which benefits from the protection of Italy with reference to its national security. Yet, San Marino maintains a small internal armed force (Forze Armate Sammarinesi), with responsibilities on border patrol and ceremonial duties. According to the tradition instated in the 1929 Lateran Treaty, Italy also provides protection to the Vatican City, a tiny enclave within Rome, which constitutes the world's smallest independent state. Nonetheless, with the exception of the Vatican City—while in practice these microstates enjoy French, Spanish, and Italian NATO umbrellas, in light of the events in Ukraine they may still wish to pursue closer coordination with the Alliance. Should they be willing to do so, they can expect to be welcome by the Alliance for an enhanced dialogue.

For the time being, other European states can most likely be ruled out in the running for a possible membership path, on account of their deep military, political, and economic ties with Russia—the Alliance's primary adversary. This reality is particularly evident with regard to NATO's relations with Belarus. After a few decades of modest ties with NATO, the Alliance suspended its dialogue with Belarus in 2021 on account of Minsk's violations of international law and respect for human rights, and recently accused the country of enabling Russia's invasion of Ukraine. Belarus entered the Partnership for Peace in 1995, and participated in NATO's Individual Partnership Program since 1997, establishing a diplomatic mission to NATO in 1998. However, the bilateral partnership between Belarus and NATO became strained after Lukashenko's third-time reelection in 2006, moving the country toward closer relations with Russia. Still, the parties were able to build progress within the framework of the 2010 NATO-Belarus Individual Partnership Program, with additional progress in the form of a 2012 package approval, extended in 2014. In August 2020, following Lukashenko's self-declared victory in the country's falsified elections, mass violent clashes between protesters and regime security forces ensued, leading to several killed, hundreds wounded and tens of thousands arrested by the regime. Lukashenko's brutal conduct was fiercely condemned by NATO Allies, severing formal ties between the country and the Alliance. The following year, as Russia planned its invasion of Ukraine, Belarus hosted Russian military forces on its soil, later allowing Russian missile launches and limited ground incursions to take place from Belarus. Despite Belarusian leader Aleksander Lukashenko denied any direct involvement of Belarusian forces in the conflict, evidence for Minsk's assistance to Russia mounted, leading several key Western countries to sanction Belarus, strongly condemning its strengthening Alliance with Russia under President Putin. The country's exiled opposition leader, Sviatlana Tsikhanouskaya, vocally condemned Lukashenko's policies, and several opposition groups led protests across Belarus to oppose the invasion, and were met with widespread arrests and violent detentions. Under these circumstances, NATO's ties with Belarus are currently the weakest in contemporary history, and it is safe to assess that until Lukashenko's regime is replaced, further bilateral advancement is effectively impossible. This reality is particularly reinforced by Lukashenko's June 2023 statements regarding his plans to place Russian tactical nuclear weapons on Belarusian soil—a strategic development that could significantly alter the nuclear architecture in the European continent.

Armenia constitutes a slightly different case study. Despite its close military and political ties with Russia, including Yerevan's participation in the Russian-led Collective Security Treaty Organization (CSTO), it also maintains a working relationship with NATO. Armenia joined the Partnership for Peace framework in 1994, and actively contributed to the NATO-led mission in Kosovo and Afghanistan. The country, which borders with NATO-Ally Turkey, cooperates with NATO based on an Individual Partnership Action Plan (IPAP), which also involves dialogue on democracy and the rule of law. Crucially, Armenia is also a founding member of the Collective Security Treaty Organization (CSTO)—a Russian-led military/political Alliance of like-minded Eurasian states, formally a NATO counterweight. Armenia also hosts two Russian military bases on its soil, occupying over two thousand troops, and takes part in the Russian-led Eurasian Economic Union (EAEU). Moreover, NATO has traditionally supported Azerbaijan's position in the dispute with Armenia over Nagorno-Karabakh, as Azerbaijan is closely aligned with Turkey—a core NATO Ally. Over the years, this support had led to constant tensions between the Alliance and Armenia, although several pro-Western political parties in the country (e.g., the European Party of Armenia and the Armenian National Movement) openly called for closer ties with the Alliance. And indeed, in 2018 Armenian Prime Minister Nikol Pashinyan attended the NATO Summit meeting in Brussels, leading to further high-level mutual visits, including a recent visit (in April 2022) from the secretary general's special representative for the Caucasus and Central Asia to Yerevan, discussing the country's ties with NATO. Yet, as Russia began its invasion of Ukraine in February 2022, Armenia—pressured by its Allies in Moscow—abstained in a UN resolution calling for Russia's withdrawal from Ukraine. While mutual high-profile visits continued (e.g., a visit by the secretary general's Special Representative for the Caucuses, Mr. Javier Colomina, in January 2023, and a visit by NATO former Secretary General Anders Fogh Rasmussen in March 2023), these exchanges are not designed to alter the strategic regional situation. A public opinion poll carried out in the country in April 2022 showed that majority of Armenians opted partnering with Russia (52 percent), while 34 percent supported forging closer ties with NATO.[83] This outlook may decrease in the future, especially after the confrontations is September 2023, which left the entire Nagorno-Karabakh region under effective Azeri control. Considering Armenia's close coordination with Russia—including past discussions over the possibility of deploying a CTSO mission to Armenia—at this time it remains highly unlikely for Yerevan to abandon its reliance on Moscow and forge a strong partnership with NATO.

Bordering Armenia to its East, Azerbaijan also maintains a working relationship with NATO through a tailor-made Individual Partnership Action Plan, and through its PfP membership (since 1994). It also joined

NATO's North Atlantic Cooperation Council in 1992, and established a representation office at NATO headquarters and a domestic Commission on Cooperation with NATO in 1997. Though it was a founding member of the Russian-led Collective Security Treaty Organization, Baku withdrew from the organization in 1999, and since President Ilham Aliyev's rise to power, he opted to maintain a neutral position, pursing membership of the Non-Aligned Movement (NAM) in 2011. The NAM is a 120-member strong group, established in Yugoslavia in 1961 as the Conference of Heads of State or Government of Non-Aligned Countries, providing a forum for consultations and dialogue for states that are not formally aligned in military/political blocs. Nonetheless, under President Aliyev, Azerbaijan maintained its cooperation with NATO, hosting several military exercises and regional consultations throughout the first decade of the 2000s, and concluding bilateral IPAP framework documents for the period between 2005 and 2016. Baku also participated in NATO-led missions in Kosovo, Iraq, and Afghanistan, demonstrating its role in support of NATO's military sphere, and recently took part in a May 2023 energy security dialogue in Brussels. In May 2023, President Aliyev stated that as a result of the country's alliance with Turkey, "Azerbaijan indirectly becomes, to a certain degree, a military Ally to NATO."[84] While NATO carefully stresses that it holds no direct role in the efforts to resolve the Nagorno-Karabakh conflict—a major regional struggle that led to several military confrontations between Azerbaijan and Armenia over the recent decades (including a major war in 2020), it openly supported Baku's territorial integrity in several North Atlantic Council declarations and high-level Summit sessions. Seemingly, however, this implicit support did not solidify a strong public sentiment toward the Alliance. According to a 2016 Gallup poll, 44 percent of Azeris considered NATO as "neither threat nor protector,"[85] a number that represents a mediocre assessment of the Alliance. With the war in Ukraine intensifying, Azerbaijan may deem it desirable to anchor its national security by enhancing its dialogue with the Alliance, but the prospects for full-fledged membership seem particularly slim, given its longtime authoritarian regime and democratic deficiencies.

Another prominent European arena in which NATO has been particularly invested is the Republic of Kosovo—a partially recognized state, which declared its independence from Serbia in February 2008. Kosovo has been recognized by the majority of NATO Allies, including the US, the UK, Germany, France, and Italy—but remains unrecognized by four member states. NATO has been instrumental in maintaining domestic security on the ground via its Kosovo Force, formed in 1999. While Kosovo's authorities eagerly call for NATO membership—including in a recent March 2022 Parliament resolution—its disputed status remains a central barrier to its membership ambitions. Serbia, which maintains a policy of military neutrality, takes part in NATO's PfP and Euro-Atlantic Partnership Council (EAPC) frameworks since 2006. It also holds an Individual Partnership Action Plan, and is in the process of transitioning to a new Individually Tailored Partnership Program (ITPP) with the Alliance. The ongoing effort to normalize and facilitate the bilateral ties with Kosovo remains a priority for the Alliance, albeit the understandable political difficulty involved in achieving such agreed framework dictates its advancement pace. A future resolution of all aspects of this relationship could lead to further enhancement in both states' ties with the Alliance, and constitutes a prerequisite for potential membership, as recently emphasized during a senior US senators' visit to Pristina in May 2023.[86]

Another politically complex arena is found in Cyprus, an EU member since 2004, whose NATO candidacy has been consistently blocked by Turkey on account of its long-standing dispute with Greece over the final status of the island. Should Ankara and Athens, with support from Nicosia, be able to harness the extraordinary courage and reach an agreed-on political resolution with regard to Cyprus—the country's road to membership would be paved.

Conclusion

Three quarters of a century since the formation of the North Atlantic Treaty Organization, the Alliance's significance in the stormy seas of global politics is experiencing a decades-high renaissance. As of late, the notion of NATO enlargement had become a centerpiece of Russia's regional security policy. As tensions on the Ukrainian border were mounting in late 2021, Russia formally issued a list of security demands for the West in order to avoid escalation. The most pivotal of these was an appeal to rule out any further NATO expansion, thus leaving Ukraine outside the Alliance's orbit, sketching a line around Russia's perceived post-Soviet influence zone. According to Moscow's narrative, NATO's so-called expansionist policies had effectively cornered Russia by constantly pushing the Alliance's membership toward its borders. As existential threats are naturally inter-subjective understandings within a political context, Moscow had become particularly fixated over this matter after NATO's announcement in 2008, according to which Ukraine and Georgia—two ex-Soviet republics—will become members of the Alliance *in the future*. A Western counternarrative emphasizes the defensive character of the Alliance, underscoring the sovereign right of European sovereign actors to autonomously navigate their security policy. Both perspectives attribute a great deal of importance to the notion of NATO enlargement, accentuating the Alliance's role in global affairs. In tandem with the narrative of NATO enlargement as a grave threat, another noteworthy concern in Moscow is the Ukrainian and Georgian aspirations for democracy and association with the West. Notably, these two scenarios are intertwined. Preserving Ukraine (and Georgia) inside Russia's sphere of influence is vital to distance NATO from Russia's borders—a notion that also traditionally obliged Moscow to act cautiously vis-à-vis its nonaligned neighbors, Finland and Sweden, who had customarily expressed negative sentiment regarding NATO membership. Ironically, however, as Russian tanks rolled into Ukraine in February 2022, Finland and Sweden unprecedently bolstered their soul-searching process with regard to NATO membership, breaking decades of nonalignment, eventually deciding to pursue full membership. The implications of the Nordic U-turn on NATO membership are expected to significantly alter the regional security architecture, strengthening the Alliance's positioning as the masthead of the Western civilization. A direct result of Russia's war in Ukraine, the Nordic accession has robustly demonstrated the enormous value of NATO's article 5 umbrella in Europe. By doing so, it has categorically positioned the once-sluggish discussion of NATO expansion back in the center of global attention, empowering the Alliance's standing in an era of a rapidly changing global balance of power. As famously stated by US Senator Richard Lugar in a June 1993 speech, "the common denominator of all new security problems in Europe is that they all lie beyond NATO's current borders."[1] This quote still rings true thirty years later. In that sense, considering French President Emmanuel Macron's November 2019 statement, according to which "what we are currently experiencing is the brain death of NATO,"[2] it is safe to assume the tables are now turned, as even the staunchest EU self-reliance enthusiasts find it difficult to decouple European security from the American pole.

Against this backdrop, considering the renewed discourse around the prospects for NATO enlargement, the book had set out to explore the concealed characteristics of the enlargement process since the Alliance's formation, contextualize its organizational framing and investigate the role that democracy plays in it. To address this theme, it developed a systematic discussion vis-à-vis the puzzle of NATO's diminishing democratic threshold, maintaining that this reality results from a gradual erosion in the prominence of democratic discourse within the organization, normalizing deviations from the Alliance core membership standards and expectations. As NATO's post–Cold War candidate pool had been mostly composed of former Soviet republics and ex-Communist regimes, whose democratic attributes failed to meet the Alliance's enlargement criteria, it eventually opted expansion over democracy. In doing so, the Alliance became oblivious to serious democratic deficiencies among many aspiring members, normalizing a suboptimal enlargement policy. The analysis of NATO's conduct in this regard relied on archival research and interviews with NATO officials and senior member states representatives, complemented by detailed case studies that scrutinize the genuine role of democracy in organizational decision-making on enlargement throughout the Alliance's history.

With this in mind, it is now feasible to identify five prototypes of possible future enlargement states and their democratic attributes, fashioned after Doris Day's 1954 classic song "Ready, Willing and Able":

1. The *ready, unwilling, and able* club—After Finland's integration, and Sweden's forthcoming accession—This group is comprised of several nonaligned European democracies, where the notion of membership conditionality is irrelevant, and the hypothetical accession process is guaranteed to run smoothly. These include Austria, Ireland, and Malta, as well as Andorra, Monaco, and San Marino (and, in a tremendously improbable scenario, Switzerland).

2. The *ready, willing, and unable* club—This group consists of those democratic European states that openly declared their interest in pursuing NATO membership, but are severely constrained by an acute political constellation that disqualifies their membership bid. These include Cyprus, on account of the long-lasting Turkish veto over its status, and to a certain extent Kosovo—awaiting a political settlement and formal recognition.

3. The *unready, unwilling, and unable* club—This group is composed of European nondemocracies that NATO deems unfit, in need of a substantial transformation in their political and democratic orientation. These include Belarus and Armenia, and to a lesser extent Azerbaijan—whose strong bond with Turkey and general political orientation may fit the Alliance's orbit, but whose regime characteristics remain deeply authoritarian.

4. The *unready, willing, and unable* club—This group consists of Ukraine and Georgia, where even a scenario of an astounding democratic transformation cannot salvage the two after the tragic events of repeated Russian invasions and land annexations, rendering them nonenlargeable. An

honest account places Moldova in this dubious club as well, as Russian military presence in its eastern Transnistria region amounts to an extremely unlikely membership scenario.

5. The *unready, willing, and able* club—This group is comprised of Bosnia and Herzegovina as its sole member. While the country is unquestionably unready in terms of its democratic characteristics, NATO's long-standing normalization of deviance is expected to eventually render the country as fit. This organizational DNA has been shaped over the course of decades of expansion, surpassing dramatic turns in global power architecture and effectively emerging victorious in the shadow of global competition. Paradoxically, Bosnia and Herzegovina can thus be emboldened with the current state of affairs in Ukraine. With NATO enlargement back on the global agenda, provided the right political constellation, the Alliance is extremely unlikely to expect the country to fully meet the organizational democracy criteria. The only tangible obstacle Sarajevo may be facing is vested in the minds of political decision-makers in Washington, London, Berlin, Paris, or Ankara.

Last, a few final words of conclusion. As NATO looks into its future, toward its hundredth anniversary in 2049, it is realistic to envision a thriving Alliance, still at work to provide collective security and protect the democratic way of life in an increasingly unstable global landscape. As challenges loom large—from AI to disruptive technologies and the rise of new global powers repeatedly threatening the rules-based international order—NATO's ability to expand its umbrella by extending its reach remains pivotal. An Alliance born with twelve founding members, reaching thirty at its seventieth anniversary (and thirty-one in 2023), can and should strive to triple its original size to thirty-six members by its platinum jubilee at 100 by 2049. To endure this test, the Alliance must constantly pursue modernization, adapt as it faces its myriad challenges, but most importantly—maintain and increase the cohesion among its member states based on its common values of democracy, respect for the rule of law, and adherence to fundamental human rights. It is by projecting its ironclad commitment to democracy and liberty that the Alliance attracted new members, and in this path lies the key for further expansion. Finland's accession (and Sweden's forthcoming membership) vividly demonstrate this notion, as their desire to join the Alliance derives not only from the its military might, but primarily from the realization that the time has come to make a bold statement regarding their identity and place under the sun, in an era of domestic and external challenges to democracy. Past expansions helped build a more prosperous Europe and strengthen the democratic camp, albeit, as this book demonstrated, this diverse group had not been regularly able to uphold the Alliance's most optimistic expectations. Further democratization is essential in additional circles across Europe, and NATO has an important role to play, by enabling these transitional states transform decades-long stalemate into rejuvenation. The alternative, undercutting democracy across the continent, destabilizing the Alliance's core values, is unbearable.

Notes

Introduction

1. "Verbatim Record of a Meeting—PART1—COR1—," NATO Archives Online, accessed November 8, 2021, https://archives.nato.int/verbatim-record-of-meeting-part1-cor1.

2. Ivan Katchanovski, "Puzzles of EU and NATO Accession of Post-Communist Countries," *Perspectives on European Politics and Society* 12, no. 3 (September 1, 2011): 304–19, https://doi.org/10.1080/15705854.2011.596308.

3. NATO, "Study on NATO Enlargement," NATO, accessed July 23, 2021, http://www.nato.int/cps/en/natohq/official_texts_24733.htm.

4. NATO, "Membership Action Plan (MAP)," NATO, accessed July 23, 2021, http://www.nato.int/cps/en/natohq/topics_37356.htm.

Chapter 1

1. Graham Allison and Philip Zelikow, *Essence of Decision: Explaining the Cuban Missile Crisis*, subsequent edition (New York: Pearson, 1999); Morton H. Halperin, Priscilla Clapp, and Arnold Kanter, *Bureaucratic Politics and Foreign Policy*, 2nd ed. (Washington, DC: Brookings Institution Press, 2006).

2. Max Weber, *Economy and Society: An Outline of Interpretive Sociology* (Berkeley: University of California Press, 1978).

3. "Long-Term EU Budget 2021–2027 and Recovery Package," accessed March 13, 2022, https://www.consilium.europa.eu/en/policies/the-eu-budget/long-term-eu-budget-2021-2027/.

4. NATO, "Structure," NATO, accessed March 13, 2022, https://www.nato.int/cps/en/natohq/structure.htm.

5. Volker Rittberger et al., *International Organization* (Macmillan International Higher Education, 2019), 36.

6. Neil Fligstein, Alina Polyakova, and Wayne Sandholtz, "European Integration, Nationalism and European Identity," *JCMS: Journal of Common Market Studies* 50, no. s1 (2012): 106–22, https://doi.org/10.1111/j.1468-5965.2011.02230.x; Franz C. Mayer and Jan Palmowski, "European Identities and the EU: The Ties That Bind the Peoples of Europe," *JCMS: Journal of Common Market Studies* 42, no. 3 (2004): 573–98, https://doi.org/10.1111/j.0021-9886.2004.00519.x; Richard K. Herrmann, Thomas Risse, and Marilynn B. Brewer, *Transnational Identities: Becoming European in the EU* (Lanham, MD: Rowman & Littlefield, 2004).

7. Steffen Eckhard and Jörn Ege, "International Bureaucracies and Their Influence on Policy-Making: A Review of Empirical Evidence," *Journal of European Public Policy* 23, no. 7 (August 8, 2016): 960–78, https://doi.org/10.1080/1 3501763.2016.1162837.

8. Ana E. Juncos and Karolina Pomorska, " 'In the Face of Adversity': Explaining the Attitudes of EEAS Officials vis-à-vis the New Service," *Journal of European Public Policy* 20, no. 9 (October 1, 2013): 1332–49, https://doi.org/10. 1080/13501763.2012.758451.

9. Roland Vaubel, Axel Dreher, and Uğurlu Soylu, "Staff Growth in International Organizations: A Principal-Agent Problem? An Empirical Analysis," *Public Choice* 133, no. 3–4 (October 30, 2007): 275–95, https://doi.org/10.1007/ s11127-007-9188-3; Eckhard and Ege, "International Bureaucracies and Their Influence on Policy-Making."

10. Ian Hurd, *After Anarchy: Legitimacy and Power in the United Nations Security Council* (Princeton, NJ: Princeton University Press, 2008).

11. Michael Barnett, Professor of Political Science Michael Barnett, and Martha Finnemore, *Rules for the World: International Organizations in Global Politics* (Ithaca, NY: Cornell University Press, 2004); Darren G. Hawkins et al., *Delegation and Agency in International Organizations* (Cambridge, UK; New York: Cambridge University Press, 2006).

12. Member states may adopt several types of tools to avoid undesirable IO autonomy, identified by Hawkins et al. (2006): Rules and guidelines to control the extent of agent discretion; Monitoring and reporting requirements; Screening and similar staff-vetting procedures; Checks and balances, constraining the IO's decision-making autonomy, and various forms of sanctions or benefits for desirable behavior. See Hawkins et al., *Delegation and Agency in International Organizations*.

13. "At Senate Foreign Relations Committee Hearing, Portman Presses Secretary Blinken on Nord Stream II, U.S. Support for a NATO Membership Action Plan for Ukraine and Georgia," Senator Rob Portman, June 8, 2021, https://www.portman.senate.gov/newsroom/press-releases/senate-foreign-relations-committee-hearing-portman-presses-secretary.

14. The White House, "Press Briefing by Press Secretary Karine Jean-Pierre and National Security Advisor Jake Sullivan, September 30, 2022," The

White House, October 1, 2022, https://www.whitehouse.gov/briefing-room/press-briefings/2022/09/30/press-briefing-by-press-secretary-karine-jean-pierre-and-national-security-advisor-jake-sullivan-september-30-2022/.

15. Julia Gray, "Life, Death, or Zombie? The Vitality of International Organizations," *International Studies Quarterly* 62, no. 1 (March 1, 2018): 1–13, https://doi.org/10.1093/isq/sqx086.

16. According to Gray (2018), over time IOs may become "zombies"—continuing their operations, but without any progress toward their mandates. The author compiled a data set of economic IOs since 1950, of which 10 percent have dissolved (i.e., died) and 38 percent can be considered zombies.

17. Leonard August Schuette, "Why NATO Survived Trump: The Neglected Role of Secretary-General Stoltenberg," *International Affairs* 97, no. 6 (November 1, 2021): 1863–81, https://doi.org/10.1093/ia/iiab167.

18. Felicia Schwartz, "U.S. Freezes $65 Million in Funding for U.N. Palestinian Refugee Agency," *Wall Street Journal*, January 16, 2018, sec. World, https://www.wsj.com/articles/u-s-freezes-65-million-in-funding-for-u-n-palestinian-refugee-agency-1516146851.

19. "United States Announces Restoration of U.S. $150 Million to Support Palestine Refugees," UNRWA, accessed July 18, 2021, https://www.unrwa.org/newsroom/press-releases/united-states-announces-restoration-us-150-million-support-palestine.

20. Daniel Carpenter, *Reputation and Power: Organizational Image and Pharmaceutical Regulation at the FDA* (Princeton, NJ: Princeton University Press, 2014), 45; Jonathan Mercer, *Reputation and International Politics* (Ithaca, NY: Cornell University Press, 2010), 16.

21. Kristina Daugirdas, "Reputation and the Responsibility of International Organizations," *European Journal of International Law* 25, no. 4 (November 1, 2014): 991–1018, https://doi.org/10.1093/ejil/chu087.

22. NATO, "The Secretary General's Annual Report 2021," NATO, accessed October 16, 2022, https://www.nato.int/cps/en/natohq/opinions_193590.htm.

23. Kenneth W. Abbott and Duncan Snidal, "International Regulation without International Government: Improving IO Performance through Orchestration," *Review of International Organizations* 5, no. 3 (September 2010): 315–44, https://doi.org/10.1007/s11558-010-9092-3.

24. NATO, "Relations with the United Nations," NATO, accessed October 16, 2022, https://www.nato.int/cps/en/natohq/topics_50321.htm.

25. Julia Gray, René Lindstädt, and Jonathan B. Slapin, "The Dynamics of Enlargement in International Organizations," *International Interactions* 43, no. 4 (July 4, 2017): 619–42, https://doi.org/10.1080/03050629.2017.1228039.

26. NATO, "Study on NATO Enlargement."

27. NATO, "Membership Action Plan (MAP)."

28. NATO, "Partnership for Peace Programme," NATO, accessed July 23, 2021, http://www.nato.int/cps/en/natohq/topics_50349.htm.

29. NATO, "Enlargement," NATO, accessed July 31, 2021, http://www.nato.int/cps/en/natohq/topics_49212.htm.

30. Christina J. Schneider and Johannes Urpelainen, "Accession Rules for International Institutions: A Legitimacy-Efficacy Trade-Off?," *Journal of Conflict Resolution* 56, no. 2 (April 1, 2012): 290–312, https://doi.org/10.1177/0022002711431422.

Chapter 2

1. NATO, "The North Atlantic Treaty," NATO, accessed August 3, 2021, http://www.nato.int/cps/en/natohq/official_texts_17120.htm.

2. NATO, "Final Communiqué of the First Session of the North Atlantic Council—(Terms of Reference and Organisation)," NATO, accessed August 3, 2021, http://www.nato.int/cps/en/natohq/official_texts_17117.htm.

3. "NATO Strategy Documents," accessed March 18, 2022, https://www.nato.int/archives/strategy.htm.

4. "Meeting 1st and 2nd November 1949," NATO Archives Online, accessed October 4, 2021, https://archives.nato.int/meeting-1st-and-2nd-november-1949.

5. "Record of a meeting of the North Atlantic Defence Committee held on Wednesday, 05 October 1949 at 1430 hours,"—NATO Archives Online, accessed November 8, 2021, https://archives.nato.int/record-of-meeting-of-north-atlantic-defence-committee-held-on-wednesday-05-october-1949-at-1430-hours.

6. NATO, "Final Communiqué Chairman: Mr. Acheson," NATO, accessed August 6, 2021, http://www.nato.int/cps/en/natohq/official_texts_17207.htm.

7. "Future development of NATO, other than in connection with defence plans," NATO Archives Online, accessed November 8, 2021, https://archives.nato.int/future-development-of-nato-other-than-in-connection-with-defence-plans.

8. Timothy Andrews Sayle, *Enduring Alliance: A History of NATO and the Postwar Global Order* (Ithaca, NY: Cornell University Press, 2019), 18.

9. Robert S. Jordan, *The Nato International Staff: Secretariat 1952–1957 : A Study in International Administration* (London: Oxford University Press, 1967), 65.

10. Hastings Lionel Ismay, *The Memoirs of General Lord Ismay* (London: Viking Adult, 1960), 454–55.

11. "Verbatim record of meeting—rev1," NATO Archives Online, accessed November 8, 2021, https://archives.nato.int/verbatim-record-of-meeting-rev1.

12. "Text of the Final Act of the Nine Power Conference in London,"—NATO Archives Online," accessed August 6, 2021, https://archives.nato.int/text-of-final-act-of-nine-power-conference-in-london.

13. "NATO Strategy Documents."

14. NATO, "Report of the Committee of Three on Non-Military Cooperation in NATO," NATO, accessed August 6, 2021, http://www.nato.int/cps/en/natohq/official_texts_17481.htm.

15. NATO, "Final Communiqué," NATO, accessed August 6, 2021, http://www.nato.int/cps/en/natohq/official_texts_17551.htm.

16. NATO, "Final Communiqué," NATO, accessed August 6, 2021, http://www.nato.int/cps/en/natohq/official_texts_26754.htm.

17. NATO, "Declaration on Atlantic Relations Issued by the North Atlantic Council ('The Ottawa Declaration')," NATO, accessed August 6, 2021, http://www.nato.int/cps/en/natohq/official_texts_26901.htm.

18. Sean Kay, *NATO and the Future of European Security* (Lanham, MD: Rowman & Littlefield, 1998), 29.

19. Ruud van Dijk and Stanley R. Sloan, "NATO's Inherent Dilemma: Strategic Imperatives vs. Value Foundations," *Journal of Strategic Studies* 43, no. 6–7 (November 9, 2020): 1014–38, https://doi.org/10.1080/01402390.2020.1824869.

20. Alexandra I. Gheciu, *NATO in the "New Europe": The Politics of International Socialization after the Cold War* (Stanford, CA: Stanford University Press, 2005), 39–40.

21. "NATO Mini. Comm. Ottawa—18th–19th June, 1974," accessed August 6, 2021, https://www.nato.int/docu/comm/49-95/c740618a.htm.

22. NATO, "Final Communiqué," NATO, accessed August 6, 2021, http://www.nato.int/cps/en/natohq/official_texts_26923.htm.

23. "NATO Mini. Comm. Washington—30th-31st May, 1978," accessed August 6, 2021, https://www.nato.int/docu/comm/49-95/c780530a.htm.

24. NATO, "Final Communiqué Chairman: Mr. J. Luns," NATO, accessed August 6, 2021, http://www.nato.int/cps/en/natohq/official_texts_27041.htm.

25. "Helsinki Final Act," accessed September 21, 2021, https://www.osce.org/helsinki-final-act.

26. "NATO Mini. Comm. Ankara—25th–26th June, 1980," accessed August 7, 2021, https://www.nato.int/docu/comm/49-95/c800625a.htm.

27. NATO, "Final Communiqué Chairman."

28. NATO, "Final Communiqué," NATO, accessed August 7, 2021, http://www.nato.int/cps/en/natohq/official_texts_23217.htm.

29. NATO, "Washington Statement on East-West Relations Issued by the Foreign Ministers at the North Atlantic Council Meeting," NATO, accessed August 9, 2021, http://www.nato.int/cps/en/natohq/official_texts_23262.htm.

30. NATO, "Declaration of the NATO Heads of State and Government Participating in the Meeting of the North Atlantic Council," NATO, accessed August 7, 2021, http://www.nato.int/cps/en/natohq/official_texts_23457.htm.

31. "NATO Secretary General Wörner Sees New Security Framework Coupling Change and Stability," NATO Archives Online, accessed November 8, 2021, https://archives.nato.int/nato-secretary-general-worner-sees-new-security-framework-coupling-change-and-stability.

32. NATO, "Declaration of the Heads of State and Government Participating in the Meeting of the North Atlantic Council," NATO, accessed August 9, 2021, http://www.nato.int/cps/en/natohq/official_texts_23554.htm.

33. "Declaration du secretaire general sur la roumanie," NATO Archives Online, accessed November 9, 2021, https://archives.nato.int/declaration-du-secretaire-general-sur-la-roumanie.

34. NATO, "Declaration on a Transformed North Atlantic Alliance ('The London Declaration')," NATO, accessed August 9, 2021, http://www.nato.int/cps/en/natohq/official_texts_23693.htm.

35. "NATO Review: Can NATO Remain an Effective Military and Political Alliance if It Keeps Growing?," *NATO Review*, March 1, 2002, https://www.nato.int/docu/review/articles/2002/03/01/can-nato-remain-an-effective-military-and-political-alliance-if-it-keeps-growing/index.html.

36. "NATO Review—The Identity of NATO," *NATO Review*, January 20, 2017, https://www.nato.int/docu/review/articles/2017/01/20/the-identity-of-nato/index.html.

37. "Charter of Paris for a New Europe," accessed January 20, 2022, https://www.osce.org/mc/39516.

38. NATO, "Partnership with the Countries of Central and Eastern Europe: Statement Issued by the North Atlantic Council," NATO, accessed August 13, 2021, http://www.nato.int/cps/en/natohq/official_texts_23858.htm.

39. NATO, "The Situation in the Soviet Union," NATO, accessed February 7, 2022, http://www.nato.int/cps/en/natohq/official_texts_23855.htm.

40. NATO, "The Alliance's New Strategic Concept (1991)," NATO, accessed August 12, 2021, http://www.nato.int/cps/en/natohq/official_texts_23847.htm.

41. NATO, "Declaration on Peace and Cooperation—('The Rome Declaration')," NATO, accessed August 13, 2021, http://www.nato.int/cps/en/natohq/official_texts_23846.htm.

42. NATO, "North Atlantic Cooperation Council (NACC) (Archived)," NATO, accessed August 10, 2021, http://www.nato.int/cps/en/natohq/topics_69344.htm.

43. NATO.

44. NATO, "Declaration of the Heads of State and Government—('The Brussels Summit Declaration')," NATO, accessed August 10, 2021, http://www.nato.int/cps/en/natohq/official_texts_24470.htm.

45. NATO, "Partnership for Peace: Invitation Document Issued by the Heads of State and Government Participating in the Meeting of the North Atlantic Council," NATO, accessed February 8, 2022, https://www.nato.int/cps/en/natohq/official_texts_24468.htm.

46. NATO, "Statement Issued at the Ministerial Meeting of the North Atlantic Cooperation Council," NATO, accessed August 11, 2021, http://www.nato.int/cps/en/natohq/official_texts_24452.htm.

47. "NATO Mini. Comm. M-NAC-1(95)51," accessed August 11, 2021, https://www.nato.int/docu/comm/49-95/c950530b.htm.

48. NATO, "Study on NATO Enlargement."

49. *NATO Review* (NATO Information Service, 1996).

50. "Summits of Heads of State and Government of the Council of Europe," Committee of Ministers, accessed January 20, 2022, https://www.coe.int/en/web/cm/summits.

51. NATO, "Final Communiqué—Meeting of the North Atlantic Council in Defence Ministers Session," NATO, accessed August 13, 2021, http://www.nato.int/cps/en/natohq/news_63927.htm.

52. "NATO Press Release M-1(97)81," accessed August 15, 2021, https://www.nato.int/docu/pr/1997/p97-081e.htm.

53. NATO, "The Alliance's Strategic Concept Approved by the Heads of State and Government Participating in the Meeting of the North Atlantic Council in Washington D.C.," NATO, accessed November 8, 2021, http://www.nato.int/cps/en/natohq/official_texts_27433.htm.

54. "NATO Press Release NAC-S(99)64—24 April 1999," accessed August 14, 2021, https://www.nato.int/docu/pr/1999/p99-064e.htm.

55. NATO, "Membership Action Plan (MAP)."

56. NATO, "Final Communiqué—Ministerial Meeting of the North Atlantic Council Held at NATO Headquarters, Brussels, on 15 December 1999," NATO, accessed August 15, 2021, http://www.nato.int/cps/en/natohq/official_texts_27405.htm.

57. NATO, " 'NATO 2020: Assured Security; Dynamic Engagement'—Analysis and Recommendations of the Group of Experts on a New Strategic Concept for NATO," NATO, accessed September 11, 2021, http://www.nato.int/cps/en/natohq/official_texts_63654.htm.

58. "NATO—Official Text: Active Engagement, Modern Defence—Strategic Concept for the Defence and Security of the Members of the North Atlantic Treaty Organisation Adopted by Heads of State and Government in Lisbon, 19 Nov. 2010," accessed September 12, 2021, https://www.nato.int/cps/en/natohq/official_texts_68580.htm.

59. "NATO2030," accessed March 19, 2022, https://www.nato.int/nato2030/.

60. "The Case for a Center for Democratic Resilience in NATO—Introduction," accessed March 19, 2022, https://nato-pa.foleon.com/coordination-centre-on-democracy-resilience/the-case-for-a-center-for-democratic-resilience-in-nato/introduction/.

61. "NATO 2022—Strategic Concept," accessed October 1, 2022, https://www.nato.int/strategic-concept/.

62. "NATO PA," NATO PA, May 22, 2023, https://www.nato-pa.int/document/declaration-481-new-nato-age-strategic-competition-accelerating-natos-adaptation-vilnius.

63. "NATO—Official Text: Vilnius Summit Communiqué Issued by NATO Heads of State and Government (2023), 11-Jul.-2023," accessed August 23, 2023, https://www.nato.int/cps/en/natohq/official_texts_217320.htm.

Chapter 3

1. Christian Bjørnskov and Martin Rode, "Regime Types and Regime Change: A New Dataset on Democracy, Coups, and Political Institutions," *Review of International Organizations* 15, no. 2 (April 1, 2020): 531–51, https://doi.org/10.1007/s11558-019-09345-1.

2. José Antonio Cheibub, Jennifer Gandhi, and James Raymond Vreeland, "Democracy and Dictatorship Revisited," *Public Choice* 143, no. 1 (April 1, 2010): 67–101, https://doi.org/10.1007/s11127-009-9491-2.

3. Michael Coppedge et al., "Conceptualizing and Measuring Democracy: A New Approach," *Perspectives on Politics* 9, no. 2 (June 2011): 247–67, https://doi.org/10.1017/S1537592711000880.

4. "Situations under Investigation," accessed December 4, 2021, https://www.icc-cpi.int/pages/situation.aspx.

5. Gerardo L. Munck, "What Is Democracy? A Reconceptualization of the Quality of Democracy," *Democratization* 23, no. 1 (January 2, 2016): 1–26, https://doi.org/10.1080/13510347.2014.918104; Haemin Jee, Hans Lueders, and Rachel Myrick, "Towards a Unified Approach to Research on Democratic Backsliding," *Democratization* 29, no. 4 (December 9, 2021): 1–14, https://doi.org/10.1080/13510347.2021.2010709.

6. Gerardo L. Munck, *Measuring Democracy: A Bridge between Scholarship and Politics*, 1st ed. (Baltimore, MD: Johns Hopkins University Press, 2009), 21.

7. Marc Bühlmann and Hanspeter Kriesi, "Models for Democracy," in *Democracy in the Age of Globalization and Mediatization*, ed. Hanspeter Kriesi et al., Challenges to Democracy in the 21st Century Series (London: Palgrave Macmillan UK, 2013), 44–68, https://doi.org/10.1057/9781137299871_3; "The Quality of Democracy: The Chain of Responsiveness," Journal of Democracy, accessed December 9, 2021, https://www.journalofdemocracy.org/articles/the-quality-of-democracy-the-chain-of-responsiveness/.

8. Bühlmann and Kriesi, "Models for Democracy."

9. Coppedge Ziblatt Michael, John Gerring, Carl Henrik Knutsen, Staffan I. Lindberg, Jan Teorell, Nazifa Alizada, David Altman, Michael Bernhard, Agnes Cornell, M. Steven Fish, Lisa Gastaldi, Haakon Gjerløw, Adam Glynn, Allen Hicken, Garry Hindle, Nina Ilchenko, Joshua Krusell, Anna Luhrmann, Seraphine F. Maerz, Kyle L. Marquardt, Kelly McMann, Valeriya Mechkova, Juraj Medzihorsky, Pamela Paxton, Daniel Pemstein, Josefine Pernes, Johannes von Römer, Brigitte Seim, Rachel Sigman, Svend-Erik Skaaning, Jeffrey Staton, Aksel Sundström, Ei-tan Tzelgov, Yi-ting Wang, Tore Wig, Steven Wilson, and Daniel Ziblatt, "V-Dem Dataset 2021" (Varieties of Democracy [V-Dem] Project, 2021), https://doi.org/10.23696/VDEMDS21.

10. Staffan I. Lindberg et al., "V-Dem: A New Way to Measure Democracy," *Journal of Democracy* 25, no. 3 (2014): 159–69, https://doi.org/10.1353/jod.2014.0040.

11. Charles Tilly, *Democracy* (Cambridge, UK: Cambridge University Press, 2007), https://doi.org/10.1017/CBO9780511804922.

12. Robert A. Dahl, "A Democratic Paradox?," *Political Science Quarterly* 115, no. 1 (2000): 35–40, https://doi.org/10.2307/2658032.

13. Sharun W. Mukand and Dani Rodrik, "The Political Economy of Liberal Democracy," *Economic Journal* 130, no. 627 (April 1, 2020): 765–92, https://doi.org/10.1093/ej/ueaa004.

14. "Populism, Pluralism, and Liberal Democracy," Journal of Democracy, accessed December 28, 2021, https://www.journalofdemocracy.org/articles/populism-pluralism-and-liberal-democracy/.

15. "Exploring 'Non-Western Democracy,'" Journal of Democracy, accessed December 28, 2021, https://www.journalofdemocracy.org/articles/exploring-non-western-democracy/.

16. The analysis is based on the indicator "regimes of the world," that distinguished between closed autocracies (where no multi-party elections, either for the legislature or the chief executive, take place at all—coded 0); electoral autocracies (where unfree or unfair elections take place—coded 1); electoral democracies (where free and fair elections take place, but visible shortcomings exist in realms of the rule of law, personal liberty, access to justice etc.—coded 2) and liberal democracies (a system with free and fair elections, guaranteed access to justice, personal liberty and sufficient levels of the rule of law—coded 3).

17. T. R. Gurr, M. G. Marshall, and K. Jaggers, "Polity IV Project: Political Regime Characteristics and Transitions, 1800–2016" (Center for Systemic Peace, n.d.), https://www.systemicpeace.org/.

18. "Democracy Index 2020," Economist Intelligence Unit, accessed November 20, 2021, https://www.eiu.com/n/campaigns/democracy-index-2020/.

19. "PolityProject," accessed November 20, 2021, https://www.systemicpeace.org/polityproject.html.

20. "Democracy Index 2020."

21. "Democracy Index 2020."

22. Ziblatt, "V-Dem Dataset 2021."

23. Coppedge et al., "Conceptualizing and Measuring Democracy."

24. "The Summit for Democracy," *United States Department of State* (blog), accessed December 9, 2021, https://www.state.gov/summit-for-democracy/.

25. Steven Feldstein, "Who's In and Who's Out From Biden's Democracy Summit," Carnegie Endowment for International Peace, accessed December 9, 2021, https://carnegieendowment.org/2021/11/22/who-s-in-and-who-s-out-from-biden-s-democracy-summit-pub-85822.

26. Christopher Fariss, Michael Kenwick, and Kevin Reuning, "Latent Human Rights Protection Scores Version 4" (Harvard Dataverse, December 10, 2020), https://doi.org/10.7910/DVN/RQ85GK.

27. "Fragile States Index/The Fund for Peace," accessed November 21, 2021, https://fragilestatesindex.org/.

28. Diane Vaughan, *The Challenger Launch Decision: Risky Technology, Culture, and Deviance at NASA* (Chicago, IL: University of Chicago Press, 1996).

29. Joseph Lorenzo Hall, "Columbia and Challenger: Organizational Failure at NASA," *Space Policy* 19, no. 4 (November 1, 2003): 239–47, https://doi.org/10.1016/j.spacepol.2003.08.013.

30. Jeffrey K. Pinto, "Project Management, Governance, and the Normalization of Deviance," *International Journal of Project Management* 32, no. 3 (April 2014): 376–87, https://doi.org/10.1016/j.ijproman.2013.06.004.

31. Kevin Bogard et al., "An Industry's Call to Understand the Contingencies Involved in Process Safety: Normalization of Deviance," *Journal of Organizational Behavior Management* 35, no. 1–2 (April 3, 2015): 70–80, https://doi.org/10.1080/01608061.2015.1031429.

32. Richard C. Prielipp et al., "The Normalization of Deviance: Do We (Un)Knowingly Accept Doing the Wrong Thing?," *Anesthesia & Analgesia* 110, no. 5 (May 2010): 1499–1502, https://doi.org/10.1213/ANE.0b013e3181d5adc5.

33. John S. Earle, Andrew Spicer, and Klara Sabirianova Peter, "The Normalization of Deviant Organizational Practices: Wage Arrears in Russia, 1991–98," *Academy of Management Journal* 53, no. 2 (2010): 218–37, https://doi.org/10.5465/AMJ.2010.49387426.

34. Barnett, Barnett, and Finnemore, *Rules for the World*, 74–120.

35. Michael N. Barnett and Martha Finnemore, "The Politics, Power, and Pathologies of International Organizations," *International Organization* 53, no. 4 (1999): 699–732, https://doi.org/10.1162/002081899551048.

36. Paul Higgins and Mitch Mackinem, *Thinking about Deviance: A Realistic Perspective* (Lanham, MD: Rowman & Littlefield Publishers, 2008).

37. Paul S. Adler, "Corporate Scandals: It's Time for Reflection in Business Schools," *Academy of Management Perspectives* 16, no. 3 (August 1, 2002): 148–49, https://doi.org/10.5465/ame.2002.8540425.

38. Yuri Mishina et al., "Why 'Good' Firms Do Bad Things: The Effects of High Aspirations, High Expectations, and Prominence on the Incidence of Corporate Illegality," *Academy of Management Journal* 53, no. 4 (August 1, 2010): 701–22, https://doi.org/10.5465/amj.2010.52814578.

39. "Challenging Complacency | APPEL Knowledge Services," accessed November 30, 2021, https://appel.nasa.gov/2006/04/01/challenging-complacency/.

40. Albert Bandura, "Moral Disengagement in the Perpetration of Inhumanities," *Personality and Social Psychology Review* 3, no. 3 (August 1, 1999): 193–209, https://doi.org/10.1207/s15327957pspr0303_3.

41. Blake E. Ashforth and Vikas Anand, "The Normalization of Corruption in Organizations," *Research in Organizational Behavior* 25 (January 1, 2003): 1–52, https://doi.org/10.1016/S0191-3085(03)25001-2.

42. Vilmos F. Misangyi, Gary R. Weaver, and Heather Elms, "Ending Corruption: The Interplay among Institutional Logics, Resources, and Institutional

Entrepreneurs," *Academy of Management Review* 33, no. 3 (July 1, 2008): 750–70, https://doi.org/10.5465/amr.2008.32465769.

43. Jiatao Li and Carmen K. Ng, "The Normalization of Deviant Organizational Practices: The Non-Performing Loans Problem in China," *Journal of Business Ethics* 114, no. 4 (June 1, 2013): 643–53, https://doi.org/10.1007/s10551-013-1710-6.

44. Martha Finnemore, "Norms, Culture, and World Politics: Insights from Sociology' Institutionalism," *International Organization* 50, no. 2 (1996): 325–47, https://doi.org/10.1017/S0020818300028587; Friedrich Kratochwil and John Gerard Ruggie, "International Organization: A State of the Art on an Art of the State," *International Organization* 40, no. 4 (1986): 753–75, https://doi.org/10.1017/S0020818300027363; Barnett, Barnett, and Finnemore, *Rules for the World*.

45. Daniel L Nielson, Michael J Tierney, and Catherine E Weaver, "Bridging the Rationalist–Constructivist Divide: Re-Engineering the Culture of the World Bank," *Journal of International Relations and Development* 9, no. 2 (June 1, 2006): 107–39, https://doi.org/10.1057/palgrave.jird.1800084.

46. Barnett and Finnemore, "The Politics, Power, and Pathologies of International Organizations."

47. Vaughan, *The Challenger Launch Decision*, 394–98.

48. Henrik B. L. Larsen, *NATO's Democratic Retrenchment: Hegemony after the Return of History* (London: Routledge, 2019), 9–10, https://doi.org/10.4324/9780429505362.

49. John W. Creswell and Vicki L. Plano Clark, *Designing and Conducting Mixed Methods Research*, Designing and Conducting Mixed Methods Research (Thousand Oaks, CA, US: Sage, 2007); Layna Mosley, *Interview Research in Political Science* (Ithaca, NY: Cornell University Press, 2013), 196–208.

50. Paul J. DiMaggio and Walter W. Powell, "The Iron Cage Revisited: Institutional Isomorphism and Collective Rationality in Organizational Fields," *American Sociological Review* 48, no. 2 (April 1983): 147, https://doi.org/10.2307/2095101; Stephen D. Krasner, *Sovereignty: Organized Hypocrisy* (Princeton, NJ: Princeton University Press, 1999).

51. Joseph Farrell, "Cheap Talk, Coordination, and Entry," *RAND Journal of Economics* 18, no. 1 (1987): 34–39.

Chapter 4

1. David Binder, "Greece, Turkey, and NATO," *Mediterranean Quarterly* 23, no. 2 (June 1, 2012): 95–106, https://doi.org/10.1215/10474552-1587883.

2. "The Greek-Turkish Relationship and NATO," Routledge & CRC Press, 30–31, accessed December 28, 2021, https://www.routledge.com/The-Greek-Turkish-Relationship-and-NATO/Moustakis/p/book/9780714683577.

3. Binder, "Greece, Turkey, and NATO."

4. Binder.

5. "NATO Review—Greece: What 60 Years in NATO Means," *NATO Review*, March 16, 2012, https://www.nato.int/docu/review/articles/2012/03/16/greece-what-60-years-in-nato-means/index.html.

6. "The Greek-Turkish Relationship and NATO," 135.

7. Sayle, *Enduring Alliance*, 22.

8. Melvyn Leffler, "5. Strategy, Diplomacy, and the Cold War: The United States, Turkey, and NATO, 1945–1952," in *5. Strategy, Diplomacy, and the Cold War: The United States, Turkey, and NATO, 1945–1952* (Princeton, NJ: Princeton University Press, 2017), 164–86, https://doi.org/10.1515/9781400888061-007.

9. "NATO—The First 5 Years 1949–1954—by Lord Ismay, Secretary General of the North Atlantic Treaty Organization," NATO Archives Online, accessed December 31, 2021, https://archives.nato.int/nato-first-5-years-1949-1954-by-lord-ismay-secretary-general-of-north-atlantic-treaty-organization.

10. "Association of the Turkish and Greek governments with the military planning of the North Atlantic Treaty Organization," NATO Archives Online, accessed December 29, 2021, https://archives.nato.int/association-of-turkish-and-greek-governments-with-military-planning-of-north-atlantic-treaty-organization.

11. Binder, "Greece, Turkey, and NATO."

12. "Records of Meetings of the Director of the Standing Group Steering Committee," NATO Archives Online, accessed December 24, 2021, https://archives.nato.int/records-of-meetings-of-director-of-standing-group-steering-committee.

13. "Association of Greece and turkey with NATO," NATO Archives Online, accessed December 29, 2021, https://archives.nato.int/association-of-greece-and-turkey-with-nato.

14. "NATO—The First 5 Years 1949–1954—by Lord Ismay, Secretary General of the North Atlantic Treaty Organization," NATO Archives Online, 39.

15. "Activities of the standing group during the last fortnight," NATO Archives Online, accessed December 29, 2021, https://archives.nato.int/activities-of-standing-group-during-last-fortnight.

16. "Verbatim record of meeting," NATO Archives Online, accessed December 27, 2021, https://archives.nato.int/verbatim-record-of-meeting.

17. "NATO Review—The Historic Document Confirming Greece and Turkey Joining NATO," *NATO Review*, February 15, 2012, https://www.nato.int/docu/review/articles/2012/02/15/the-historic-document-confirming-greece-and-turkey-joining-nato/index.html.

18. "Record of meeting," NATO Archives Online, accessed December 27, 2021, https://archives.nato.int/record-of-meeting-586.

19. "Building A New NATO | Foreign Affairs," accessed December 28, 2021, https://www.foreignaffairs.com/articles/southeastern-europe/1993-09-01/building-new-nato.

20. Süleyman Demirel, "Turkey and NATO at the Threshold of a New Century," *Perceptions: Journal of International Affairs* 4, no. 1 (March 1, 1999).

21. Tarık Oğuzlu, "Turkey's Eroding Commitment to NATO: From Identity to Interests," *Washington Quarterly* 35, no. 3 (August 1, 2012): 153–64, https://doi.org/10.1080/0163660X.2012.706578.

22. "Basic Law for the Federal Republic of Germany," accessed March 28, 2022, https://www.gesetze-im-internet.de/englisch_gg/englisch_gg.html.

23. Michael Bernhard, "Democratization in Germany: A Reappraisal," *Comparative Politics* 33, no. 4 (2001): 379–400, https://doi.org/10.2307/422440.

24. NATO, " 'Germany's Accession to NATO: 50 Years on' by Helga Haftendorn, Free University of Berlin," NATO, accessed January 1, 2022, http://www.nato.int/cps/en/natohq/opinions_22005.htm.

25. "NATO—The First 5 Years 1949–1954—by Lord Ismay, Secretary General of the North Atlantic Treaty Organization," NATO Archives Online, 32.

26. Sayle, *Enduring Alliance*, 18.

27. "Fourth session—second meeting—verbatim," NATO Archives Online, accessed January 4, 2022, https://archives.nato.int/fourth-session-second-meeting-verbatim.

28. "Foreign Relations of the United States, 1951, European Security and the German Question, Volume III, Part 1—Office of the Historian," accessed January 6, 2022, https://history.state.gov/historicaldocuments/frus1951v03p1/pg_1306.

29. "German contribution to the defence of Western Europe—statement made by the French deputy at the 28th meeting of the council deputies held on the 13th November 1950," NATO Archives Online, accessed January 5, 2022, https://archives.nato.int/german-contribution-to-defence-of-western-europe-statement-made-by-french-deputy-at-28th-meeting-of-council-deputies-held-on-13th-november-1950.

30. "NATO—The First 5 Years 1949–1954—by Lord Ismay, Secretary General of the North Atlantic Treaty Organization," NATO Archives Online, 34.

31. "German memorandum concerning a German defence contribution," NATO Archives Online, accessed January 5, 2022, https://archives.nato.int/german-memorandum-concerning-german-defence-contribution.

32. "NATO Mini. Comm. Lisbon, 20–25 February 1952," accessed January 7, 2022, https://www.nato.int/docu/comm/49-95/c520225a.htm.

33. "Record of meeting," NATO Archives Online, accessed January 1, 2022, https://archives.nato.int/record-of-meeting-632.

34. "Schuman Declaration May 1950," accessed March 30, 2022, https://european-union.europa.eu/principles-countries-history/history-eu/1945-59/schuman-declaration-may-1950_en.

35. Sayle, *Enduring Alliance*, 25.

36. "Record of meeting," NATO Archives Online, accessed January 4, 2022, https://archives.nato.int/record-of-meeting-688.

37. "Record of meeting," NATO Archives Online, accessed January 4, 2022, https://archives.nato.int/record-of-meeting-711.

38. "Final communiqué—approved by the North Atlantic Council on 23rd April 1954," NATO Archives Online, accessed January 5, 2022, https://archives.nato.int/final-communique-approved-by-north-atlantic-council-on-23rd-april-1954.

39. "Declaration Inviting Italy and the Federal Republic of Germany to Accede to the Brussels Treaty," NATO Archives Online, accessed January 1, 2022, https://archives.nato.int/declaration-inviting-italy-and-federal-republic-of-germany-to-accede-to-brussels-treaty-2.

40. "Text of the final act of the nine-power conference in London," NATO Archives Online, accessed August 6, 2021, https://archives.nato.int/text-of-final-act-of-nine-power-conference-in-london.

41. NATO, "Protocol to the North Atlantic Treaty on the Accession of the Federal Republic of Germany," NATO, accessed January 1, 2022, http://www.nato.int/cps/en/natohq/official_texts_17411.htm.

42. "VERBATIM RECORD OF MEETING—COR1," NATO Archives Online, accessed January 5, 2022, https://archives.nato.int/verbatim-record-of-meeting-cor1-10.

43. "NATO Speech: Address to the North Atlantic Council on the Occasion of German Unification," accessed May 6, 2022, https://www.nato.int/docu/speech/1990/s901003a_e.htm.

44. "Not One Inch: America, Russia, and the Making of Post-Cold War Stalemate: Sarotte, M. E.: 9780300259933: Books," accessed May 6, 2022.

45. "Not One Inch: America, Russia, and the Making of Post-Cold War Stalemate: Sarotte, M. E.; "Promises Made, Promises Broken? What Yeltsin Was Told About NATO in 1993 and Why It Matters," War on the Rocks, July 12, 2016, https://warontherocks.com/2016/07/promises-made-promises-broken-what-yeltsin-was-told-about-nato-in-1993-and-why-it-matters/.

46. van Dijk and Sloan, "NATO's Inherent Dilemma."

47. "Record of meeting," NATO Archives Online.

48. Thomas Carothers, "Spain, Nato and Democracy," *World Today* 37, no. 7/8 (1981): 298–303.

49. "Shape History Volume I—Origin and Development of SHAPE," NATO Archives Online, accessed December 27, 2021, https://archives.nato.int/shape-history-volume-i.

50. "AXP-1:—PROVISION OF NATO DOCUMENTS TO SPAIN," NATO Archives Online, accessed November 7, 2022, https://archives.nato.int/axp-1-provision-of-nato-documents-to-spain.

51. "Release of NATO air forces personnel classification manual stanag 3152 to include aap-10 to Spain," NATO Archives Online, accessed November 8, 2022, https://archives.nato.int/release-of-nato-air-forces-personnel-classification-manual-stanag-3152-to-include-aap-10-to-spain.

52. "Release of certain documents to Spain," NATO Archives Online, accessed November 8, 2022, https://archives.nato.int/release-of-certain-documents-to-spain.

53. "Record of meeting," NATO Archives Online, accessed November 8, 2022, https://archives.nato.int/record-of-meeting-142.

54. "Historical record on the iberlant command," NATO Archives Online, accessed November 8, 2022, https://archives.nato.int/historical-record-on-iberlant-command.

55. Carothers, "Spain, Nato and Democracy."

56. Alfred Tovias, "The International Context of Democratic Transition," *West European Politics* 7, no. 2 (April 1, 1984): 158–71, https://doi.org/10.1080/014023884 08424476.

57. "Speech of Minister Perez Lorca before the Atlantic Council," NATO Archives Online, accessed December 31, 2021, https://archives.nato.int/speech-of-minister-perez-llorca-before-atlantic-council.

58. "Final Communiqué—NAC meeting in ministerial session in Luxembourg, 17th and 18th May 1982," NATO Archives Online, accessed December 31, 2021, https://archives.nato.int/final-communique-nac-meeting-in-ministerial-session-in-luxembourg-17th-and-18th-may-1982.

59. "Statement made by the President of the Spanish Government at the opening ceremony of the NAC with the participation of the Heads of State and Government in Bonn on 10 June 1982," NATO Archives Online, accessed December 31, 2021, https://archives.nato.int/statement-made-by-president-of-spanish-government-at-opening-ceremony-of-nac-with-participation-of-heads-of-state-and-government-in-bonn-on-10-june-1982.

Chapter 5

1. NATO, "Address given at the 35th Annual Session of the North Atlantic Assembly," NATO, accessed January 16, 2022, http://www.nato.int/cps/en/natohq/opinions_23565.htm.

2. M. E. Sarotte, *Not One Inch: America, Russia, and the Making of Post–Cold War Stalemate* (Yale University Press: 2021), 31.

3. Gheciu, *NATO in the "New Europe,"* 232.

4. James M. Goldgeier, *Not Whether but When: The U.S. Decision to Enlarge NATO*, 1st ed. (Washington, DC: Brookings Institution Press, 1999).

5. Data for the Economist Democracy Index was not available for the said period.

6. Zoltan Barany, *The Future of NATO Expansion: Four Case Studies* (Cambridge, UK; New York: Cambridge University Press, 2003), 23.

7. "Not One Inch: America, Russia, and the Making of Post-Cold War Stalemate: Sarotte, M. E.: 9780300259933: Books," 109.

8. *Not One Inch: America, Russia, and the Making of Post-Cold War Stalemate,* 109.

9. "NATO Press Release (1999)," accessed January 17, 2022, https://www.nato.int/docu/pr/1999/p99-035e.htm.

10. "NATO Review—Can NATO Remain an Effective Military and Political Alliance if It Keeps Growing?"

11. Goldgeier, *Not Whether but When,* 78.

12. "NATO Press Release M-NAC-1(2000)52—24 May 2000," accessed February 8, 2022, https://www.nato.int/docu/pr/2000/p00-052e.htm.

13. "NATO Speech: NATO HQ—June 2001," accessed November 3, 2021, https://www.nato.int/docu/speech/2001/s010613l.htm.

14. Gheciu, *NATO in the "New Europe,"* 7; Gheciu, 70.

15. Thomas C. Bruneau and Steven C. Boraz, *Reforming Intelligence: Obstacles to Democratic Control and Effectiveness* (Austin: University of Texas Press, 2007), 219.

16. Gheciu, *NATO in the "New Europe,"* 160.

17. Barany, *The Future of NATO Expansion,* 24.

18. Gheciu, *NATO in the "New Europe,"* 185.

19. Barany, *The Future of NATO Expansion,* 139.

20. Barany, 173.

21. Mary Kaldor and Ivan Vejvoda, "Democratization in Central and East European Countries," *International Affairs* 73, no. 1 (1997): 59–82, https://doi.org/10.2307/2623550.

22. Freedom House Survey Team Staff, ed., *Freedom in the World 1993–94: The Annual Survey of Political Rights and Civil Liberties 1993–1994* (New York: Freedom House, 1994).

23. Federico Matías Rossi, "The Elite Coup: The Transition to Democracy in Bulgaria," working paper, 2012, https://cadmus.eui.eu//handle/1814/26183.

24. European Parliament, Briefing no. 13, "Slovakia and the Enlargement of the European Union," accessed January 29, 2022, https://www.europarl.europa.eu/enlargement/briefings/13a2_en.htm.

25. Gheciu, *NATO in the "New Europe,"* 72.

26. Barany, *The Future of NATO Expansion,* 24.

27. Barany, 62.

28. The Freedom House Survey Team, *Freedom in the World 1995–96: Annual Survey of Political Rights and Civil Liberties: The Annual Survey of Political Rights and Civil Liberties, 1995–1996* (New York: Freedom House, 1996).

29. Barany, *The Future of NATO Expansion,* 63.

30. Anton Bebler, "Slovenia's Smooth Transition," *Journal of Democracy* 13, no. 1 (2002): 127–40, https://doi.org/10.1353/jod.2002.0001.

31. Sabrina P. Ramet and Danica Fink-Hafner, eds., *Democratic Transition in Slovenia: Value Transformation, Education, and Media,* Illustrated ed. (College Station: Texas A&M University Press, 2006).

32. Ramet and Fink-Hafner.

33. Barany, *The Future of NATO Expansion*, 90.

34. Bebler, "Slovenia's Smooth Transition."

35. R. Bruce McColm, Dale Bricker, and James Finn, *Freedom in the World 1992–1993: The Annual Survey of Political Rights and Civil Liberties* (New York: Freedom House, 1993), accessed March 11, 2022, https://www.amazon.com/Freedom-World-Political-Liberties-1992-1993/dp/0932088791.

36. Ramet and Fink-Hafner, *Democratic Transition in Slovenia*, 240.

37. Barany, *The Future of NATO Expansion*, 103.

38. Ryan Hendrickson, "Expanding NATO: The Case for Slovenia," November 1, 2002, 14.

39. Barany, *The Future of NATO Expansion*, 24.

40. Warren Christopher, "NATO PLUS," *Washington Post*, January 9, 1994, https://www.washingtonpost.com/archive/opinions/1994/01/09/nato-plus/88b3d1a6-8111-4491-bbf0-e6267b0dae95/.

41. Katchanovski, "Puzzles of EU and NATO Accession of Post-Communist Countries."

42. Gheciu, *NATO in the "New Europe,"* 73.

43. Paul Poast and Johannes Urpelainen, *Organizing Democracy: How International Organizations Assist New Democracies*, 2018, 130, https://doi.org/10.7208/chicago/9780226543512.001.0001.

44. Poast and Urpelainen, 134.

45. Poast and Urpelainen, 142.

46. Dizaino Kryptis, "Lithuania's Membership in the North Atlantic Treaty Organization (NATO)," accessed January 23, 2022, https://www.urm.lt/default/en/foreign-policy/lithuania-in-the-region-and-the-world/lithuanias-security-policy/lithuanian-membership-in-nato.

47. Ronald D. Asmus, *Opening NATO's Door: How the Alliance Remade Itself for a New Era* (New York: Columbia University Press, 2004), 161–63.

48. "The Baltic Charter," accessed January 22, 2022, https://1997-2001.state.gov/www/regions/eur/ch_9801_baltic_charter.html.

49. "Freedom in the World 1997," Freedom House, accessed March 11, 2022, https://freedomhouse.org/report/freedom-world/1997/freedom-world-1997.

50. "NATO Press Release NAC-S(99)64—24 April 1999."

51. NATO, "Prague Summit Declaration," NATO, accessed August 16, 2021, http://www.nato.int/cps/en/natohq/official_texts_19552.htm.

52. Karen Dawisha and Bruce Parrott, *Politics, Power and the Struggle for Democracy in South-East Europe* (Cambridge, UK; New York: Cambridge University Press, 1997).

53. Dawisha and Parrott.

54. Fred C. Abrahams, *Modern Albania: From Dictatorship to Democracy in Europe*, Reprint ed. (New York: NYU Press, 2016), 143.

55. Abrahams, 270.

56. NATO, "Prague Summit Declaration."

57. "NATO Press Release (2003)152—4 Dec. 2003," accessed August 16, 2021, https://www.nato.int/docu/pr/2003/p03-152e.htm.

58. Freedom House, *Freedom in the World 2005: The Annual Survey of Political Rights and Civil Liberties* (New York: Rowman & Littlefield Publishers, 2005).

59. "History of NATO-Albania Relations," accessed February 2, 2022, https://www.mod.gov.al/eng/index.php/security-policies/relations-withinato/88-history-of-nato-albania-relations.

60. "Albania," U.S. Department of State, accessed April 8, 2022, https://2009-2017.state.gov/j/drl/rls/hrrpt/2009/eur/136016.htm.

61. "NATO: Enlargement and Effectiveness," accessed April 8, 2022, https://www.govinfo.gov/content/pkg/CHRG-110shrg44537/html/CHRG-110shrg44537.htm.

62. "C-SPAN Transcript Viewer," accessed April 8, 2022, https://www.c-span.org/video/cc/?progid=196372.

63. "Democracy in Croatia: From Stagnant 1990s to Rapid Change 2000–2011—Victoria Finn, 2021," accessed February 16, 2022, https://journals.sage-pub.com/doi/full/10.1177/0192512119863140?casa_token=QDZ6MIdGNHcAAAAA%3A-XowIsoBHTxB2fUpLNaVy9doXZ2hD27bLGhZ0tCzlPOOLtdBwfis41F69vG7V8GQRg7RqPkUBGA.

64. Nenad Zakošek, "Democratization, State-Building and War: The Cases of Serbia and Croatia," *Democratization* 15, no. 3 (June 1, 2008): 588–610, https://doi.org/10.1080/13510340801991130.

65. "NATO Topics: NATO's Relations with Croatia," accessed February 16, 2022, https://www.nato.int/summit2009/topics_en/08-croatia.html.

66. NATO, "The Euro-Atlantic Partnership: Refocusing and Renewal," NATO, accessed February 18, 2022, https://www.nato.int/cps/en/natohq/official_texts_21015.htm.

67. NATO, "Final Communiqué of the Ministerial Meeting of the North Atlantic Council Held at NATO Headquarters," NATO, accessed August 25, 2021, http://www.nato.int/cps/en/natohq/official_texts_21006.htm.

68. NATO, "Final Communiqué: Ministerial Meeting of the North Atlantic Council Held at NATO Headquarters, Brussels," NATO, accessed August 25, 2021, http://www.nato.int/cps/en/natohq/official_texts_46356.htm.

69. NATO, "Bucharest Summit Declaration: Issued by the Heads of State and Government Participating in the Meeting of the North Atlantic Council in Bucharest on 3 April 2008," NATO, accessed August 25, 2021, http://www.nato.int/cps/en/natohq/official_texts_8443.htm.

70. "Montenegro: A Miracle in the Balkans?," *Journal of Democracy*, accessed February 16, 2022, https://www.journalofdemocracy.org/articles/montenegro-a-miracle-in-the-balkans/.

71. NATO, "Lisbon Summit Declaration Issued by the Heads of State and Government Participating in the Meeting of the North Atlantic Council in Lis-

bon," NATO, accessed September 12, 2021, http://www.nato.int/cps/en/natohq/official_texts_68828.htm.

72. NATO, "Relations with the Republic of North Macedonia (Archived)," NATO, accessed February 14, 2022, https://www.nato.int/cps/en/natohq/topics_48830.htm.

73. NATO.

74. NATO, "Relations with Finland," NATO, accessed March 8, 2022, https://www.nato.int/cps/en/natohq/topics_49594.htm.

75. "Suomi Lähettää Aseita Ukrainalle—Pääministeri Marin: "Päätös on Historiallinen," *Helsingin Sanomat*, "Politiikka," accessed March 8, 2022, https://www.hs.fi/politiikka/art-2000008647428.html.

76. NATO, "Secretary General Welcomes NATO's Close Cooperation with Finland," NATO, accessed March 8, 2022, https://www.nato.int/cps/en/natohq/news_187609.htm.

77. NATO, "Secretary General: NATO, Finland and Sweden Share the Same Security Interests," NATO, accessed March 8, 2022, https://www.nato.int/cps/en/natohq/news_188061.htm.

78. MFA Russia, "#Zakharova: We Regard the Finnish Government's Commitment to a Military Non-Alignment Policy as an Important Factor in Ensuring Security and Stability in Northern Europe. Finland's Accession to @NATO Would Have Serious Military and Political Repercussions. Https://T.Co/ECY5oG23rL," Tweet, *@mfa_russia* (blog), February 25, 2022, https://twitter.com/mfa_russia/status/1497234734765780997.

79. "The Effects of Finland's Possible NATO Membership," Ministry for Foreign Affairs, accessed March 8, 2022, https://um.fi/publications/-/asset_publisher/TVOLgBmLyZvu/content/arvio-suomen-mahdollisen-nato-jasenyyden-vaikutuksista.

80. Ministry for Foreign Affairs of Finland, "Government Report on Changes in the Security Environment," Sarjajulkaisu (Valtioneuvosto, April 13, 2022), https://julkaisut.valtioneuvosto.fi/handle/10024/164002.

81. NATO, "Relations with Sweden," NATO, accessed March 9, 2022, https://www.nato.int/cps/en/natohq/topics_52535.htm.

82. NATO, "NATO Secretary General Discusses Security Challenges with Swedish Foreign Minister," NATO, accessed March 9, 2022, https://www.nato.int/cps/en/natohq/news_178235.htm.

83. NATO, "Secretary General Stresses Strength of NATO's Partnership with Sweden," NATO, accessed March 9, 2022, https://www.nato.int/cps/en/natohq/news_188069.htm.

84. NATO, "Secretary General Welcomes NATO's Close Cooperation with Finland."

85. NATO, "Secretary General Discusses Russian Military Build-up, NATO's Open Door Policy with Finland and Sweden," NATO, accessed March 9, 2022, https://www.nato.int/cps/en/natohq/news_191037.htm.

86. *51 Procent Av Svenskarna Vill Gå Med i Nato: Aftonbladet TV*, accessed March 10, 2022, https://tv.aftonbladet.se/video/339793/51-procent-av-svenskarna-vill-gaa-med-i-nato.

87. "48 Prosenttia Suomalaisista, Vastustajien Määrä Painui Noin Neljäsosaan," *Helsingin Sanomat*, "HS Gallup," March 4, 2022, https://www.hs.fi/politiikka/art-2000008659067.html.

88. "Sweden's Ruling Social Democrats to Review Party Policy on NATO," *Reuters*, accessed April 13, 2022, https://www.reuters.com/world/europe/swedens-ruling-social-democrats-review-party-policy-nato-2022-04-11/.

89. Jon Henley and Julian Borger, "Russia Warns of Nuclear Weapons in Baltic if Sweden and Finland Join Nato," *Guardian*, April 14, 2022, sec. World news, https://www.theguardian.com/world/2022/apr/14/russia-says-it-will-reinforce-borders-if-sweden-and-finland-join-nato.

90. NATO, "Press Statement Following the Meeting between Türkiye, Sweden, and the NATO Secretary General," NATO, accessed August 27, 2023, https://www.nato.int/cps/en/natohq/news_217147.htm.

91. "NATO—Official Text: Vilnius Summit Communiqué Issued by NATO Heads of State and Government (2023), 11-Jul.-2023," accessed August 23, 2023, https://www.nato.int/cps/en/natohq/official_texts_217320.htm.

92. Hanna Ojanen, Nato Defense College: Research, "Finland and Sweden in NATO: The Potential of New Security Providers," NDC Policy Brief No. 18,November 2022, accessed November 25, 2022, https://www.ndc.nato.int/research/research.php?icode=6.

93. Katherine Kjellström Elgin and Alexander Lanoszka, "Sweden, Finland, and the Meaning of Alliance Membership (Spring 2023)," 2023, https://doi.org/10.26153/tsw/46144.

Chapter 6

1. NATO, "Relations with Ukraine," NATO, accessed February 22, 2022, https://www.nato.int/cps/en/natohq/topics_37750.htm.

2. NATO, "Madrid Declaration on Euro-Atlantic Security and Cooperation on Euro-Atlantic Security and Cooperation Issued by the Heads of State and Government at the Meeting of the North Atlantic Council," NATO, accessed February 20, 2022, http://www.nato.int/cps/en/natohq/official_texts_25460.htm.

3. NATO, "The Alliance's Strategic Concept Approved by the Heads of State and Government Participating in the Meeting of the North Atlantic Council in Washington D.C."

4. NATO, "NATO-Ukraine Action Plan," NATO, accessed February 23, 2022, https://www.nato.int/cps/en/natohq/official_texts_19547.htm.

5. NATO, "Statement Meeting of the NATO-Ukraine Commission in Ambassadorial Session Brussels, 26 November 2003," NATO, accessed February 20, 2022, http://www.nato.int/cps/en/natohq/official_texts_20304.htm.

6. "President Bush Participates in Joint Press Availability with President Viktor Yushchenko of Ukraine," accessed November 16, 2022, https://george wbush-whitehouse.archives.gov/news/releases/2008/04/20080401-1.html.

7. NATO, "Strasbourg/Kehl Summit Declaration Issued by the Heads of State and Government Participating in the Meeting of the North Atlantic Council in Strasbourg/Kehl," NATO, accessed September 12, 2021, http://www.nato.int/cps/en/natohq/news_52837.htm.

8. Steven Pifer, "Ukraine's Perilous Balancing Act," *Brookings* (blog), November 30, 1AD, https://www.brookings.edu/articles/ukraines-perilous-balancing-act/.

9. NATO, "NATO Foreign Ministers' Statement on Ukraine," NATO, accessed February 20, 2022, http://www.nato.int/cps/en/natohq/news_105435.htm.

10. NATO, "Wales Summit Declaration Issued by the Heads of State and Government Participating in the Meeting of the North Atlantic Council in Wales," NATO, accessed September 15, 2021, http://www.nato.int/cps/en/natohq/official_texts_112964.htm.

11. "The Democratic Leadership Gap," Freedom House, accessed March 5, 2022, https://freedomhouse.org/report/freedom-world/2014/democratic-leadership-gap.

12. "NATO—Official Text: Joint Statement of the NATO-Ukraine Commission, 02-Dec.-2014," accessed February 22, 2022, https://www.nato.int/cps/en/natohq/official_texts_115474.htm.

13. NATO, "Joint Statement of the NATO-Ukraine Commission," NATO, accessed February 22, 2022, https://www.nato.int/cps/en/natohq/official_texts_119425.htm.

14. NATO, "Relations with Ukraine."

15. "Constitution of Ukraine: Verkhovna Rada of Ukraine," accessed February 22, 2022, https://www.rada.gov.ua/en/news/Constitution_of_Ukraine/.

16. NATO, "Statement of the NATO-Ukraine Commission: Kyiv, 31 October 2019," NATO, accessed February 22, 2022, https://www.nato.int/cps/en/natohq/official_texts_170408.htm.

17. NATO, "NATO Recognises Ukraine as Enhanced Opportunities Partner," NATO, accessed February 25, 2022, http://www.nato.int/cps/en/natohq/news_176327.htm.

18. NATO, "Brussels Summit Communiqué Issued by the Heads of State and Government Participating in the Meeting of the North Atlantic Council in Brussels 14 June 2021," NATO, accessed February 25, 2022, https://www.nato.int/cps/en/natohq/news_185000.htm.

19. "Ukraine: Civilian Casualty Update 22 May 2023," OHCHR, accessed June 15, 2023, https://www.ohchr.org/en/news/2023/05/ukraine-civilian-casualty-update-22-may-2023.

20. Andrew Carey LeBlanc Oleksandra Ochman,Kylie Atwood,Paul, "Zelensky Signals He Doesn't Expect Ukraine to Join NATO Anytime Soon," CNN, March 16, 2022, https://www.cnn.com/2022/03/15/europe/ukraine-nato-zelensky-shift/index.html.

21. NATO, "Statement by NATO Heads of State and Government (Brussels 2022)," NATO, accessed November 18, 2022, https://www.nato.int/cps/en/natohq/official_texts_193719.htm.

22. "New Format of Ukraine-NATO Relations May Begin from Vilnius Summit: Ukraine's Defence Minister," Yahoo News, June 15, 2023, https://news.yahoo.com/format-ukraine-nato-relations-may-214335438.html.

23. NATO, "NATO Defence Ministers Conclude Two Days of Meetings, Pledging Increased Support for Ukraine," NATO, accessed June 17, 2023, https://www.nato.int/cps/en/natohq/news_215691.htm.

24. NATO, "Opening Remarks by NATO Secretary General Jens Stoltenberg at the Meeting of the NATO-Ukraine Council at the Level of Heads of State and Government, with Sweden," NATO, accessed August 27, 2023, https://www.nato.int/cps/en/natohq/opinions_217096.htm.

25. NATO, "NATO-Ukraine Council," NATO, accessed August 27, 2023, https://www.nato.int/cps/en/natohq/topics_217652.htm.

26. NATO, "Relations with Georgia," NATO, accessed March 2, 2022, https://www.nato.int/cps/en/natohq/topics_38988.htm.

27. NATO, "NATO-Georgia Commission (NGC)," NATO, accessed February 26, 2022, https://www.nato.int/cps/en/natohq/topics_52131.htm.

28. NATO, "NATO-Georgia Joint Press Statement on the Occasion of the North Atlantic Council Visit to Georgia and the Inaugural Meeting of the NATO-Georgia Commission," NATO, accessed February 26, 2022, http://www.nato.int/cps/en/natohq/news_46438.htm.

29. NATO, "Lisbon Summit Declaration Issued by the Heads of State and Government Participating in the Meeting of the North Atlantic Council in Lisbon."

30. NATO, "Joint Statement: Meeting of the NATO-Georgia Commission at the Level of Ambassadors, with the Participation of the Prime Minister of Georgia, 9 November 2011, Tbilisi, Georgia," NATO, accessed February 26, 2022, https://www.nato.int/cps/en/natohq/official_texts_80593.htm.

31. NATO, "Chicago Summit Declaration Issued by the Heads of State and Government Participating in the Meeting of the North Atlantic Council in Chicago on 20 May 2012," NATO, accessed September 15, 2021, http://www.nato.int/cps/en/natohq/official_texts_87593.htm.

32. NATO, "Joint Statement of the NATO-Georgia Commission at the Level of Defence Ministers," NATO, accessed February 27, 2022, http://www.nato.int/cps/en/natohq/official_texts_117221.htm.

33. NATO, "Statement by NATO Foreign Ministers on Open Door Policy," NATO, accessed September 16, 2021, http://www.nato.int/cps/en/natohq/official_texts_125591.htm.

34. "Caucasus Barometer Time-Series Dataset Georgia," accessed November 27, 2022, https://caucasusbarometer.org/en/cb-ge/NATOSUPP/.

35. NATO, "Warsaw Summit Communiqué: Issued by the Heads of State and Government Participating in the Meeting of the North Atlantic Council in Warsaw, 8–9 July 2016," NATO, accessed September 16, 2021, http://www.nato.int/cps/en/natohq/official_texts_133169.htm.

36. NATO, "Brussels Summit Declaration Issued by the Heads of State and Government Participating in the Meeting of the North Atlantic Council in Brussels, 11–12 July 2018," NATO, accessed September 16, 2021, http://www.nato.int/cps/en/natohq/official_texts_156624.htm.

37. NATO, "NATO-Georgia Commission Declaration at the Brussels Summit," NATO, accessed February 27, 2022, https://www.nato.int/cps/en/natohq/official_texts_156627.htm.

38. "Georgia Is Not Trying to Appease Russia, Its President Tells Euronews," *euronews*, March 15, 2022, https://www.euronews.com/2022/03/15/georgia-not-in-the-same-situation-as-nato-countries-president-says.

39. NATO, "NATO Military Committee Discusses NATO-Georgia Military Cooperation," NATO, accessed June 17, 2023, https://www.nato.int/cps/en/natohq/news_211438.htm.

40. "NATO—Official Text: Vilnius Summit Communiqué Issued by NATO Heads of State and Government (2023), 11 July 2023," accessed August 23, 2023, https://www.nato.int/cps/en/natohq/official_texts_217320.htm.

41. NATO, "Relations with Bosnia and Herzegovina," NATO, accessed February 23, 2022, https://www.nato.int/cps/en/natohq/topics_49127.htm.

42. NATO, "Bosnia and Herzegovina and Membership Action Plan," NATO, accessed September 12, 2021, http://www.nato.int/cps/en/natohq/news_62811.htm.

43. NATO, "Statement by NATO Foreign Ministers on Open Door Policy."

44. NATO, "Relations with Bosnia and Herzegovina."

45. "PM Novalic: I Am Proud of What I Saw during the Military Exercise Held under the Auspices of NATO," *Sarajevo Times*," accessed February 23, 2022, https://sarajevotimes.com/pm-novalic-i-am-proud-of-what-i-saw-during-the-military-exercise-held-under-the-auspices-of-nato/.

46. NATO, "Brussels Summit Communiqué Issued by the Heads of State and Government Participating in the Meeting of the North Atlantic Council in Brussels 14 June 2021," NATO, accessed September 18, 2021, http://www.nato.int/cps/en/natohq/news_185000.htm.

47. NATO, "Relations with Bosnia and Herzegovina."

48. "Russian Embassy Accuses West of 'NATOisation' of Bosnia," *Balkan Insight* (blog), August 17, 2022, https://balkaninsight.com/2022/08/17/russian-embassy-accuses-west-of-natoisation-of-bosnia/.

49. EWB, "Bosnia and Herzegovina and the Western Balkans Included in NATO Strategic Concept 2022," *European Western Balkans* (blog), July 1, 2022, https://europeanwesternbalkans.com/2022/07/01/bosnia-and-herzegovina-and-the-western-balkans-included-in-nato-strategic-concept-2022/.

50. "Bosnia's New Presidency Takes Office, Vows to Resolve Mounting Crises," euronews, November 16, 2022, https://www.euronews.com/2022/11/16/bosnias-new-presidency-takes-office-and-vows-to-resolve-mounting-crises.

51. NATO, "NATO Strengthens Political Dialogue with Serbia and Bosnia and Herzegovina," NATO, accessed November 19, 2022, https://www.nato.int/cps/en/natohq/news_209051.htm.

52. NATO, "NATO Secretary General Meets with the Chair of the Tri-Presidency of Bosnia and Herzegovina Sefik Džaferović," NATO, accessed November 19, 2022, https://www.nato.int/cps/en/natohq/news_195739.htm.

53. NATO, "NATO Secretary General Meets with Member of the Presidency of Bosnia and Herzegovina," NATO, accessed June 17, 2023, https://www.nato.int/cps/en/natohq/news_210670.htm.

54. Denis Bećirović, "NATO Must Fast Track Bosnia's Membership," Just Security, April 13, 2023, https://www.justsecurity.org/85938/nato-must-fast-track-bosnias-membership/.

55. NATO, "Joint Press Conference by NATO Secretary General Jens Stoltenberg, the Minister of Foreign Affairs Wopke Hoekstra, and the Minister of Defence of the Netherlands Kajsa Ollongren," NATO, accessed November 19, 2022, https://www.nato.int/cps/en/natohq/opinions_209006.htm.

56. "NATO—Official Text: Vilnius Summit Communiqué Issued by NATO Heads of State and Government (2023), 11 July 2023."

57. "Send NATO Troops to Help Stabilize Bosnia and Herzegovina," War on the Rocks, August 12, 2022, https://warontherocks.com/2022/08/send-nato-troops-to-help-stabilize-bosnia-and-herzegovina/.

58. "1955—State Treaty and Neutrality | Austrian Parliament," accessed November 22, 2022, https://www.parlament.gv.at/ENGL/PERK/HIS/REP2/1955/index.shtml.

59. "Will Austria Abandon Neutrality to Join NATO?,"DW, May 32, 2022, accessed November 22, 2022, https://www.dw.com/en/will-austria-abandon-neutrality-to-join-nato/a-61880804.

60. von Thomas Mayr-Harting, "Neutralität oder Nato? Diese Debatte greift zu kurz," *Die Presse*, July 4, 2022, https://www.diepresse.com/6161239/neutralitaet-oder-nato-diese-debatte-greift-zu-kurz.

61. "With Finland and Sweden Set to Join NATO, Austria Seeks Neutral Allies," *euronews*, October 13, 2022, http://www.euronews.com/2022/10/13/with-finland-and-sweden-set-to-join-nato-austria-seeks-neutral-allies.

62. "Neutral Austria under Pressure to Get Tougher on Russia," *AP News*, February 12, 2023, https://apnews.com/article/russia-ukraine-politics-government-austria-moscow-cd43bd689dfbd8c674c1b6d9d214d86f.

63. "Majority of Austrians Reject Joining NATO," *Local Austria* (blog), May 6, 2022, https://www.thelocal.at/20220506/majority-of-austrians-reject-joining-nato/.

64. "Survey: Most of Austrians Oppose NATO Accession," www.euractiv.com, May 4, 2023, https://www.euractiv.com/section/politics/news/survey-most-of-austrians-oppose-nato-accession/.

65. "Unseresicherheit.Org," Unseresicherheit.org, accessed June 20, 2023, https://unseresicherheit.org/.

66. Chiara Swaton, "Austrian FM Defends Military Neutrality amid International Criticism," www.euractiv.com, August 22, 2023, https://www.euractiv.com/section/politics/news/austrian-fm-defends-military-neutrality-amid-international-criticism/.

67. Nick Cumming-Bruce, "Switzerland and Austria, Both Traditionally Neutral, Join a German-Led Air Defense Initiative," *New York Times*, July 7, 2023, sec. World, https://www.nytimes.com/2023/07/07/world/europe/switzerland-austria-sky-shield-germany-russia.html.

68. NATO, "Relations with Ireland," NATO, accessed May 5, 2022, https://www.nato.int/cps/en/natohq/topics_51979.htm.

69. "Report of the Commission on the Defence Forces," accessed November 23, 2022, https://www.gov.ie/en/publication/eb4c0-report-of-the-commission-on-defence-forces/.

70. "Poll: More Irish Want to Join NATO in Wake of Ukraine Invasion," *Politico*, accessed November 23, 2022, https://www.politico.eu/article/poll-more-irish-want-to-join-nato/.

71. "Public Divided on Nato Membership, Survey Finds," *Irish Times*, accessed November 23, 2022, https://www.irishtimes.com/ireland/2022/10/18/public-divided-on-nato-membership-survey-finds/.

72. Louise Burne and Eithne Dodd, "Ireland Will Give 'Deep Consideration' to Joining NATO, Says Taoiseach," *Buzz.ie*, June 2, 2023, https://www.buzz.ie/news/politics/hybrid-security-threats-joining-nato-30136936.

73. "March—Tánaiste Announces Plans for a Consultative Forum on International Security Policy—Department of Foreign Affairs," accessed August 29, 2023, https://www.dfa.ie/news-and-media/press-releases/press-release-archive/2023/march/tanaiste-announces-plans-for-a-consultative-forum-on-international-security-policy.php.

74. "Malta 1964 (Rev. 2016)." Constitution-*Constitute*, accessed November 25, 2022, https://www.constituteproject.org/constitution/Malta_2016?lang=en.

75. "Two in Three Maltese Strongly Support Neutrality: Survey," *Times of Malta*, accessed November 25, 2022, https://timesofmalta.com/articles/view/two-in-three-maltese-strongly-support-neutrality-survey.933304.

76. "Neutrality Needs to Be Debated, Not Discarded," MaltaToday.com.mt, accessed November 25, 2022, http://www.maltatoday.com.mt/comment/editorial/116481/neutrality_needs_to_be_debated_not_discarded?fbclid=IwAR1EfLrRnzgxQmhjtvzyEscBtqjFi_LcBT6pCSs_pponNFcgyJAlRBpYz4A.

77. Mario Borg, "Malta Takes Political U-Turn on NATO's PFP Membership: A Shift in Neutrality Stance," *Lovin Malta* (blog), June 5, 2023, https://lovinmalta.com/news/malta-takes-political-u-turn-on-natos-pfp-membership-a-shift-in-neutrality-stance/.

78. "Brussels Playbook: Where Are the Leaders?: Foreign Affairs Council—€500M for Ukraine," *Politico* (blog), January 23, 2023, https://www.politico.eu/newsletter/brussels-playbook/where-are-the-leaders-foreign-affairs-council-e500m-for-ukraine/.

79. swissinfo.ch/Reuters/ts, "Small Majority of Swiss Back Re-Exporting Arms to Ukraine," SWI swissinfo.ch, January 29, 2023, https://www.swissinfo.ch/eng/politics/small-majority-of-swiss-back-re-exporting-arms-to-ukraine/48242050.

80. Cumming-Bruce, "Switzerland and Austria, Both Traditionally Neutral, Join a German-Led Air Defense Initiative."

81. Keystone-SDA/sb, "Most Swiss Support Closer Ties with NATO, Survey Reveals," SWI swissinfo.ch, March 16, 2023, https://www.swissinfo.ch/eng/politics/most-swiss-support-closer-ties-with-nato—survey-reveals/48366004.

82. *Légimonaco*, "Non-Codified Texts: Ordinance of 08/09/1919 Promulgating the Treaty Establishing the Principality's Relations with France," accessed November 25, 2022, https://www.legimonaco.mc/305/legismclois.nsf/db3b0488a44ebcf9c12574c7002a8e84/cf98c1484c39d9eac125773f003778d0!OpenDocument&Highlight=0,1919.

83. "Arminfo: Survey: Security Policy Priorities Are Divided in Armenian Society," accessed November 27, 2022, https://arminfo.info/full_news.php?id=68709&lang=3.

84. "Aliyev: Azerbaijan 'Indirectly Becomes NATO's Military Ally,'" *mediamax.am*, accessed June 23, 2023, https://mediamax.am/en/news/region/51181/.

85. Gallup, "Most NATO Members in Eastern Europe See It as Protection," Gallup.com, February 10, 2017, https://news.gallup.com/poll/203819/nato-members-eastern-europe-protection.aspx.

86. Fatos Bytyci, "Kosovo Must Implement Serbia Peace Deal before It Can Join NATO-US Senators," *Reuters*, May 22, 2023, sec. Europe, https://www.reuters.com/world/europe/kosovo-must-implement-serbia-peace-deal-before-it-can-join-nato-us-senators-2023-05-22/.

Conclusion

1. James M. Goldgeier, *Not Whether but When: The U.S. Decision to Enlarge NATO*, 1st ed. (Washington, DC: Brookings Institution Press, 1999), 35.

2. "Emmanuel Macron Warns Europe: NATO Is Becoming Brain-Dead," *Economist*, accessed May 3, 2022, https://www.economist.com/europe/2019/11/07/emmanuel-macron-warns-europe-nato-is-becoming-brain-dead.

Bibliography

51 Procent Av Svenskarna Vill Gå Med i Nato: Aftonbladet TV. n.d. Accessed March 10, 2022. https://tv.aftonbladet.se/video/339793/51-procent-av-svenskarna-vill-gaa-med-i-nato.

Abbott, Kenneth W., Philipp Genschel, Duncan Snidal, and Bernhard Zangl. 2015. *International Organizations as Orchestrators.* Cambridge, UK: Cambridge University Press.

Abbott, Kenneth W., and Duncan Snidal. 1998. "Why States Act through Formal International Organizations." *Journal of Conflict Resolution* 42 (1): 3–32. https://doi.org/10.1177/0022002798042001001.

———. 2010. "International Regulation without International Government: Improving IO Performance through Orchestration." *Review of International Organizations* 5 (3): 315–44. https://doi.org/10.1007/s11558-010-9092-3.

Abrahams, Fred C. 2016. *Modern Albania: From Dictatorship to Democracy in Europe.* Reprint ed. New York: NYU Press.

Adler, Emanuel, and Michael Barnett, eds. 1998. *Security Communities.* Cambridge, UK: Cambridge University Press. https://doi.org/10.1017/CBO9780511598661.

Adler, Paul S. 2002. "Corporate Scandals: It's Time for Reflection in Business Schools." *Academy of Management Perspectives* 16 (3): 148–49. https://doi.org/10.5465/ame.2002.8540425.

Adler-Nissen, Rebecca, and Vincent Pouliot. 2014. "Power in Practice: Negotiating the International Intervention in Libya." *European Journal of International Relations* 20 (4): 889–911. https://doi.org/10.1177/1354066113512702.

"Albania." n.d. U.S. Department of State. Accessed April 8, 2022. https://2009-2017.state.gov/j/drl/rls/hrrpt/2009/eur/136016.htm.

Allison, Graham, and Philip Zelikow. 1999. *Essence of Decision: Explaining the Cuban Missile Crisis.* Subsequent edition. New York: Pearson.

Alvarez, Mike, José Antonio Cheibub, Fernando Limongi, and Adam Przeworski. 1996. "Classifying Political Regimes." *Studies in Comparative International Development* 31 (2): 3–36. https://doi.org/10.1007/BF02719326.

McColm, R. Bruce, Dale Bricker, and James Finn. 1993. *Freedom in the World 1992–1993: The Annual Survey of Political Rights and Civil Liberties.* Washington, DC: Freedom House, n.d. Accessed March 11, 2022. https://www.amazon.com/Freedom-World-Political-Liberties-1992-1993/dp/0932088791.

Aras, B. 2013. *The New Geopolitics of Eurasia and Turkey's Position.* New York and London: Routledge.

Archer, Clive. 2014. *International Organizations.* New York: Routledge.

Armstrong, C. K. 2013. *The Koreas.* New York and London: Routledge.

Ashforth, Blake E, and Vikas Anand. 2003. "The Normalization of Corruption in Organizations." *Research in Organizational Behavior* 25 (January): 1–52. https://doi.org/10.1016/S0191-3085(03)25001-2.

Asmus, Ronald D. 2004. *Opening NATO's Door: How the Alliance Remade Itself for a New Era.* New York: Columbia University Press.

"At Senate Foreign Relations Committee Hearing, Portman Presses Secretary Blinken on Nord Stream II, U.S. Support for a NATO Membership Action Plan for Ukraine and Georgia." 2021. Senator Rob Portman. June 8, 2021. https://www.portman.senate.gov/newsroom/press-releases/senate-foreign-relations-committee-hearing-portman-presses-secretary.

Axelrod, Robert, and Robert O. Keohane. 1985. "Achieving Cooperation under Anarchy: Strategies and Institutions." *World Politics* 38 (1): 226–54. https://doi.org/10.2307/2010357.

Bäckstrand, Karin, and Jonathan W. Kuyper. 2017. "The Democratic Legitimacy of Orchestration: The UNFCCC, Non-State Actors, and Transnational Climate Governance." *Environmental Politics* 26 (4): 764–88. https://doi.org/10.1080/09644016.2017.1323579.

Bandura, Albert. 1999. "Moral Disengagement in the Perpetration of Inhumanities." *Personality and Social Psychology Review* 3 (3): 193–209. https://doi.org/10.1207/s15327957pspr0303_3.

Barany, Zoltan. 2003. *The Future of NATO Expansion: Four Case Studies.* Cambridge, UK; New York: Cambridge University Press.

———. 2009. "Stretching the Umbrella: NATO's Eastern Expansion." *European View* 8 (2): 231–38. https://doi.org/10.1007/s12290-009-0087-5.

Barnett, Michael, Michael Barnett, and Martha Finnemore. 2004. *Rules for the World: International Organizations in Global Politics.* Ithaca, NY: Cornell University Press.

Barnett, Michael N., and Martha Finnemore. 1999. "The Politics, Power, and Pathologies of International Organizations." *International Organization* 53 (4): 699–732. https://doi.org/10.1162/002081899551048.

"Basic Law for the Federal Republic of Germany." n.d. Accessed March 28, 2022. https://www.gesetze-im-internet.de/englisch_gg/englisch_gg.html.

Bauer, Michael W., and Jörn Ege. 2016. "Bureaucratic Autonomy of International Organizations' Secretariats." *Journal of European Public Policy* 23 (7): 1019–37. https://doi.org/10.1080/13501763.2016.1162833.

Bebler, Anton. 2002. "Slovenia's Smooth Transition." *Journal of Democracy* 13 (1): 127–40. https://doi.org/10.1353/jod.2002.0001.

Bećirović, Denis. 2023. "NATO Must Fast Track Bosnia's Membership." Just Security. April 13, 2023. https://www.justsecurity.org/85938/nato-must-fast-track-bosnias-membership/.

Beland, Daniel, and Robert Henry Cox. 2010. *Ideas and Politics in Social Science Research*. New York: Oxford University Press.

Bernhard, Michael. 2001. "Democratization in Germany: A Reappraisal." *Comparative Politics* 33 (4): 379–400. https://doi.org/10.2307/422440.

Binder, David. 2012. "Greece, Turkey, and NATO." *Mediterranean Quarterly* 23 (2): 95–106. https://doi.org/10.1215/10474552-1587883.

Bjørnskov, Christian, and Martin Rode. 2020. "Regime Types and Regime Change: A New Dataset on Democracy, Coups, and Political Institutions." *Review of International Organizations* 15 (2): 531–51. https://doi.org/10.1007/s11558-019-09345-1.

Bogard, Kevin, Timothy D. Ludwig, Chris Staats, and Danielle Kretschmer. 2015. "An Industry's Call to Understand the Contingencies Involved in Process Safety: Normalization of Deviance." *Journal of Organizational Behavior Management* 35 (1–2): 70–80. https://doi.org/10.1080/01608061.2015.103 1429.

Borg, Mario. 2023. "Malta Takes Political U-Turn on NATO's PFP Membership: A Shift in Neutrality Stance." *Lovin Malta* (blog). June 5, 2023. https://lovinmalta. com/news/malta-takes-political-u-turn-on-natos-pfp-membership-a-shift-in-neutrality-stance/.

Börzel, Tanja A., and Michael Zürn. 2021. "Contestations of the Liberal International Order: From Liberal Multilateralism to Postnational Liberalism." *International Organization* 75 (2): 282–305. https://doi.org/10.1017/S0020818320000570.

"Bosnia's New Presidency Takes Office, Vows to Resolve Mounting Crises." 2022. *Euronews*. November 16, 2022. https://www.euronews.com/2022/11/16/bosnias-new-presidency-takes-office-and-vows-to-resolve-mounting-crises.

Bouchard, Caroline, and John Peterson. 2010. "Multilateralism: Dead or Alive?," Mercury Working Paper, vol. 1, no. 1, 19. "Bridging the Rationalist–Constructivist Divide: Re-Engineering the Culture of the World Bank." SpringerLink. n.d. Accessed December 8, 2021. https://link.springer.com/article/10.1057/palgrave.jird.1800084.

Bruneau, Thomas C., and Steven C. Boraz. 2007. *Reforming Intelligence: Obstacles to Democratic Control and Effectiveness*. Austin: University of Texas Press.

"Brussels Playbook: Where Are the Leaders?—Foreign Affairs Council—€500M for Ukraine." 2023. *Politico* (blog). January 23, 2023. https://www.politico. eu/newsletter/brussels-playbook/where-are-the-leaders-foreign-affairs-council-e500m-for-ukraine/.

Bühlmann, Marc, and Hanspeter Kriesi. 2013. "Models for Democracy." In *Democracy in the Age of Globalization and Mediatization*, edited by Hanspeter

Kriesi, Sandra Lavenex, Frank Esser, Jörg Matthes, Marc Bühlmann, and Daniel Bochsler, 44–68. Challenges to Democracy in the 21st Century Series. London: Palgrave Macmillan UK. https://doi.org/10.1057/9781137299871_3.

"Building A New NATO." *Foreign Affairs*. n.d. Accessed December 28, 2021. https://www.foreignaffairs.com/articles/southeastern-europe/1993-09-01/building-new-nato.

Burne, Louise, and Eithne Dodd. 2023. "Ireland Will Give 'Deep Consideration' to Joining NATO, Says Taoiseach." Buzz.Ie. June 2, 2023. https://www.buzz.ie/news/politics/hybrid-security-threats-joining-nato-30136936.

Bytyci, Fatos. 2022. "Kosovo Must Implement Serbia Peace Deal before It Can Join NATO—US Senators," *Reuters*, May 22, sec. Europe, https://www.reuters.com/world/europe/kosovo-must-implement-serbia-peace-deal-before-it-can-join-nato-us-senators-2023-05-22/.

Campbell, John L. 1998. "Institutional Analysis and the Role of Ideas in Political Economy." *Theory and Society* 27 (3): 377–409. https://doi.org/10.1023/A:1006871114987.

Caporaso, James A. 1992. "International Relations Theory and Multilateralism: The Search for Foundations." *International Organization* 46 (3): 599–632.

Carothers, Thomas. 1981. "Spain, Nato and Democracy." *World Today* 37 (7/8): 298–303.

Carpenter, Daniel. 2014. *Reputation and Power: Organizational Image and Pharmaceutical Regulation at the FDA*. Princeton, NJ: Princeton University Press.

"Caucasus Barometer Time-Series Dataset Georgia." n.d. Accessed November 27, 2022. https://caucasusbarometer.org/en/cb-ge/NATOSUPP/.

"Challenging Complacency | APPEL Knowledge Services." n.d. Accessed November 30, 2021. https://appel.nasa.gov/2006/04/01/challenging-complacency/.

"Charter of Paris for a New Europe." n.d. Accessed January 20, 2022. https://www.osce.org/mc/39516.

Cheibub, José Antonio, Jennifer Gandhi, and James Raymond Vreeland. 2010. "Democracy and Dictatorship Revisited." *Public Choice* 143 (1): 67–101. https://doi.org/10.1007/s11127-009-9491-2.

Christopher, Warren. 1994. "NATO PLUS." *Washington Post*, January 9, 1994. https://www.washingtonpost.com/archive/opinions/1994/01/09/nato-plus/88b3d1a6-8111-4491-bbf0-e6267b0dae95/.

Cumming-Bruce. July 2023. "Switzerland and Austria, Both Traditionally Neutral, Join a German-Led Air Defense Initiative." *New York Times*, sec. World. https://www.nytimes.com/2023/07/07/world/europe/switzerland-austria-sky-shield-germany-russia.html.

Downs, George W. 1994. *Collective Security beyond the Cold War*. Ann Arbor: University of Michigan Press. "Constitution of Ukraine: Verkhovna Rada of Ukraine." n.d. Accessed February 22, 2022. https://www.rada.gov.ua/en/news/Constitution_of_Ukraine/.

Copelovitch, Mark S., and David Ohls. 2012. "Trade, Institutions, and the Timing of GATT/WTO Accession in Post-Colonial States." *Review of International Organizations* 7 (1): 81–107. https://doi.org/10.1007/s11558-011-9129-2.

Coppedge, Michael, John Gerring, David Altman, Michael Bernhard, Steven Fish, Allen Hicken, Matthew Kroenig, et al. 2011. "Conceptualizing and Measuring Democracy: A New Approach." *Perspectives on Politics* 9 (2): 247–67. https://doi.org/10.1017/S1537592711000880.

Coppedge, Michael, John Gerring, Carl Henrik Knutsen, Staffan I. Lindberg, Jan Teorell, Nazifa Alizada, David Altman, Michael Bernhard, Agnes Cornell, M. Steven Fish, Lisa Gastaldi, Haakon Gjerløw, Adam Glynn, Allen Hicken, Garry Hindle, Nina Ilchenko, Joshua Krusell, Anna Luhrmann, Seraphine F. Maerz, Kyle L. Marquardt, Kelly McMann, Valeriya Mechkova, Juraj Medzihorsky, Pamela Paxton, Daniel Pemstein, Josefine Pernes, Johannes von Römer, Brigitte Seim, Rachel Sigman, Svend-Erik Skaaning, Jeffrey K. Staton, Aksel Sundström, Ei-tan Tzelgov, Yi-ting Wang, Tore Wig, Steven Wilson, and Daniel Ziblatt. 2021. "V-Dem Dataset 2021." Varieties of Democracy (V-Dem) Project. https://doi.org/10.23696/VDEMDS21. N.d. Accessed January 7, 2023.

Cox, Robert W. 1997. "An Alternative Approach to Multilateralism for the Twenty-First Century." *Global Governance* 3 (1): 103–16.

Creswell, John W., and Vicki L. Plano Clark. 2007. *Designing and Conducting Mixed Methods Research.* Thousand Oaks, CA: Sage Publications.

"Crises and Crisis Generations: The Long-Term Impact of International Crises on Military Political Participation." *Security Studies* 26, (4): n.d. Accessed December 28, 2022. https://www.tandfonline.com/doi/abs/10.1080/09636412.2017.1336388.

"C-SPAN Transcript Viewer." n.d. Accessed April 8, 2022. https://www.c-span.org/video/cc/?progid=196372.

"CspRandD." n.d. Accessed November 20, 2021. https://www.systemicpeace.org/csprandd.html.

Dahl, Robert A. 1999. "Can International Organizations Be Democratic? A Skeptic's View." In *Democracy's Edges*, edited by Casiano Hacker-Cordón and Ian Shapiro, 19–36. *Contemporary Political Theory.* Cambridge, UK: Cambridge University Press. https://doi.org/10.1017/CBO9780511586361.003.

———. 2000. "A Democratic Paradox?" *Political Science Quarterly* 115 (1): 35–40. https://doi.org/10.2307/2658032.

Daugirdas, Kristina. 2014. "Reputation and the Responsibility of International Organizations." *European Journal of International Law* 25 (4): 991–1018. https://doi.org/10.1093/ejil/chu087.

Davis, Christina. 2014. "Membership Conditionality and Institutional Reform: The Case of the OECD." 110th annual Meeting of the American Political Science Association, Washington, DC.

Davis, Christina L., and Meredith Wilf. 2017. "Joining the Club: Accession to the GATT/WTO." *Journal of Politics* 79 (3): 964–78. https://doi.org/10.1086/691058.

Dawisha, Karen, and Bruce Parrott. 1997. *Politics, Power and the Struggle for Democracy in South-East Europe.* Cambridge, UK: Cambridge University Press.

De Silva, Nicole. 2017. "Intermediary Complexity in Regulatory Governance: The International Criminal Court's Use of NGOs in Regulating International Crimes." *ANNALS of the American Academy of Political and Social Science* 670 (1): 170–88. https://doi.org/10.1177/0002716217696085. https://archives.nato.int/declaration-inviting-italy-and-federal-republic-of-germany-to-accede-to-brussels-treaty-2.

"Declaration of the Council of Europe's First Summit (Vienna, 9 October 1993)." n.d., 12.

Demirel, Süleyman. 1999. "Turkey and Nato at the Threshold of a New Century." *Perceptions: Journal of International Affairs* 4 (1).

"Democracy in Croatia: From Stagnant 1990s to Rapid Change 2000–2011: Victoria Finn, 2021." n.d.

"Democracy Index 2020." n.d. Economist Intelligence Unit. Accessed November 20, 2021a. https://www.eiu.com/n/campaigns/democracy-index-2020/.

———. n.d. Economist Intelligence Unit. Accessed November 24, 2021b. https://www.eiu.com/n/campaigns/democracy-index-2020/.

"Democracy Index 2020 Download Success." n.d. Economist Intelligence Unit. Accessed November 24, 2021. https://www.eiu.com/n/campaigns/democracy-index-2020-download-success/.

"Democratic Leadership Gap." n.d. Freedom House. Accessed March 5, 2022. https://freedomhouse.org/report/freedom-world/2014/democratic-leadership-gap.

"Democratic Transition in Slovenia: Value Transformation, Education, and Media—Peace Research Institute Oslo." n.d. Accessed January 30, 2022. https://www.prio.org/publications/3492.

Diebold, William, ed. 1988. *Bilateralism, Multilateralism and Canada in U.S. Trade Policy.* English Language edition. Cambridge, MA: Ballinger/Harper & Row.

Dijk, Ruud van, and Stanley R. Sloan. 2020. "NATO's Inherent Dilemma: Strategic Imperatives vs. Value Foundations." *Journal of Strategic Studies* 43 (6–7): 1014–38. https://doi.org/10.1080/01402390.2020.1824869.

DiMaggio, Paul J., and Walter W. Powell. 1983. "The Iron Cage Revisited: Institutional Isomorphism and Collective Rationality in Organizational Fields." *American Sociological Review* 48 (2): 147. https://doi.org/10.2307/2095101.

Downs, George W. 1994. *Collective Security beyond the Cold War.* Ann Arbor: University of Michigan Press.

"Draft Government Proposal on Finland's Accession to NATO Sent out for Comments." n.d. Ministry for Foreign Affairs. Accessed November 20, 2022. https://um.fi/press-releases/-/asset_publisher/ued5t2wDmr1C/content/suomen-liittymista-natoon-koskeva-hallituksen-esitysluonnos-lausuntokierrokselle/35732.

Duffield, John S. 1992. "International Regimes and Alliance Behavior: Explaining NATO Conventional Force Levels." *International Organization* 46 (4): 819–55.

Earle, John S., Andrew Spicer, and Klara Sabirianova Peter. 2010. "The Normalization of Deviant Organizational Practices: Wage Arrears in Russia, 1991–98." *Academy of Management Journal* 53 (2): 218–37. https://doi.org/10.5465/amj.2010.49387426.

Eckhard, Steffen, and Jörn Ege. 2016. "International Bureaucracies and Their Influence on Policy-Making: A Review of Empirical Evidence." *Journal of European Public Policy* 23 (7): 960–78. https://doi.org/10.1080/13501763.2016.1162837.

"The Effects of Finland's Possible NATO Membership." n.d. Ministry for Foreign Affairs. Accessed March 8, 2022. https://um.fi/publications/-/asset_publisher/TVOLgBmLyZvu/content/arvio-suomen-mahdollisen-nato-jasenyyden-vaikutuksista.

Eilstrup-Sangiovanni, Mette. 2020. "Death of International Organizations. The Organizational Ecology of Intergovernmental Organizations, 1815–2015." *Review of International Organizations* 15 (2): 339–70. https://doi.org/10.1007/s11558-018-9340-5.

Elgin, Katherine Kjellström, and Alexander Lanoszka. 2023. "Sweden, Finland, and the Meaning of Alliance Membership." *Texas National Security Review* (Spring). https://doi.org/10.26153/tsw/46144.

"Emmanuel Macron Warns Europe: NATO Is Becoming Brain-Dead." *Economist.* n.d. Accessed May 3, 2022. https://www.economist.com/europe/2019/11/07/emmanuel-macron-warns-europe-nato-is-becoming-brain-dead.

"Enduring Alliance by Timothy Andrews Sayle." n.d. *Cornell University Press* (blog). Accessed November 6, 2021. https://www.cornellpress.cornell.edu/book/9781501735509/enduring-alliance/.

Evans, Tony, and Peter Wilson. 1992. "Regime Theory and the English School of International Relations: A Comparison." *Millennium* 21 (3): 329–51. https://doi.org/10.1177/03058298920210030701.

EWB. 2022. "Bosnia and Herzegovina and the Western Balkans Included in NATO Strategic Concept 2022." *European Western Balkans* (blog). July 1, 2022. https://europeanwesternbalkans.com/2022/07/01/bosnia-and-herzegovina-and-the-western-balkans-included-in-nato-strategic-concept-2022/.

"Expanding NATO: The Case for Slovenia." ProQuest. n.d. Accessed January 30, 2022. https://www.proquest.com/docview/198038202?pq-origsite=gscholar&fromopenview=true.

Fariss, Christopher, Michael Kenwick, and Kevin Reuning. 2020. "Latent Human Rights Protection Scores Version 4." Harvard Dataverse. https://doi.org/10.7910/DVN/RQ85GK.

Farrell, Joseph. 1987. "Cheap Talk, Coordination, and Entry." *RAND Journal of Economics* 18 (1): 34–39.

Feldstein, Steven. n.d. "Who's In and Who's Out from Biden's Democracy Summit." Carnegie Endowment for International Peace. Accessed December 9, 2021. https://carnegieendowment.org/2021/11/22/who-s-in-and-who-s-out-from-biden-s-democracy-summit-pub-85822.

"Final Act of the Nine-Power Conference." Nine-Power Conference, London, 28 September–October 3, 1954 [online]. [Brussels]: Western European Union. (06.10.2000). http://www.weu.int/index.html.

Finland, Ministry for Foreign Affairs of. 2022. "Government Report on Changes in the Security Environment." Sarjajulkaisu. Valtioneuvosto. April 13, 2022. https://julkaisut.valtioneuvosto.fi/handle/10024/164002.

Finnemore, Martha. 1996. "Norms, Culture, and World Politics: Insights from Sociology's Institutionalism." *International Organization* 50 (2): 325–47. https://doi.org/10.1017/S0020818300028587.

Finnish Government "Report on Changes in the Security Environment." 2022. https://julkaisut.valtioneuvosto.fi/handle/10024/164002

Fligstein, Neil, Alina Polyakova, and Wayne Sandholtz. 2012. "European Integration, Nationalism and European Identity." *JCMS: Journal of Common Market Studies* 50 (s1): 106–22. https://doi.org/10.1111/j.1468-5965.2011.02230.x.

"Foreign Relations of the United States, 1951, European Security and the German Question," vol. III, pt. 1. Office of the Historian." n.d. Accessed January 6, 2022. https://history.state.gov/historicaldocuments/frus1951v03p1/pg_1306.

"Fragile States Index: The Fund for Peace." n.d. Accessed November 21, 2021. https://fragilestatesindex.org/.

"Fragile States Index 2019: The Fund for Peace." n.d. Accessed November 21, 2021. https://fundforpeace.org/2019/04/10/fragile-states-index-2019/.

Freedom House Survey Team, ed. 1994. *Freedom in the World 1993–94: The Annual Survey of Political Rights and Civil Liberties 1993–1994*. New York: Freedom House.

Freedom House Survey Team, ed. 1996. *Freedom in the World 1995–96: Annual Survey of Political Rights and Civil Liberties: The Annual Survey of Political Rights and Civil Liberties, 1995–1996*. New York: Freedom House.

"Freedom in the World." n.d. Freedom House. Accessed November 20, 2021. https://freedomhouse.org/report/freedom-world.

"Freedom in the World 1997." n.d. Freedom House. Accessed March 11, 2022. https://freedomhouse.org/report/freedom-world/1997/freedom-world-1997.

Explaining Civil-Military Relations in Complex Political Environments: India and Pakistan in Comparative Perspective." n.d.

———. n.d. Accessed December 28, 2022b. https://www.tandfonline.com/doi/full/10.1080/09636410802099022.

What Is Democracy? A Reconceptualization of the Quality of Democracy." n.d.

"Future Development of NATO, Other than in Connection with Defence Plans." NATO Archives Online. n.d. Accessed November 8, 2021. https://archives.nato.int/future-development-of-nato-other-than-in-connection-with-defence-plans.

Gallup. 2017. "Most NATO Members in Eastern Europe See It as Protection." Gallup.Com. February 10, 2017. https://news.gallup.com/poll/203819/nato-members-eastern-europe-protection.aspx.

Gateva, Eli. 2016. *European Union Enlargement Conditionality*. London: Palgrave Macmillan.

"Georgia Is Not Trying to Appease Russia, Its President Tells Euronews." 2022. Euronews. March 15, 2022. https://www.euronews.com/2022/03/15/georgia-not-in-the-same-situation-as-nato-countries-president-says.

Gheciu, Alexandra I. 2005. *NATO in the "New Europe": The Politics of International Socialization after the Cold War*. Stanford, CA: Stanford University Press.

"GlobalReport." n.d. Accessed November 20, 2021. http://www.systemicpeace.org/globalreport.html.

Goldgeier, James M. 1999. *Not Whether but When: The U.S. Decision to Enlarge NATO*. 1st ed. Washington, DC: Brookings Institution Press.

Gray, Julia. 2018. "Life, Death, or Zombie? The Vitality of International Organizations." *International Studies Quarterly* 62 (1): 1–13. https://doi.org/10.1093/isq/sqx086.

Gray, Julia, René Lindstädt, and Jonathan B. Slapin. 2017. "The Dynamics of Enlargement in International Organizations." *International Interactions* 43 (4): 619–42. https://doi.org/10.1080/03050629.2017.1228039.

Gross, Oren, and Fionnuala Ní Aoláin. 2006. *Law in Times of Crisis: Emergency Powers in Theory and Practice*. Cambridge, UK: Cambridge University Press.

Gurr, T. R, M. G. Marshall, and K. Jaggers. n.d. "Polity IV Project: Political Regime Characteristics and Transitions, 1800–2016." Center for Systemic Peace. https://www.systemicpeace.org/.

Hale, Henry. 2011. Review of *Measuring Democracy: A Bridge between Scholarship and Politics*, by Gerardo L. Munck. *Perspectives on Politics* 9 (June): 417–18. https://doi.org/10.1017/S153759271100082X.

Hall, Joseph Lorenzo. 2003. "Columbia and Challenger: Organizational Failure at NASA." *Space Policy* 19 (4): 239–47. https://doi.org/10.1016/j.spacepol.2003.08.013.

Halperin, Morton H., Priscilla Clapp, and Arnold Kanter. 2006. *Bureaucratic Politics and Foreign Policy*. 2nd ed. Washington, DC: Brookings Institution Press.

Hawkins, Darren G., David A. Lake, Daniel L. Nielson, and Michael J. Tierney. 2006. *Delegation and Agency in International Organizations*. New York: Cambridge University Press.

"Helsinki Final Act." n.d. Accessed September 21, 2021. https://www.osce.org/helsinki-final-act.

Hendrickson, Ryan C. 2002. "Expanding NATO: the Case for Slovenia." *US Army War College Quarterly: Parameters* 32 (4): 7.

Henley, Jon, and Julian Borger. 2022. "Russia Warns of Nuclear Weapons in Baltic if Sweden and Finland Join Nato." *Guardian*, April 14, 2022, sec. World news. https://www.theguardian.com/world/2022/apr/14/russia-says-it-will-reinforce-borders-if-sweden-and-finland-join-nato.

Herrmann, Richard K., Thomas Risse, and Marilynn B. Brewer. 2004. *Transnational Identities: Becoming European in the EU*. Rowman & Littlefield.

Higgins, Paul, and Mitch Mackinem. 2008. *Thinking About Deviance: A Realistic Perspective*. Lanham, MD: Rowman & Littlefield.

"History of NATO-Albania Relations." n.d. Accessed February 2, 2022. https://www.mod.gov.al/eng/index.php/security-policies/relations-withinato/88-history-of-nato-albania-relations.

Hovhannisyan, Alina. "Arminfo: Survey: Security Policy Priorities Are Divided in Armenian Society." ArmInfo. n.d. Accessed November 27, 2022. https://arminfo.info/full_news.php?id=68709&lang=3.

"HS-Gallup: Nato-Jäsenyyttä Kannattaa 48 Prosenttia Suomalaisista, Vastustajien Määrä Painui Noin Neljäsosaan." 2022. *Helsingin Sanomat*. March 4. https://www.hs.fi/politiikka/art-2000008659067.html.

Hurd, Ian. 2008. *After Anarchy: Legitimacy and Power in the United Nations Security Council*. Princeton, NJ: Princeton University Press.

Ismay, Hastings Lionel. 1960. *The Memoirs of General Lord Ismay*. London: Viking.

"Israel's Security Networks." n.d. Accessed December 28, 2022. https://www.cambridge.org/core/books/israels-security-networks/799D331632DE27ED513F708032EF69FA.

Jee, Haemin, Hans Lueders, and Rachel Myrick. 2021. "Towards a Unified Approach to Research on Democratic Backsliding." *Democratization* 29 (4): 1–14. https://doi.org/10.1080/13510347.2021.2010709.

Jones, Kent. 2009. "The Political Economy of WTO Accession: The Unfinished Business of Universal Membership." *World Trade Review* 8 (2): 279–314. https://doi.org/10.1017/S1474745609004261.

Jordan, Robert S. 1967. *The NATO International Staff: Secretariat 1952–1957: A Study in International Administration*. London: Oxford University Press.

Juncos, Ana E., and Karolina Pomorska. 2013. "'In the Face of Adversity': Explaining the Attitudes of EEAS Officials vis-à-vis the New Service." *Journal of European Public Policy* 20 (9): 1332–49. https://doi.org/10.1080/13501763.2012.758451.

Kaldor, Mary, and Ivan Vejvoda. 1997. "Democratization in Central and East European Countries." *International Affairs* 73 (1): 59–82. https://doi.org/10.2307/2623550.

Katchanovski, Ivan. 2011. "Puzzles of EU and NATO Accession of Post-Communist Countries." *Perspectives on European Politics and Society* 12 (3): 304–19. https://doi.org/10.1080/15705854.2011.596308.

Kattenburg, Paul M. 1992. *The Vietnam Trauma in American Foreign Policy: 1945–75*. New Brunswick, NJ: Transaction Publishers.

Kay, Sean. 1998. *NATO and the Future of European Security*. Lanham, MD: Rowman & Littlefield.

Keohane, Robert O. 1969. "Lilliputians' Dilemmas: Small States in International Politics." *International Organization* 23 (2): 291–310. https://doi.org/10.1017/S002081830003160X.

———. 1986. "Reciprocity in International Relations." *International Organization* 40 (1): 1–27. https://doi.org/10.1017/S0020818300004458.

———. 1990. "Multilateralism: An Agenda for Research." *International Journal* 45 (4): 731–64. https://doi.org/10.1177/002070209004500401.

Keohane, Robert O., Stephen Macedo, and Andrew Moravcsik. 2009. "Democracy-Enhancing Multilateralism." *International Organization* 63 (1): 1–31. https://doi.org/10.1017/S0020818309090018.

Klotz, Audie. 2018. *Norms in International Relations: The Struggle against Apartheid*. Ithaca, NY: Cornell University Press.

"Kraftigt Ökat Stöd För Nato: 57 Procent Vill Gå Med." n.d. Accessed May 12, 2022. https://www.aftonbladet.se/a/1O90qq.

Krasner, Stephen D. 1999. *Sovereignty: Organized Hypocrisy*. Princeton, NJ: Princeton University Press.

Kratochwil, Friedrich, and John Gerard Ruggie. 1986. "International Organization: A State of the Art on an Art of the State." *International Organization* 40 (4): 753–75. https://doi.org/10.1017/S0020818300027363.

Lake, David A., Lisa L. Martin, and Thomas Risse. 2021. "Challenges to the Liberal Order: Reflections on International Organization." *International Organization* 75 (2): 225–57. https://doi.org/10.1017/S0020818320000636.

Larsen, Henrik B. L. 2019. *NATO's Democratic Retrenchment: Hegemony after the Return of History*. London: Routledge. https://doi.org/10.4324/9780429505362.

Le Matin. 2022. "Sondage Tamedia/20 minutes: Trois quarts des Suisses approuvent les sanctions européennes contre la Russie," March 23, 2022. https://www.lematin.ch/story/trois-quarts-des-suisses-approuvent-les-sanctions-europeennes-971374128302.

Lee, W. (2019). "*The Enforcement of Human Rights Treaties in Korean Courts*." In *Asian Yearbook of International Law, Volume 23 (2017)*. Leiden, Netherlands: Brill Nijhoff, 95–136.

Andrew Carey, Oleksandra Ochman, Kylie Atwood, and Paul LeBlanc. 2022. "Zelensky Signals He Doesn't Expect Ukraine to Join NATO Anytime Soon." CNN. March 16, 2022. https://www.cnn.com/2022/03/15/europe/ukraine-nato-zelensky-shift/index.html.

Leffler, Melvyn. 2017. "5. Strategy, Diplomacy, and the Cold War: The United States, Turkey, and NATO, 1945—1952." In *5. Strategy, Diplomacy, and the Cold*

War: The United States, Turkey, and NATO, 1945—1952, 164–86. Princeton, NJ: Princeton University Press. https://doi.org/10.1515/9781400888061-007.

"Légimonaco: Non-Codified Texts—Ordinance of 08/09/1919 Promulgating the Treaty Establishing the Principality's Relations with France." n.d. Accessed November 25, 2022. https://www.legismclois.mc/305/legismclois.nsf/db3b0488a44ebcf9c12574c7002a8e84/cf98c1484c39d9eac125773f003778d0!OpenDocument&Highlight=0,1919.

Li, Jiatao, and Carmen K. Ng. 2013. "The Normalization of Deviant Organizational Practices: The Non-Performing Loans Problem in China." *Journal of Business Ethics* 114 (4): 643–53. https://doi.org/10.1007/s10551-013-1710-6.

Lieberman, Robert C. 2002. "Ideas, Institutions, and Political Order: Explaining Political Change." *American Political Science Review* 96 (4): 697–712. https://doi.org/10.1017/S0003055402000394.

Lindberg, Staffan I., Michael Coppedge, John Gerring, and Jan Teorell. 2014. "V-Dem: A New Way to Measure Democracy." *Journal of Democracy* 25 (3): 159–69. https://doi.org/10.1353/jod.2014.0040.

"Lithuania's Membership in the North Atlantic Treaty Organization (NATO)." Accessed January 23, 2022. https://www.urm.lt/default/en/foreign-policy/lithuania-in-the-region-and-the-world/lithuanias-security-policy/lithuanian-membership-in-nato.

"Long-Term EU Budget 2021–2027 and Recovery Package." n.d. Accessed March 13, 2022. https://www.consilium.europa.eu/en/policies/the-eu-budget/long-term-eu-budget-2021-2027/.

Lopes, Rui. 2016. "Accommodating and Confronting the Portuguese Dictatorship within NATO, 1970–4." *International History Review* 38 (3): 505–26. https://doi.org/10.1080/07075332.2015.1046388.

"Majority of Austrians Reject Joining NATO." 2022. *The Local Austria* (blog). May 6, 2022. https://www.thelocal.at/20220506/majority-of-austrians-reject-joining-nato/.

"Malta 1964 (Rev. 2016) Constitution: Constitute." n.d. Accessed November 25, 2022. https://www.constituteproject.org/constitution/Malta_2016?lang=en.

Mansfield, Edward D., Helen V. Milner, and B. Peter Rosendorff. 2002. "Why Democracies Cooperate More: Electoral Control and International Trade Agreements." *International Organization* 56 (3): 477–513. https://doi.org/10.1162/002081802760199863.

Marshall, M. G., and K. Jaggers. 2009). *Polity IV Dataset Version 2007 and Dataset Users' Manual.* Fairfax, VA: Center for Systemic Peace and Center for Global Policy, George Mason University.

Marten, Kimberly. 2020. "NATO Enlargement: Evaluating Its Consequences in Russia." *International Politics* 57 (3): 401–26. https://doi.org/10.1057/s41311-020-00233-9.

Martin, Lisa L. 2003. "Multilateral Organizations after the U.S.-Iraq War." In *The Iraq War and Its Consequences*. London: World Scientific. https://doi.org/10.1142/9789812387554_0029.

Mayer, Franz C., and Jan Palmowski. 2004. "European Identities and the EU: The Ties That Bind the Peoples of Europe." *JCMS: Journal of Common Market Studies* 42 (3): 573–98. https://doi.org/10.1111/j.0021-9886.2004.00519.x.

Mayr-Harting, Thomas. 2022. "Neutralität oder Nato? Diese Debatte greift zu kurz." *Die Presse*. July 4. https://www.diepresse.com/6161239/neutralitaet-oder-nato-diese-debatte-greift-zu-kurz.

McDonald, Matt. 2008. "Securitization and the Construction of Security." *European Journal of International Relations* 14 (4): 563–87. https://doi.org/10.1177/1354066108097553.

Mercer, Jonathan. 2010. *Reputation and International Politics*. Ithaca, NY: Cornell University Press.

MFA Russia. 2022. "#Zakharova: We Regard the Finnish Government's Commitment to a Military Non-Alignment Policy as an Important Factor in Ensuring Security and Stability in Northern Europe. Finland's Accession to @NATO Would Have Serious Military and Political Repercussions. Https://T.Co/ECY5oG23rL." Tweet. *@mfa_russia* (blog). February 25, 2022. https://twitter.com/mfa_russia/status/1497234734765780997.

Michta, Andrew A. 2009. "NATO Enlargement Post-1989: Successful Adaptation or Decline?" *Contemporary European History* 18 (3): 363–76. https://doi.org/10.1017/S0960777309005098.

Misangyi, Vilmos F., Gary R. Weaver, and Heather Elms. 2008. "Ending Corruption: The Interplay among Institutional Logics, Resources, and Institutional Entrepreneurs." *Academy of Management Review* 33 (3): 750–70. https://doi.org/10.5465/amr.2008.32465769.

Mishina, Yuri, Bernadine J. Dykes, Emily S. Block, and Timothy G. Pollock. 2010. "Why 'Good' Firms Do Bad Things: The Effects of High Aspirations, High Expectations, and Prominence on the Incidence of Corporate Illegality." *Academy of Management Journal* 53 (4): 701–22. https://doi.org/10.5465/amj.2010.52814578.

Moller, Sara Bjerg. 2020. "Twenty Years After: Assessing the Consequences of Enlargement for the NATO Military Alliance." *International Politics* 57 (3): 509–29. https://doi.org/10.1057/s41311-020-00230-y.

"Montenegro: A Miracle in the Balkans?" n.d. *Journal of Democracy*. Accessed February 16, 2022. https://www.journalofdemocracy.org/articles/montenegro-a-miracle-in-the-balkans/.

Morgenthau, H. (1948). Politics among Nations: The Struggle for Power and Peace. New York: Knopf. Mosley, Layna. 2013. *Interview Research in Political Science*. Ithaca, NY: Cornell University Press.

Mukand, Sharun W., and Dani Rodrik. 2020. "The Political Economy of Liberal Democracy." *Economic Journal* 130 (627): 765–92. https://doi.org/10.1093/ej/ueaa004.

Munck, Gerardo L. 2009. *Measuring Democracy: A Bridge between Scholarship and Politics.* 1st ed. Baltimore, MD: Johns Hopkins University Press.

———. 2016. "What Is Democracy? A Reconceptualization of the Quality of Democracy." *Democratization* 23 (1): 1–26. https://doi.org/10.1080/13510347.2014.918104.

Moustakis, F. (2004). *The Greek-Turkish Relationship and NATO.* New York: Routledge. Accessed December 28, 2021. https://www.routledge.com/The-Greek-Turkish-Relationship-and-NATO/Moustakis/p/book/9780714683577.

NATO. n.d. "1949." NATO Archives Online. n.d. Accessed November 8, 2021. https://archives.nato.int/1949-6.

———. n.d. "Activities of the Standing Group during the Last Fortnight." NATO Archives Online. n.d. Accessed December 29, 2021. https://archives.nato.int/activities-of-standing-group-during-last-fortnight.

———. n.d. "Association of Greece and Turkey with NATO." NATO Archives Online. n.d. Accessed December 29, 2021. https://archives.nato.int/association-of-greece-and-turkey-with-nato.

———. n.d. "Association of the Turkish and Greek Governments with the Military Planning of the North Atlantic Treaty Organization." NATO Archives Online. n.d. Accessed December 29, 2021. https://archives.nato.int/association-of-turkish-and-greek-governments-with-military-planning-of-north-atlantic-treaty-organization.

———. n.d. "AXP-1: Provision of NATO Documents to Spain." NATO Archives Online. n.d. Accessed November 7, 2022. https://archives.nato.int/axp-1-provision-of-nato-documents-to-spain.

———. n.d. "Compte-rendu de la premiere reunion comite de Defense de l'Atlantique Nord LE 5 Octobre 1949 2:30 PMP. Le Pentagone Washington DC." NATO Archives Online." n.d. Accessed November 8, 2021. https://archives.nato.int/compte-rendu-de-la-premiere-reunion-comite-de-defense-de-latlantique-nord-le-5-octobre-1949-2-30-pmp-le-pentagone-washington-d-c.

———. n.d. "Declaration du Secretaire General sur la Roumanie." NATO Archives Online. n.d. Accessed November 9, 2021. https://archives.nato.int/declaration-du-secretaire-general-sur-la-roumanie.

———. n.d. "Final Communiqué: Approved by the North Atlantic Council on 23rd April 1954." NATO Archives Online. n.d. Accessed January 5, 2022. https://archives.nato.int/final-communique-approved-by-north-atlantic-council-on-23rd-april-1954.

———. n.d. "Final Communiqué: NAC Meeting in Ministerial Session in Luxembourg, 17th and 18th May 1982." NATO Archives Online. n.d.

Accessed December 31, 2021. https://archives.nato.int/final-communique-nac-meeting-in-ministerial-session-in-luxembourg-17th-and-18th-may-1982.

———. n.d. "Fourth Session, Second Meeting, Verbatim." NATO Archives Online. n.d. Accessed January 4, 2022. https://archives.nato.int/fourth-session-second-meeting-verbatim.

———. n.d. "German Contribution to the Defence of Western Europe: Statement Made by the French Deputy at the 28th Meeting of the Council Deputies Held on the 13th November 1950." NATO Archives Online. n.d. Accessed January 5, 2022. https://archives.nato.int/german-contribution-to-defence-of-western-europe-statement-made-by-french-deputy-at-28th-meeting-of-council-deputies-held-on-13th-november-1950.

———. n.d. "German Memorandum Concerning a German Defence." NATO Archives Online. n.d. Accessed January 5, 2022. https://archives.nato.int/german-memorandum-concerning-german-defence-contribution.

———. n.d. "Historical Record on the Iberlant Command." NATO Archives Online. n.d. Accessed November 8, 2022. https://archives.nato.int/historical-record-on-iberlant-command.

———. n.d. "NATO-Ukraine Council," NATO. Accessed August 27, 2023. https://www.nato.int/cps/en/natohq/topics_217652.htm.

———. n.d. "NATO - Official Text: Vilnius Summit Communiqué Issued by NATO Heads of State and Government (2023), 11-Jul.-2023." Accessed August 23, 2023. https://www.nato.int/cps/en/natohq/official_texts_217320.htm.

———. n.d. "Opening Remarks by NATO Secretary General Jens Stoltenberg at the Meeting of the NATO-Ukraine Council at the Level of Heads of State and Government, with Sweden," NATO. Accessed August 27, 2023. https://www.nato.int/cps/en/natohq/opinions_217096.htm.

———. 2022. NATO Parliamentary Assembly. "The Case for a Center for Democratic Resilience in NATO." Introduction." Accessed March 19, 2022. https://nato-pa.foleon.com/coordination-centre-on-democracy-resilience/the-case-for-a-centre-for-democratic-resilience-in-nato/.

———. n.d. "Release of NATO Air Forces Personnel Classification Manual Stanag 3152 to Include AAP-10 to Spain," NATO Archives Online. n.d. Accessed November 8, 2022. https://archives.nato.int/release-of-nato-air-forces-personnel-classification-manual-stanag-3152-to-include-aap-10-to-spain.

———. n.d. "Verbatim Record of Meeting - COR1." NATO Archives Online. n.d. Accessed January 5, 2022. https://archives.nato.int/verbatim-record-of-meeting-cor1-10.

———. n.d. "Verbatim Record of Meeting." NATO Archives Online. n.d. Accessed December 27, 2021. https://archives.nato.int/verbatim-record-of-meeting.

———. n.d. "Verbatim Record of Meeting - PART1 - COR1." NATO Archives Online. n.d. Accessed November 8, 2021. https://archives.nato.int/verbatim-record-of-meeting-part1-cor1.

———. n.d. "Verbatim Record of Meeting - REV1." NATO Archives Online." n.d. Accessed November 8, 2021. https://archives.nato.int/verbatim-record-of-meeting-rev1.

"NATO Archives." n.d. Accessed August 6, 2021. https://www.nato.int/archives/1st5years/appendices/1b.htm.

"Nato Macedonia Veto Stokes Tension." April 4, 2008. http://news.bbc.co.uk/2/hi/europe/7329963.stm.

"NATO Mini. Comm. Ankara, 25th–26th June, 1980." n.d. Accessed August 7, 2021. https://www.nato.int/docu/comm/49-95/c800625a.htm.

"NATO Mini. Comm. Lisbon, 20th–25th February 1952." n.d. Accessed January 7, 2022. https://www.nato.int/docu/comm/49-95/c520225a.htm.

"NATO Mini. Comm. M-NAC-1(95)51." n.d. Accessed August 11, 2021. https://www.nato.int/docu/comm/49-95/c950530b.htm.

"NATO Mini. Comm. Ottawa,- 18th–19th June, 1974." n.d. Accessed August 6, 2021. https://www.nato.int/docu/comm/49-95/c740618a.htm.

"NATO Mini. Comm. Washington, 30th–31st May, 1978." n.d. Accessed August 6, 2021. https://www.nato.int/docu/comm/49-95/c780530a.htm.

"NATO, Official Text: Active Engagement, Modern Defence: Strategic Concept for the Defence and Security of the Members of the North Atlantic Treaty Organisation Adopted by Heads of State and Government in Lisbon, 19 Nov. 2010." n.d. Accessed September 12, 2021. https://www.nato.int/cps/en/natohq/official_texts_68580.htm.

"NATO, Official Text: Joint Statement of the NATO-Ukraine Commission, 02 Dec. 2014." n.d. Accessed February 22, 2022. https://www.nato.int/cps/en/natohq/official_texts_115474.htm.

"NATO PA." 2023. NATO PA. May 22, 2023. https://www.nato-pa.int/document/declaration-481-new-nato-age-strategic-competition-accelerating-natos-adaptation-vilnius.

"NATO Press Release (1999)035." n.d. Accessed January 17, 2022. https://www.nato.int/docu/pr/1999/p99-035e.htm.

"NATO Press Release (2003)152, 4 Dec. 2003." n.d. Accessed August 16, 2021. https://www.nato.int/docu/pr/2003/p03-152e.htm.

"NATO Press Release M-1(97)81." n.d. Accessed August 15, 2021. https://www.nato.int/docu/pr/1997/p97-081e.htm.

"NATO Press Release M-NAC-1(2000)52, 24 May 2000." n.d. Accessed February 8, 2022. https://www.nato.int/docu/pr/2000/p00-052e.htm.

"NATO Press Release NAC-S(99)64 - 24 April 1999." n.d. Accessed August 14, 2021. https://www.nato.int/docu/pr/1999/p99-064e.htm.

NATO Review. 2002. "Can NATO Remain an Effective Military and Political Alliance if It Keeps Growing?" 2002. *NATO Review.* March 1, 2002. https://

www.nato.int/docu/review/articles/2002/03/01/can-nato-remain-an-effective-military-and-political-alliance-if-it-keeps-growing/index.html.

NATO Review. 2012. "Greece: What 60 Years in NATO Means." *NATO Review.* March 16, 2012. https://www.nato.int/docu/review/articles/2012/03/16/greece-what-60-years-in-nato-means/index.html.

NATO Review. 2012. "The Historic Document Confirming Greece and Turkey Joining NATO." 2012. *NATO Review.* February 15, 2012. https://www.nato.int/docu/review/articles/2012/02/15/the-historic-document-confirming-greece-and-turkey-joining-nato/index.html.

NATO Review. 2017. "The Identity of NATO." *NATO Review.* January 20, 2017. https://www.nato.int/docu/review/articles/2017/01/20/the-identity-of-nato/index.html.

NATO Review. 1996. NATO Information Service.

"NATO Secretary General Wörner Sees New Security Framework Coupling Change and Stability." 2021 NATO Archives Online. n.d. Accessed November 8, 2021. https://archives.nato.int/nato-secretary-general-worner-sees-new-security-framework-coupling-change-and-stability.

"NATO Speech: Address to the North Atlantic Council on the Occasion of German Unification." n.d. Accessed May 6, 2022. https://www.nato.int/docu/speech/1990/s901003a_e.htm.

"NATO Speech: NATO HQ, June 2001." n.d. Accessed November 3, 2021. https://www.nato.int/docu/speech/2001/s010613l.htm.

"NATO Strategy Documents." n.d. Accessed March 18, 2022. https://www.nato.int/archives/strategy.htm.

"NATO, The First 5 Years 1949–1954, by Lord Ismay, Secretary General of the North Atlantic Treaty Organization, NATO Archives Online. n.d. Accessed December 31, 2021. https://archives.nato.int/nato-first-5-years-1949-1954-by-lord-ismay-secretary-general-of-north-atlantic-treaty-organization.

"NATO, Topic: Relations with the Republic of Moldova." n.d. Accessed May 10, 2022. https://www.nato.int/cps/en/natohq/topics_49727.htm.

"NATO Topics: NATO's Relations with Croatia." n.d. Accessed February 16, 2022. https://www.nato.int/summit2009/topics_en/08-croatia.html.

"NATO 2022, Strategic Concept." n.d. Accessed October 1, 2022. https://www.nato.int/strategic-concept/.

"NATO 2030." n.d. Accessed March 19, 2022. https://www.nato.int/nato2030/.

"NDC - Research." n.d. Accessed November 25, 2022. https://www.ndc.nato.int/research/research.php?icode=6.

———. n.d. Accessed November 25, 2022. https://www.ndc.nato.int/research/research.php?icode=0.

Neary, Ian. 2022. *Human Rights in Japan, South Korea and Taiwan.* 1st ed. London and New York: Routledge. Accessed December 28, 2022. https://www.routledge.com/Human-Rights-in-Japan-South-Korea-and-Taiwan/Neary/p/book/9780415406697.

Neumayer, Eric. 2013. "Strategic Delaying and Concessions Extraction in Accession Negotiations to the World Trade Organization: An Analysis of Working Party Membership." *World Trade Review* 12 (4): 669–92. https://doi.org/10.1017/S147474561300013X.

"Neutral Austria under Pressure to Get Tougher on Russia." 2023. AP NEWS. February 12, 2023. https://apnews.com/article/russia-ukraine-politics-government-austria-moscow-cd43bd689dfbd8c674c1b6d9d214d86f.

"Neutrality Needs to Be Debated, Not Discarded." n.d. MaltaToday.Com.Mt.

"New Format of Ukraine-NATO Relations May Begin from Vilnius Summit: Ukraine's Defence Minister." 2023. *Yahoo News*. June 15, 2023. https://news.yahoo.com/format-ukraine-nato-relations-may-214335438.html.

Nieburg, H. L. 1970. *In the Name of Science*. Rev. ed./3rd printing. Chicago, IL: Quadrangle.

Nielson, Daniel L., Michael J. Tierney, and Catherine E. Weaver. 2006. "Bridging the Rationalist–Constructivist Divide: Re-Engineering the Culture of the World Bank." *Journal of International Relations and Development* 9 (2): 107–39. https://doi.org/10.1057/palgrave.jird.1800084.

"North Atlantic Council, 1st to 9th Sessions," NATO Archives Online. n.d. Accessed October 4, 2021. https://archives.nato.int/north-atlantic-council-1st-to-9th-sessions.

OECD. "Accession to the Organisation," n.d. Accessed July 31, 2021. https://www.oecd.org/legal/accession-process.htm.

OECD. "OECD and Enlargement, OECD." n.d. Accessed July 31, 2021. https://www.oecd.org/about/document/enlargement.htm#_msocom_1.

Oğuzlu, Tarık. 2012. "Turkey's Eroding Commitment to NATO: From Identity to Interests." *Washington Quarterly* 35 (3): 153–64. https://doi.org/10.1080/0163660X.2012.706578.

Parlament Österreich "1955—State Treaty and Neutrality: Austrian Parliament." n.d. Accessed November 22, 2022. https://www.parlament.gv.at/ENGL/PERK/HIS/REP2/1955/index.shtml.

Pedaliu, Effie G. H. 2011. "'A Discordant Note': NATO and the Greek Junta, 1967–1974." *Diplomacy & Statecraft* 22 (1): 101–20. https://doi.org/10.1080/09592296.2011.549745.

Pevehouse, Jon, Timothy Nordstrom, and Kevin Warnke. 2004. "The Correlates of War 2 International Governmental Organizations Data Version 2.0." *Conflict Management and Peace Science* 21 (2): 101–19. https://doi.org/10.1080/07388940490463933.

Piano, Aili, and Arch Puddington, eds. 2005. *Freedom in the World 2005: The Annual Survey of Political Rights and Civil Liberties*. New York: Rowman & Littlefield.

Pifer, Steven. 1AD. "Ukraine's Perilous Balancing Act." *Brookings* (blog). November 30, 1AD. https://www.brookings.edu/articles/ukraines-perilous-balancing-act/.

Pinto, Jeffrey K. 2014. "Project Management, Governance, and the Normalization of Deviance." *International Journal of Project Management* 32 (3): 376–87. https://doi.org/10.1016/j.ijproman.2013.06.004.

"PM Novalic: I Am Proud of What I Saw during the Military Exercise Held under the Auspices of NATO—Sarajevo Times." n.d. Accessed February 23, 2022. https://sarajevotimes.com/pm-novalic-i-am-proud-of-what-i-saw-during-the-military-exercise-held-under-the-auspices-of-nato/.

Poast, Paul, and Johannes Urpelainen. 2018. *Organizing Democracy: How International Organizations Assist New Democracies.* https://doi.org/10.7208/chicago/9780226543512.001.0001.

Political-Military Relations and the Stability of Arab Regimes. 2013. London: Routledge. https://doi.org/10.4324/9781315000930.

"PolityProject." n.d. Accessed November 20, 2021. https://www.systemicpeace.org/polityproject.html.

"Poll: More Irish Want to Join NATO in Wake of Ukraine Invasion—POLITICO." n.d. Accessed November 23, 2022. https://www.politico.eu/article/poll-more-irish-want-to-join-nato/.

Pollack, Mark A. 2003. *The Engines of European Integration: Delegation, Agency, and Agenda Setting in the EU.* New York: Oxford University Press.

"Populism, Pluralism, and Liberal Democracy." n.d. *Journal of Democracy.* Accessed December 28, 2021. https://www.journalofdemocracy.org/articles/populism-pluralism-and-liberal-democracy/.

"President Bush Participates in Joint Press Availability with President Viktor Yushchenko of Ukraine." n.d. Accessed November 16, 2022. https://georgewbush-whitehouse.archives.gov/news/releases/2008/04/20080401-1.html.

Pridham, G. 2005. *Designing Democracy: EU Enlargement and Regime Change in Post-Communist Europe.* New York: Palgrave Macmillan.

Prielipp, Richard C., Maria Magro, Robert C. Morell, and Sorin J. Brull. 2010. "The Normalization of Deviance: Do We (Un)Knowingly Accept Doing the Wrong Thing?" *Anesthesia & Analgesia* 110 (5): 1499–1502. https://doi.org/10.1213/ANE.0b013e3181d5adc5.

"Project Management, Governance, and the Normalization of Deviance, Science Direct." n.d.

"Project MUSE, Democracy's Past and Future: Populism, Pluralism, and Liberal Democracy." n.d.

"Project MUSE, Montenegro: A Miracle in the Balkans?" n.d.

"Project MUSE, Slovenia's Smooth Transition." n.d. Accessed January 30, 2022. https://muse.jhu.edu/article/17171.

"Project MUSE, The Quality of Democracy: The Chain of Responsiveness." n.d.

"Promises Made, Promises Broken? What Yeltsin Was Told about NATO in 1993 and Why It Matters." 2016. *War on the Rocks.* July 12, 2016. https://

warontherocks.com/2016/07/promises-made-promises-broken-what-yeltsin-was-told-about-nato-in-1993-and-why-it-matters/.

Przeworski, Adam, Michael E. Alvarez, Jose Antonio Cheibub, and Fernando Limongi. 2000. *Democracy and Development: Political Institutions and Well-Being in the World, 1950–1990*. New York: Cambridge University Press.

"Public Divided on Nato Membership, Survey Finds." n.d. *Irish Times*. Accessed November 23, 2022. https://www.irishtimes.com/ireland/2022/10/18/public-divided-on-nato-membership-survey-finds/.

Puddington, Arch. 2014. "The Democratic Leadership Gap." *Journal of Democracy* 25 (2): 77–92. https://doi.org/10.1353/jod.2014.0025.

Ramet, Sabrina P., and Danica Fink-Hafner, eds. 2006. *Democratic Transition in Slovenia: Value Transformation, Education, and Media*. Illustrated ed. College Station: Texas A&M University Press.

"Record of a Meeting of the North Atlantic Defence Committee Held on Wednesday, 05 October 1949 at 1430 Hours," NATO Archives Online. n.d. Accessed November 8, 2021. https://archives.nato.int/record-of-meeting-of-north-atlantic-defence-committee-held-on-wednesday-05-october-1949-at-1430-hours.

"Record of Meeting," NATO Archives Online. n.d. Accessed December 27, 2021a. https://archives.nato.int/record-of-meeting-586.

———. n.d. Accessed December 27, 2021b. https://archives.nato.int/record-of-meeting-632.

———. n.d. Accessed December 31, 2021c. https://archives.nato.int/record-of-meeting-586.

———. n.d. Accessed January 1, 2022d. https://archives.nato.int/record-of-meeting-632.

———. n.d. Accessed January 4, 2022e. https://archives.nato.int/record-of-meeting-688.

———. n.d. Accessed January 4, 2022f. https://archives.nato.int/record-of-meeting-711.

———. n.d. Accessed November 8, 2022g. https://archives.nato.int/record-of-meeting-142.

"Records of Meetings of the Director of the Standing Group Steering Committee," NATO Archives Online. n.d. Accessed December 24, 2021. https://archives.nato.int/records-of-meetings-of-director-of-standing-group-steering-committee.

"Release of Certain Documents to Spain," NATO Archives Online. n.d. Accessed November 8, 2022. https://archives.nato.int/release-of-certain-documents-to-spain.

"Report of the Commission on the Defence Forces." n.d. Accessed November 23, 2022. https://www.gov.ie/en/publication/eb4c0-report-of-the-commission-on-defence-forces/.

Reuters. 2022. "Russia Warns West over Risk of Conflict with NATO." *Reuters*, May 12, 2022, sec. World. https://www.reuters.com/world/russia-warns-west-over-risk-conflict-with-nato-2022-05-12/.

Revill, John. 2022. "Analysis: Neutral Switzerland Leans Closer to NATO in Response to Russia." *Reuters*, May 16, 2022, sec. European Markets. https://www.reuters.com/markets/europe/neutral-switzerland-leans-closer-nato-response-russia-2022-05-15/.

Rittberger, Volker, Bernhard Zangl, Andreas Kruck, and Hylke Dijkstra. 2019. *International Organization*. London: Macmillan.

Roger, Charles B. 2020. *The Origins of Informality: Why the Legal Foundations of Global Governance Are Shifting, and Why It Matters*. New York: Oxford University Press.

"Rome Statute of the International Criminal Court." n.d. Accessed July 31, 2021. https://www.icc-cpi.int/resourcelibrary/official-journal/rome-statute.aspx.

Rossi, Federico Matías. 2012. "The Elite Coup: The Transition to Democracy in Bulgaria." Working paper. https://cadmus.eui.eu//handle/1814/26183.

Rothstein, Robert L. 1968. *Alliances and Small Powers*. New York: Columbia University Press.

Ruggie, John Gerard. 1992. "Multilateralism: The Anatomy of an Institution." *International Organization* 46 (3): 561–98. https://doi.org/10.1017/S00208 18300027831.

"Russia Warns West over Risk of Conflict with NATO | Reuters." n.d. Accessed May 13, 2022. https://www.reuters.com/world/russia-warns-west-over-risk-conflict-with-nato-2022-05-12/.

"Russian Embassy Accuses West of 'NATOisation' of Bosnia." 2022. *Balkan Insight* (blog). August 17, 2022. https://balkaninsight.com/2022/08/17/russian-embassy-accuses-west-of-natoisation-of-bosnia/.

Sanders, David, Paolo Bellucci, Gábor Tóka, and Mariano Torcal. 2012. *The Europeanization of National Polities?: Citizenship and Support in a Post-Enlargement Union*. Oxford, UK: Oxford University Press.

Sayle, Timothy Andrews. 2019. *Enduring Alliance: A History of NATO and the Postwar Global Order*. Ithaca, NY: Cornell University Press.

Schimmelfennig, Frank, and Ulrich Sedelmeier. 2002. "Theorizing EU Enlargement: Research Focus, Hypotheses, and the State of Research." *Journal of European Public Policy* 9 (4): 500–528. https://doi.org/10.1080/13501760210152411.

Schmidt, Vivien. 2010. "Taking Ideas and Discourse Seriously: Explaining Change through Discursive Institutionalism as the Fourth 'New Institutionalism.'" *European Political Science Review* 2 (March): 1–25. https://doi.org/10.1017/S175577390999021X.

Schmidt, Vivien A. 2008. "Discursive Institutionalism: The Explanatory Power of Ideas and Discourse." *Annual Review of Political Science* 11 (1): 303–26. https://doi.org/10.1146/annurev.polisci.11.060606.135342.

Schneider, Christina J. 2020. "Public Commitments as Signals of Responsiveness in the European Union." *Journal of Politics* 82 (1): 329–44. https://doi.org/10.1086/705924.

Schneider, Christina J., and Johannes Urpelainen. 2012. "Accession Rules for International Institutions: A Legitimacy-Efficacy Trade-Off?" *Journal of Conflict Resolution* 56 (2): 290–312. https://doi.org/10.1177/0022002711431422.

Schuette, Leonard August. 2021. "Why NATO Survived Trump: The Neglected Role of Secretary-General Stoltenberg." *International Affairs* 97 (6): 1863–81. https://doi.org/10.1093/ia/iiab167.

———. 2022. "Shaping Institutional Overlap: NATO's Responses to EU Security and Defence Initiatives since 2014." *British Journal of Politics and International Relations*, March, 13691481221079188. https://doi.org/10.1177/13691481221079188.

"Schuman Declaration May 1950." n.d. Accessed March 30, 2022. https://european-union.europa.eu/principles-countries-history/history-eu/1945-59/schuman-declaration-may-1950_en.

Schwartz, Felicia. 2018. "U.S. Freezes $65 Million in Funding for U.N. Palestinian Refugee Agency." *Wall Street Journal*, January 16, 2018, sec. World. https://www.wsj.com/articles/u-s-freezes-65-million-in-funding-for-u-n-palestinian-refugee-agency-1516146851.

Schweickert, Rainer, Inna Melnykovska, Ansgar Belke, and Ingo Bordon. 2011. "Prospective NATO or EU Membership and Institutional Change in Transition Countries1." *Economics of Transition and Institutional Change* 19 (4): 667–92. https://doi.org/10.1111/j.1468-0351.2011.00415.x.

"Send NATO Troops to Help Stabilize Bosnia and Herzegovina." 2022. *War on the Rocks*. August 12, 2022. https://warontherocks.com/2022/08/send-nato-troops-to-help-stabilize-bosnia-and-herzegovina/.

"Shape History, Volume I, Origin and Development of SHAPE," NATO Archives Online. n.d. Accessed December 27, 2021. https://archives.nato.int/shape-history-volume-i.

"Situations under Investigation." n.d. Accessed December 4, 2021. https://www.icc-cpi.int/pages/situation.aspx.

"Slovakia and the Enlargement of the European Union (1)." n.d. Accessed January 29, 2022. https://www.europarl.europa.eu/enlargement/briefings/13a2_en.htm.

"Slovenia's Smooth Transition." n.d. Journal of Democracy. Accessed January 30, 2022. https://www.journalofdemocracy.org/articles/slovenias-smooth-transition/.

Smith, M. 2000. *NATO Enlargement during the Cold War: Strategy and System in the Western Alliance.* 2000th ed. Houndmills, Basingstoke, Hampshire, UK; New York: Palgrave Macmillan.

Sotomayor, Arturo C. 2014. *The Myth of the Democratic Peacekeeper: Civil-Military Relations and the United Nations.* Baltimore, MD: Johns Hopkins University Press.

"Sovereign Debt and Supersanctions in Emerging Markets: Evidence from Four Southeast European Countries, 1878–1913." n.d. Accessed October 4, 2021. https://ideas.repec.org/p/hes/wpaper/0216.html.

"Speech of Minister Perez Llorca before the Atlantic Council," NATO Archives Online. n.d. Accessed December 31, 2021. https://archives.nato.int/speech-of-minister-perez-llorca-before-atlantic-council.

"Statement Made by the President of the Spanish Government at the Opening Ceremony of the NAC with the Participation of the Heads of State and Government in BONN on 10 June 1982." NATO Archives Online. n.d. Accessed December 31, 2021. https://archives.nato.int/statement-made-by-president-of-spanish-government-at-opening-ceremony-of-nac-with-participation-of-heads-of-state-and-government-in-bonn-on-10-june-1982.

"Statute of the Council of Europe (London, 5 May 1949)." 2014. Text. CVCE.EU by UNI.LU. CVCE.EU by UNI.LU. June 13, 2014. https://www.cvce.eu/en/obj/statute_of_the_council_of_europe_london_5_may_1949-en-4aa0bc88-cea9-48b2-902d-a19e5bbf2c82.html.

Subramaniam, Tara, Andrew Raine, Sana Noor Haq, and Adrienne Vogt. n.d. "September 30, 2022 Russia-Ukraine News." CNN. n.d. Accessed October 2, 2022. https://www.cnn.com/europe/live-news/russia-ukraine-war-news-09-30-22/index.html.

"Summits of Heads of State and Government of the Council of Europe." n.d. Committee of Ministers. Accessed January 20, 2022. https://www.coe.int/en/web/cm/summits.

"Suomi Lähettää Aseita Ukrainalle—Pääministeri Marin: "Päätös on Historiallinen." Politiikka| HS.Fi. n.d. Accessed March 8, 2022. https://www.hs.fi/politiikka/art-2000008647428.html.

"Survey: Most of Austrians Oppose NATO Accession." 2023. Www.Euractiv.Com. May 4, 2023. https://www.euractiv.com/section/politics/news/survey-most-of-austrians-oppose-nato-accession/.

Swaton, Chiara. "Austrian FM Defends Military Neutrality amid International Criticism," www.euractiv.com. August 22, 2023. https://www.euractiv.com/section/politics/news/austrian-fm-defends-military-neutrality-amid-international-criticism.

"Sweden's Ruling Social Democrats to Review Party Policy on NATO." Reuters. n.d. Accessed April 13, 2022. https://www.reuters.com/world/europe/swedens-ruling-social-democrats-review-party-policy-nato-2022-04-11/.

swissinfo.ch/Reuters/ts. 2023. "Small Majority of Swiss Back Re-Exporting Arms to Ukraine." SWI Swissinfo.Ch. January 29, 2023. https://www.swissinfo.ch/eng/politics/small-majority-of-swiss-back-re-exporting-arms-to-ukraine/48242050."Tánaiste Announces Plans for a Consultative Forum on International Security Policy." 2023. Department of Foreign Affairs. Accessed August 29, 2023. https://www.dfa.ie/news-and-media/press-releases/press-release-archive/2023/march/tanaiste-announces-plans-for-a-consultative-forum-on-international-security-policy.php.

Thorhallsson, Baldur. 2017. *The Role of Small States in the European Union*. London: Routledge. https://doi.org/10.4324/9781315237268.

"[Ticker] Finland Won't Join Nato without Sweden: Niinistö." 2022. *EUobserver*. June 13, 2022. https://euobserver.com/tickers/155194.

Tierney, Michael. n.d. "Principles and Principals? The Possibilities for Theoretical Synthesis and Scientific Progress in the Study of International Organizations," 31.

Tilly, Charles. 2007. *Democracy*. Cambridge, UK: Cambridge University Press. https://doi.org/10.1017/CBO9780511804922.

Tovias, Alfred. 1984. "The International Context of Democratic Transition." *West European Politics* 7 (2): 158–71. https://doi.org/10.1080/01402388408424476.

"Treaties Pending in the Senate." n.d. *United States Department of State* (blog). Accessed July 28, 2021. https://www.state.gov/treaties-pending-in-the-senate/.

"Two in Three Maltese Strongly Support Neutrality—Survey." n.d. *Times of Malta*. Accessed November 25, 2022. https://timesofmalta.com/articles/view/two-in-three-maltese-strongly-support-neutrality-survey.933304.

"Ukraine: Civilian Casualty Update 22 May 2023." n.d. OHCHR. Accessed June 15, 2023. https://www.ohchr.org/en/news/2023/05/ukraine-civilian-casualty-update-22-may-2023.

"Ukraine's Parliament Backs Changes to Constitution Confirming Ukraine's Path toward EU, NATO." n.d. Accessed September 18, 2021. https://www.unian.info/politics/10437570-ukraine-s-parliament-backs-changes-to-constitution-confirming-ukraine-s-path-toward-eu-nato.html.

"Ukraine's Perilous Balancing Act - ProQuest." n.d. Accessed September 18, 2021. https://www.proquest.com/openview/d1e4dbac642ec3eff1b8e54c2c25cce5/1.pdf?pq-origsite=gscholar&cbl=41559.

United Nations. "United Nations Charter (Full Text)." Accessed July 25, 2021. https://www.un.org/en/about-us/un-charter/full-text.

"United States Announces Restoration of U.S. $150 Million to Support Palestine Refugees." n.d. UNRWA. Accessed July 18, 2021. https://www.unrwa.org/newsroom/press-releases/united-states-announces-restoration-us-150-million-support-palestine.

"United States Senate Committee on Foreign Relations." n.d. Accessed April 8, 2022. https://www.foreign.senate.gov/publications/download/testimony-of-daniel-fried-from-protocols-to-the-north-atlantic-treaty.

"Unseresicherheit.Org." n.d. Unseresicherheit.Org. Accessed June 20, 2023. https://unseresicherheit.org/.

U.S. Department of State. "The Summit for Democracy." n.d. *United States Department of State* (blog). Accessed December 9, 2021. https://www.state.gov/summit-for-democracy/.

U.S. Department of State Archive. "The Baltic Charter." n.d. Accessed January 22, 2022. https://1997-2001.state.gov/www/regions/eur/ch_9801_baltic_charter.html.

U.S. Department of State Archive. "The North Atlantic Cooperation Council." n.d. Accessed March 18, 2022. https://1997-2001.state.gov/regions/eur/nato_fsnacc.html.

Váli, Ferenc A. 1972. *The Turkish Straits and NATO.* 1st ed. Stanford, CA: Hoover Institution Press.

Vaubel, Roland, Axel Dreher, and Uğurlu Soylu. 2007. "Staff Growth in International Organizations: A Principal-Agent Problem? An Empirical Analysis." *Public Choice* 133 (3–4): 275–95. https://doi.org/10.1007/s11127-007-9188-3.

Vaughan, Diane. 1996. *The Challenger Launch Decision: Risky Technology, Culture, and Deviance at NASA.* Chicago, IL: University of Chicago Press.

Waltz, Kenneth N. 1993. "The Emerging Structure of International Politics." *International Security* 18 (2): 44. https://doi.org/10.2307/2539097.

Weber, Max. 1978. *Economy and Society: An Outline of Interpretive Sociology.* Berkeley: University of California Press.

Wendt, Alexander. 1999. *Social Theory of International Politics.* Cambridge, UK: Cambridge University Press.

White House. 2022. "Press Briefing by Press Secretary Karine Jean-Pierre and National Security Advisor Jake Sullivan, September 30, 2022." White House. October 1, 2022. https://www.whitehouse.gov/briefing-room/press-briefings/2022/09/30/press-briefing-by-press-secretary-karine-jean-pierre-and-national-security-advisor-jake-sullivan-september-30-2022/.

"Will Austria Abandon Neutrality to Join NATO?"DW May 21, 2022. Dw.Com. Accessed November 22, 2022. https://www.dw.com/en/will-austria-abandon-neutrality-to-join-nato/a-61880804.

Williams, Michael C., and Iver B. Neumann. 2000. "From Alliance to Security Community: NATO, Russia, and the Power of Identity." *Millennium* 29 (2): 357–87. https://doi.org/10.1177/03058298000290020801.

"With Finland and Sweden Set to Join NATO, Austria Seeks Neutral Allies." 2022. Euronews. October 13, 2022. http://www.euronews.com/2022/10/13/with-finland-and-sweden-set-to-join-nato-austria-seeks-neutral-allies.

WTO. "Legal Texts—Marrakesh Agreement." n.d. Accessed July 31, 2021. https://www.wto.org/english/docs_e/legal_e/gatt47_01_e.htm.

Yarbrough, Beth V., and Robert M. Yarbrough. 1992. *Cooperation and Governance in International Trade: The Strategic Organizational Approach.* Princeton, NJ: Princeton University Press. https://www.jstor.org/stable/j.ctt7zvsw5.

"Yle Poll: Support for Nato Membership Soars to 76%." 2022. *Yle News.* May 9, 2022. https://yle.fi/news/3-12437506.

"Ylen kysely: Enemmistö suomalaisista kannattaa Suomen Nato-jäsenyyttä." 2022. *Yle Uutiset.* February 28, 2022. https://yle.fi/uutiset/3-12336530.

Youngs, R. (2015). "Exploring Non-Western Democracy." *Journal of Democracy* 26: 140.

Zakošek, Nenad. 2008. "Democratization, State-Building and War: The Cases of Serbia and Croatia." *Democratization* 15 (3): 588–610. https://doi.org/10.1080/13510340801991130.

Index